T0073096

ESSENTIAL TOPICS OF MANAGING INFORMATION SYSTEMS

ESSENTIAL TOPICS OF MANAGING INFORMATION SYSTEMS

Jun Xu

Southern Cross University, Australia

W⊖ World Scientific

NEW JERSEY · LONDON · SINGAPORE · BEIJING · SHANGHAI · HONG KONG · TAIPEI · CHENNAI · TOKYO

Published by

World Scientific Publishing Co. Pte. Ltd.

5 Toh Tuck Link, Singapore 596224

USA office: 27 Warren Street, Suite 401-402, Hackensack, NJ 07601

UK office: 57 Shelton Street, Covent Garden, London WC2H 9HE

British Library Cataloguing-in-Publication Data
A catalogue record for this book is available from the British Library.

ESSENTIAL TOPICS OF MANAGING INFORMATION SYSTEMS

ISBN 978-981-121-355-7

For any available supplementary material, please visit
https://www.worldscientific.com/worldscibooks/10.1142/11647#t=suppl

Printed in Singapore

Preface

Information systems have become an essential part and a major resource of the organization; and they can radically affect the structure of an organisation, the way it serves customers, and the way it helps people in the organization to communicate both internally and externally, and the way an organisation runs its business. Managing information systems effectively and efficiently has become an important part of the life of 21st century managers. This book is about managing information systems and focuses on relationships between information, information systems, people and business. The impacts, roles, risks, challenges as well as emerging trends of information systems are an important element of the book. At the same time, many strategic and contemporary uses of information systems such as implementing enterprise planning systems for improving internal operation, adopting customer relationship management systems and supply chain management systems to enhance relations with customers and suppliers/partners respectively, and establishing knowledge management systems for better managing organizational knowledge resources as well as using different information systems for supporting managers' decision making in all levels are an integral part of the book. In addition, essential and critical information systems management skills including using information systems for competitive advantages, planning and evaluating information systems, developing & implementing information systems, and managing information systems operation are a critical part of the book.

This book has ten chapters. Chapter 1 looks at foundations of information system/information technology and discusses topics such as the importance of information systems, key concepts of information systems, information systems competence for managers, critical issues of information systems, and emerging trends & future directions of information systems. In Chapter 2 an important dimension of managing information systems, how information systems can help organisations gain competitive advantages, is discussed. Organisations can apply strategic planning tools such as Porter's five forces and value chain to analyse their competitive position, examine their competitive advantages, and identify relevant competitive strategies. Information systems can play a very important role in the success of an organisation's identified competitive strategies.

Chapter 3 studies the importance of good information systems strategy, which is critical for the strategic use and success of information systems in the organization. Chapter 3 also looks at another important aspect of information systems management: evaluation of initiatives/investments of information systems. There is an old saying: 'If you cannot measure it, you cannot manage it'. Through systematic assessment of their information systems initiatives/investments, organizations can be effective in choosing right information systems projects and managing their chosen initiatives/investments. In order to measure the performance of information systems, organisations could use a set of metrics (such as net present value, return of investment, internal rate of return, payback period, and total cost of ownership). Meanwhile organisations should look beyond financial metrics, and take into consideration of financial and non-financial data, qualitative and quantitative information, tangible and intangible costs/benefits, and formal and informal processes.

Chapter 4 looks at developing and implementing information systems. Correctly developed and deployed information systems can significantly contribute to the success of the business (e.g., enhancing competitive advantages, improving business performance). On the other hand, a poorly developed and implemented information system can have a damaging effect on business performance and can even cause a business to fail. To ensure successfully develop and implement information systems organizations need to adopt systems development life cycle (or its variations), which includes such activities as systems planning, analysis, design, development, testing, implementation, and maintenance. In addition, while organizations are developing and implementing information systems they have to pay close attention to such areas as project management, change management, and risk management, these areas are critically associated with the success of information systems development and implementation.

Chapter 5 discusses the importance of managing organization's knowledge resources/assets. Effectively managing and leveraging knowledge assets, has critical implications for business performance and sustainable business growth. Information systems such as knowledge management systems could assist in organization's efforts of capturing, storing, disseminating, utilizing and creating knowledge. On a related note, Chapter 5 also discusses data resources management. As a result of global connectedness, the wide adoption of computing tools & mobile devices, the rapid advancement of Internet technologies, and more powerful computing capability, gathering and analysing large (or very large) volume of data is quickly becoming popular among organizations for reasons such as better understanding customers, better utilizing data resources & computing infrastructure, designing new business models, and creating new revenue streams.

Chapter 6 touches on the information systems infrastructure management and discusses hardware, software, networks and telecommunications management. Hardware is a vital part of computer systems and provides the underlying physical foundation for firms' information systems infrastructure. Other infrastructure components of software, networks and telecommunications require hardware for their storage and operation. To be useful, hardware needs software, which gives instructions that control the operation of a computer system. Networks and Telecommunications enable large and small businesses to communicate internally between staff and externally with customers, suppliers, business partners, strategic alliances and others. Making the right decision in relation to information systems infrastructure is vital to the success of the business.

Chapter 7 deals with functional information systems and discusses cross-functional information systems. Traditionally businesses are operated by dividing the organisation into various functions (e.g., accounting, marketing, finance, productions/operations management, human resources management) in a silo structure with each having its own information systems and tending to work in isolation. In order to deal with these problems of silo approach (e.g., information recreation, information errors, communication gaps among departments, loss of information arising from inaccurate information and not-timely shared information, and lack of consistent services to customers), managers need to think beyond the walls of the organisation. Thus there is a need for a cross-functional approach, which focuses on business process and customer services.

Cross-functional information systems are a strategic way to use information systems to share information resources and focus on accomplishing fundamental business processes in concert with the company's customer, supplier, partner, and employee stakeholders. Some typical examples of cross-functional information systems include: enterprise resource planning systems, customer relationship management systems, supply chain management systems, and knowledge management systems. These four systems have different focuses: enterprise resource planning systems emphasize on internal efficiency; customer relationship management systems concentrate on customer relations; supply chain management systems focus on managing relations with suppliers and business partners; and knowledge management systems facilitate managing tacit and explicit knowledge of the organization. Meanwhile these four systems are inter-related (e.g., accurate information is critical to the success of supply chain management systems and enterprise planning systems; knowledge sharing facilitated by knowledge management systems is important to all the aspect of business including the success of supply chain management systems, enterprise planning systems, customer relationship management systems). Chapter 7 also has a close look at enterprise planning systems and discusses implementation issues and emerging trends of enterprise resource planning systems. Chapter 8 looks at various aspects of customer relationship management systems and supply chain management systems, including benefits, types of systems/applications, challenges & issues of implementation, and future trends.

Chapter 9 reviews information systems for supporting decision making. Organisations today can no longer use a 'cook book' approach to decision making. In order to succeed in business today, companies need information systems that support the diverse decision-making needs of their operations. The massive volume of available data generated by billions of connected devices and human minds has further strengthened the role of information systems for decision-making support. Providing information and support for all levels of management decision making is no easy task. Therefore, information systems must be designed to produce a variety of information products to meet the changing needs of decision makers at all levels throughout the organisation. Examples of information systems for decision making cover management information systems, decision support systems, executive information systems, data warehousing & data mining, business intelligence/business analytics, and artificial intelligence.

Chapter 10 looks at managing information systems function and operation. The success of information systems in the organization heavily rely on good management. Good information systems management examines and works on enterprise information systems operation/function management, information systems governance & service management, information skills & talent management, information systems in mergers and acquisitions, global information systems management, virtual workforce, and roles of chief information officer

(CIO). Chapter 10 also discusses information systems outsourcing management by looking at insourcing, outsourcing, multi-sourcing, offshore outsourcing, and partnership.

In this edition of the book (*previous edition titled "Managing Information Systems: Ten Essential Topics" published by Atlantis Press*), the following changes and highlights have been included:

• Re-organizing the flow and the content of the book.

• Providing more comprehensive discussion and/or updated information for topics such as Information Systems Competence for Managers, Emerging Technologies & Future Trends, Competitive Strategies, Business Ecosystems, Innovation Strategy, Information Systems Strategy, Information Systems Investment Evaluation, Information Systems Development, Big Data & Data Analytics, Hardware Management, Software Management, Telecommunication Management, The Internet of Things, Cloud Computing, Mobile Computing, Social Technologies, ICT Management Challenges, Enterprise Resource Planning Systems, Customer Relationship Management Systems, Supply Chain Management Systems, Artificial Intelligence, Information Systems Governance & Service Management, Information Systems Skills & Talent Management, The Roles of CIO, and Outsourcing.

• Bringing in new topics such as Digital Platforms, Agile Organization, Digital Transformation, Agile Methodology, DevOPs, Microservices, The Lean Start-up Approach, Open Source Approach, Design Thinking, Data Center, Blockchain, 5G, Self-driving Vehicles, Edge Computing, and Quantum Computing.

I would like to thank Mr John Hammond, Dr Reza Ghanbarzadeh, Dr Nicky Antonius, Dr Chad Lin, and Dr Daniel O'Sheedy, for their suggestions and assistance. Finally I would like to thank World Scientific for opportunity of working on the book, and thank Steven Patt, Editor at World Scientific, for overseeing the publishing process of the book and for giving me such a wonderful publishing experience.

Jun Xu
Gold Coast, Australia
September 2019

Contents

Chapter 1

Foundation

This chapter will explain the importance of management of information resources, discuss the key concepts of information systems, explain information systems competence for managers, discuss critical issues of information systems, and discuss emerging trends and future directions of information systems.

1.1 Managing Information as a Strategic Resource

Efficient and strategic use of information holds the key to enhanced competitiveness, increased efficiency, better resource allocation, and improved effectiveness. Information resource is different with traditional tangible resources. Eaton and Bawden (1991) suggest some key distinctions between information as a resource and traditional tangible resources:

• Value of information: it is difficult to quantify the value of information. For example, the same piece of information (e.g., information about the share price of Google) could lead to different impacts (positive or neutral or negative), and could have different values (small or large).

• Consumption of information: information has the characteristics of 'self-multiplicative', which basically says the information will not be lost or diminished when it is provided to others. This feature makes information resources fundamentally different with other (tangible and commodity) resources. For example, if I have a piece of information, I will still have it even after I share it with you; but if I have a tangible item (e.g., five dollars, one apple), if I share with others, then I won't have the same item (e.g., less than five dollars, not having the same whole apple I had before).

• Dynamics of information: information is a dynamic source for change. We need information to make changes and improve the way we do things. For example, by collecting and analysing customer information, we can have better understanding customers' needs and concerns, thus are able to provide better products and services to customers.

•   Life cycle of information: the life cycle of information is unpredictable; and information can have multiple life cycles. For example, how do you predict the information demand?; how do you predict the peaks and the troughs of information demand?; and how do you predict the declining and exit of information resources?. Information can be in one life cycle (being useful) then leaves (becoming irrelevant), but come back again in another life cycle later or enter other life cycles of information (for different stakeholders in different areas across various areas).

•   Individuality of information: information has situational uniqueness. Information can come from different approaches (e.g., first-hand and second-hand information) and can exist in various formats (e.g., digital and non-digital formats). Other tangible resources tend to have the identifiable format and sources (e.g., petroleum in liquid formats and coming from the underground or the bottom of the ocean).

1.2 Key Concepts of Information Systems

The concept of information systems (IS)/information technology (IT)

An information system includes all components and resources necessary to deliver information and information processing functions to the organisation and can be any organised combination of people, hardware, software, communication networks and data resources that collects, transforms and disseminates information within an organisation. Business professionals rely on many types of information systems that use a variety of information technologies, from simple manual (pen-and-pencil) hardware devices and informal (word-of-mouth) communication channels to complex computer-based systems (e.g., enterprise resource planning systems). However, in today's environment, when we talk about an information system, we refer to computer-based information systems, that use computer hardware and software, the Internet, telecommunication networks, and computer-based data resource management techniques to gather, manage and distribute information. The terms Information Technology (IT) and Information Systems (IS) will be used interchangeably in this book.

So far there is no universal classification of information systems. For example, information systems can be classified for the purpose of either serving business operations or supporting managerial decision making (O'Brien & Marakas 2011, p. 13). On the other hand, information systems can be classified according to different needs at different organisational levels (e.g., strategic, management and operational levels) across various functions (e.g., sales and marketing, manufacturing and production, finance and accounting and human resources) (Laudon & Laudon 2005, p. 43). People at different levels of an organisation have different information needs. The structure of a typical organisation is similar to a pyramid. The array of organisational activities occurs at different levels of the pyramid. People in the organisation have unique information needs and thus require various sets of information systems tools. For example information systems such as management information systems, decision support systems, executive information systems, suit different information needs of operational managers, middle managers, and senior managers. Functional information systems, such as accounting information systems, finance information systems, marketing information systems, productions/operations information systems, and human resource information systems, serve different business functions.

Organisations are increasingly using cross-functional information systems, which focus on cross-functional business processes and emphasize customer services. Examples of cross-functional information systems include enterprise resource planning systems, customer relationship management systems, supply chain management systems, and knowledge management systems.

The concept of strategic information systems

Strategic information systems are any kind of information systems that 'support or shape the competitive position and strategies of a business enterprise' (O'Brien & Marakas 2011, p. 46), and they play strategic roles and provide effective support to organisations' efforts for achieving competitive advantages (e.g., cost leadership, differentiation, innovation, growth, strategic alliance/partnership) (O'Brien & Marakas 2011, p. 49). Some examples of strategic applications of information systems include:

•   use of enterprise resources planning systems for improving internal efficiency.

•   use of customer relationship management systems for acquiring, enhancing and retaining customers and supply chain management systems for managing supply chains.

- use of management information systems, decision support systems, executive information systems, and other information systems for supporting decision support.
- use of collaboration systems and knowledge management systems for intra-organisational and inter-organisational collaboration and knowledge sharing.

1.3 Information Systems Competence for Managers

Information systems are a vital component for business success and a major functional area in business and therefore an essential field of study in many MBA programs. Information systems are an essential body of knowledge for business managers, professionals, and business students. As we argue information systems need to have a business view, business managers should participate in information systems decision-making for the following reasons (Pearlson & Saunders 2016, p. 3):

- Information systems have to be managed as a critical resource
- Information systems provide an opportunity to make changes in the way people work together
- Information systems work with almost every aspect of business
- Information systems create business opportunities and new strategies
- Information systems can assist in combating business challenges from competitors.

Based on a survey of information systems competence for MBA graduates among executives in 1995 (Ramakrishna et al. 1995), it is recommended that MBA graduates should equip themselves with such skills and knowledge as: general skills and knowledge of information systems, hardware skills, software skills, knowledge of applications, systems development, and knowledge of related topics including privacy, security, legal aspects, and ethical issues. The focus on soft skills (e.g., project management and information skills/talent management), is the trend identified in the survey. The same trend can be observed in today's business environment. On a related note, for information systems/information technology (IS/IT) professionals, soft skills are also critical to their profession. A recent of survey of members of Society for Information Management (SIM) (reported in Kappelman et al. 2018) unveils that some important soft skills for IS/IT professionals are (in the order): Critical thinking, Strategic planning, Leadership, Business knowledge, Systems thinking, Being innovative, Change management,

Emotional intelligence, Problem solving, Communication, Business analysis, and Collaboration/Teamwork.

Meanwhile, business managers need to be able to discuss and examine the roles and consequences of information systems in the organization. Some dimensions and questions they should look at and ask include (Silver, et al. 1995, p. 376):

- What are an information system's features? What does it do?
- How does the information system match with the firm's external environment?
- How does the information system support the firm's strategy?
- How does the information system facilitate the firm's business processes?
- How does the information system work with the organisational structure and culture?
- Is the organisation's existing computing infrastructure suitable for the information system?
- Does the information system enhance the infrastructure? Does it extend it?
- How and how effectively was the system implemented?
- Who are the users of the system and how do they use it? as intended?
- What are the consequences of the information system for performance, people, and future flexibility? Did the system achieve its objectives?
- Do we want to use the information system to improve our business process or reengineer our business processes?

The ten chapters of this book cover a set of information systems competence for managers:

Table 1.1. Information Systems Competence for Managers

Topics	Key Knowledge Areas	Corresponding Chapter(s) in the Book
Information Systems Foundation	Key Concepts of Information and Information Systems; Information Systems Competence for Managers; Critical Issues of Information Systems Management (including Security and Privacy Concerns, Governance Issues, Societal Considerations, Legal Implications, Responsible Computing); Emerging Trends & Future Directions.	Chapter 1
Information Systems for Competitive Advantages	Applying Information Systems for Enhancing Competitiveness; Information Systems Supported	Chapter 2

Topics	Key Knowledge Areas	Corresponding Chapter(s) in the Book
	Competitive Strategies; Using Information Systems for Value Creation or Added Value; Information Systems Enabled/Supported Innovation Strategies; Digital Platforms; Ecosystems; Collaboration and Coopetition; Information System Supported/Enabled Innovation Strategy; Business Design; Agile Organization.	
Information Systems Strategy and Investment	Information Systems Strategy; Alignment between Information Systems Plan/Strategy and Business Strategy; Justifying Information Systems Projects/Investments; Measuring the Success of Information Systems Investments; Digital Transformation.	Chapter 3
Development and Implementation of Information Systems	Systems Approach; Information Systems Development Processes; Information Systems Development Life Cycle; Agile Method; Design Thinking; DevOPs; Microservices; Component-based Approach; Lean Startup; Open Source; System Analysis and Design; Conversion Approaches; Project Management; Project Change Management; Project Risk Management; Information Systems Development Approaches; Internal Development; Outsourcing Information Systems Development; Acquisition and Merger of Information Systems ; Use of Application Service Provider.	Chapter 4
Managing Organization's Data, Information and Knowledge Resources;	Data, Information and Knowledge; Database, Data Warehouse and Data Centre; Big Data; Blockchain Technology; Knowledge Management and Knowledge Management Systems.	Chapter 5
Managing Infrastructure for Information Systems	Hardware and Software Management; Managing Networks, Wireless Communication; BYOD	Chapter 6

Topics	Key Knowledge Areas	Corresponding Chapter(s) in the Book
	(Bring Your Own Device) Management; 4G, 5G and 6G; Mobile Computing; Web-based Computing; Cloud Computing; Edge Computing; Quantum Computing; Self-driving/ Driverless Vehicles; Internet of Things (IoTs); IPV6; Internet 2; Integration Issues; Global ICT Trends; Decentralization and Centralization of Computing Resources and Capabilities; Critical Issues of Managing Information Systems Infrastructure.	
Using Information Systems for Enhancing Internal Operations	Functional and Cross-functional Information Systems; Enterprise Resource Planning Systems; Costs and Benefits of Enterprise Resource Planning Systems; Challenges and Critical Issues of Enterprise Planning Systems; Integration Issues of Enterprise Resource Planning Systems; Emerging Trends and Future Directions of Enterprise Resource Planning Systems.	Chapter 7
Using Information Systems for Improving External Operations	Customer-Focused Business Strategy; Good Understanding of Customers and Their Decision-making Process; Strategies and Technologies for Attracting, Assisting, Serving and Retaining Customers; Customer Relation Management; Customer Relation Management Systems; Challenges and Issues of Managing Relations with Customers and Implementing Customer Relation Management Systems; Emerging Trends and Future Directions of Customer Relation Management and Customer Relationship Management Systems; Good Understanding of Parts and Stakeholders of Supply Chains; Supply Chain Management; Technologies and Systems for Supply Chain Management;	Chapter 8

Topics	Key Knowledge Areas	Corresponding Chapter(s) in the Book
	Challenges and Issues of Supply Chains and Supply Chain Management Systems; Emerging Trends and Future Directions of Supply Chain Management and Supply Chain Management Systems.	
Using Information Systems for Supporting Decision Making	Enabling the Organization's Decision Making; Quality of the Information for Decision Making; Information Systems for Supporting Decision Making; Data/Business Analytics and Business Intelligence; Data-driven Decision Making; Artificial Intelligence; Challenges and Issues of Using Information Systems for Decision Making.	Chapter 9
Information Systems Operation Management	Enterprise Information Systems Operation Management; Chief Information Officer and other Senior Information Systems Roles; Information Systems Talent Management; Outsourcing Information Systems Operations; Global Information Systems Operation Management; Managing Global Virtual Teams; Information Systems Governance; Information Systems Service Management Standards; Information Systems and Acquisition & Merger; Information Systems Contingency Plan and Disaster Recovery Plan.	Chapter 10

(Source: Developed by the Author)

1.4 Critical Issues of Information Systems Management

Organisations face various information systems management issues. Understanding these issues is very critical to the success of information systems in business. According to a recent study in 2017 conducted by the Society of Information Management (SIM) (reported in Kappelman et al. 2018), ten top IS/IT management concerns are (in the order): (1) Security/Cybersecurity/Privacy; (2) Alignment of IT with the business; (3) Data analytics/Data management;

(4) Compliance & Regulations; (5) Cost reduction/Cost controls (IT); (6) Cost reduction/Cost controls (Business); (7) Innovation; (8) Digital transformation; (9) Agility/Flexibility (Business); and (10) Agility/Flexibility (IT). In the same study, top application and technology developments were also identified. Top ten application and technology developments include (in the order): (1) Analytics/Business intelligence/Data mining/Forecasting/Big data; (2) Security/Cybersecurity; (3) Cloud computing; (4) App/Software development/ Maintenance; (5) Enterprise Resource Planning (ERP); (6) Customer relationship management (CRM); (7) Data center/infrastructure; (8) Network/ Telecommunications; (9) Legacy systems replacing/re-platforming; and (10) Legacy systems maintenance/update/consolidate.

Meanwhile even though the key information systems management issues could be varied for different organisations in various countries (e.g., arising from the differences in types of companies, industries, governments & regulations, IS/IT infrastructures, levels of sophistication, and cultures) and in different studies (e.g., resulting from differences in data collection methods, research subjects involved, and sample sizes), some common factors, which are common to all businesses, can be identified as: (1) focusing on customers; (2) building and enhancing relationships with business partners and suppliers; (3) fostering collaboration among people and teams across the organisation; (4)improving operational efficiency and effectiveness; (5) enhancing business performance; (6) managing, developing and evaluating information systems; (7) protecting information resources; (8) using information systems ethically; and (9) managing information systems organisation.

In addition, according to one recent global survey of 1,469 senior executives of firms with different sizes and from different sectors and regions (reported in Brown & Sikes 2012), some challenges organizations faced for the success of digital technologies include:
- Organizational structure for successful deployment of digital technologies
- Lack of technology and information systems
- Lack of quality data
- Lack of internal leadership
- Difficulty in finding functional talent
- Inappropriate business processes to take advantages of opportunities created by digital technologies
- Lack of senior management support
- Difficulty in finding technical talent.

Management security & ethical issues

Security and ethical implications of information systems are a must for strategic management and use of information systems and are the biggest challenge for board directors (Cheng & Groysberg 2017; Kappelman et al. 2018). In a recent McKinsey global study of 400 executives and experts on Internet of Things (reported in Bauer et al. 2017), 75% participants indicated that cybersecurity is a top concern for their organizations, but only 16% believed that their organizations are well prepared. They are critical issues for organizations and could cause serious damage financially to the organization (for example, according to RSA Anti-Fraud Command Center (reported in Enterprise Management Associates 2012), phishing attacks alone cost businesses US$ 1.3 billion in 2011). It is reported that some firms are investing up to $500 million on cybersecurity and globally more than 100 billion lines of security codes are created every year (Poppensieker & Riemenschnitter 2018). Organisations have to take them seriously; otherwise they may face the consequence of going out of business. Today's attackers are well organized and well informed, and they take advantages of latest advances in crimeware and hacking skills (Enterprise Management Associates 2012).

While the global connectedness has provided us with many benefits, it also has made managing security and ethical issues a much more challenging task. For example, the latest video surveillance and facial recognition systems on the one hand could help us monitor criminals' movement, assist in looking for missing persons, but on the other hand it will impose significant ethical issues. And as a result of the wider adoption and Internet of Things (IoT) applications and networks, the connecting points on the large corporate networks has increased from between 50,000 and 500, 000 to millions or tens of millions. By 2020 the IoT networks may consist of as many as 30 billion devices; 46% of Internet connections will be machine-to-machine and many of those connecting points (if not most) are beyond the control of the corporate (Poppensieker & Riemenschnitter 2018). Laseter and Johnson (2011) suggest that there are more than 5 billion devices connected to the Internet (a perpetrator needs only a single weakness in order to attack a system), accessing and serving up to 500 billion gigabytes of information and transmitting 2 trillion emails per day, furthermore 75% of emails are spam even though spam rate has been dropping in recent years. Every minute 42 new strains of malware (short for malicious software including viruses, worms, and Trojans) are generated, an average of 8,600 new websites with malicious code are developed each day, and half of the results for the top 100 daily search terms lead to malicious sites. Deloitte (2019) suggests that by 2026, 463 billion GB of data will be generated daily. Poppensieker and Riemenschnitter (2018) point out that several billion data sets are breached every year and many companies are experiencing thousand attacks every month. Some major cyber technical attacks include: Malware, Unauthorized access, Denial of Services attack, Spam & Spyware, Hijacking (servers and pages), and Botnets (Turban et al. 2012, p. 500; Laudon & Laudon 2012, p.246). Malware is one of the significant cyber security concerns, and every year some 120 million new variants of malware are generated by hackers (Poppensieker & Riemenschnitter 2018). Another major issue is SPAM. Even though we do have solutions (e.g., Junk-mail filters, Automatic junk-mail deleters, Blocking certain URLs and e-mail addresses), it has been really challenging for controlling spamming since spammers send millions of e-mails, shifting Internet accounts to avoid detection and use different methods to find their victims. Some top security concerns associated with mobile enterprise applications include: Malware on devices, Data leaks, Compromised credentials or configurations, Lost or stolen devices, Movement of data to unauthorized or consumer applications (e.g., dropbox), Unsecure network access, and Unsecure Wifi (IDG 2015). Meanwhile some top cloud security considerations consist of: Data encryption, Protection of data at rest, Protection data in transit, Data security between cloud and end user, User identity and access management, File integrity monitoring, Data security between cloud providers, Mapping the correct workload to respective cloud environment, and data classification (Telstra 2019, p. 44). In addition, state-sponsored actor attacks, large-scale data provider (e.g., data center, cloud provider, telecom) attacks, and monetary extortion cases (e.g., cryptocurrency) are rising in recent years (Meeker 2019, p. 207).

Some attacks require sophisticated techniques and technologies, most attacks are not sophisticated (e.g., preying on poor security practice and human weaknesses), and insiders' breach could be more frequent and more harmful than that of outsiders. Effective security risk management procedures can be used to minimize their probability and impact. We as a society, which consists of individuals, institutions, businesses, and governments, need to work together to create an open but safe global community.

Effective security management of information technology is critical to the success of a business. Security of today's networked enterprises is a major management challenge. Networked computer systems are highly vulnerable to various threats and failures, ranging from natural failure of hardware and software to misuse by information systems professionals and end users; and security weaknesses could be identified and explored in many parts of business operations and many perspectives of the organization (Bailey, Kaplan & Weinberg 2012;

Laudon & Laudon 2005, p. 523). For example the threats can be looked at from perspectives of data assets (e.g., data breach, misuse or manipulation of information, data corruption), people perspectives (e.g., identity theft, social engineering, authorization abuse), infrastructure (e.g., denial of service, botnets, network intrusion), and applications (e.g., software manipulation, unauthorized installation of software, misuses) (Chinn, Hannigan & London 2019). The explosive growth of the Internet uses by businesses and individuals has been accompanied by rising concerns of security breach and identity theft. Corporate and personal information is at a higher risk of theft and misuse than ever before as a result of the global connectedness.

However organizations have not given sufficient attention to security issues or don't feel knowledgeable about security issues (Bauer et al. 2017; Chinn, Hannigan & London 2019). According to Carnegie Mellon 2012 CyLab's global survey on how boards and senior management are governing their organizations' information assets (digital assets) (cited in Westby 2012, p.5), "57% of them are not analysing the adequacy of cyber insurance coverage or undertaking key activities related to cyber risk management to help them manage reputational and financial risks associated with the theft of confidential and proprietary data and security breaches". In addition, on top of potential legal implications (more and sophisticated regulations for protecting information and privacy are being established around the world), the reputational and financial losses arising from a breach could be significant. The results of the survey also show that the majority of organizations still lag in establishing key positions for properly looking at privacy, risk and security risks (such as Chief Information Security Officer, Chief Security Officer, Chief Privacy Officer, and Chief Risk Officer). The 2011 U.S. Cost of a Data Breach Study by Symantec and the Ponemom Institute (cited in Westby 2012, p.11) indicate that the data breach cost firms an average of US$ 5.5 million per incident, and another recent study by Ponemom Institute (cited in Westby 2012, p. 11) point out a data breach could cost organizations 17-30% loss of brand and reputation, and such damage to corporate image could take them more than a year to recover. Deloitte 2019 Future of Cyber Survey unveils that biggest impacts of cyber incidents or breaches on organizations include (in the order): Loss of revenue, Loss of customer trust, Change in leadership, Reputational loss, Regulatory fines, and Drop in share price.

To deal with various security challenges arising from the use of information technology and protect our information resources, a variety of security tools and defensive measures and a coordinated security management program are required, including hardware, software, policies, and procedures. Some security measures and tools adopted by organizations include: Biometrics (e.g., Vein ID, finger prints, Iris Scan, face recognition, speech recognition), Password, Swipe card & other tools for physical access control, Endpoint detection and response, Video surveillance analytics, Antivirus software/applications, Virtual private networks, Firewalls, Identity management and access control systems, Tokenization & Key Management, Intrusion detection systems, Online access control, Network security protocols, Data encryption, Data recovery ability, Data backup, Data loss prevention systems (for monitoring data moving on the corporate network), Regular security plan testing, Continuous vulnerability test, Security plan compliance audit, Automated control system testing, Information systems control & audit, Cyber forensics, Threat hunting, Security for IoT devices, Cloud access security broker, Cloud security policy enforcement, AI-assisted security platforms, DevOps for security, Mobile threat detection, User behavior analytics, Risk Management & Cyber Risk Insurance, Information Security Plan, Security & Privacy risks committees, and C-level positions (e.g., Chief Information Officer, Chief Security/Information Security Officer, Chief Privacy Officer, Chief Risk Officer, Chief Trust Officer) (Chinn, Hannigan & London 2019; Laudon & Laudon 2005; p.542; Laseter & Johnson 2011; O'Brien & Marakas 2011, p. 534 & 538; Telstra 2019;, The Author's own knowledge; Westby 2012). On a related note, Cyber insurance is getting popular. Meanwhile, the larger the organisation and the more sensitive of the information (e.g., information in certain government intelligence gathering agencies), the increased risk and costs of security breaches, and thus more comprehensive, systematic, integrated and sophisticated security (and privacy) measures need to be put into place. On a related note, spending on security alone can't guarantee effective security management (Choi et al. 2017), which requires sufficient funding & resources and other perspectives of security management discussed above.

Some barriers to establishing effective security defenses include (CyberEdge Group 2016; Deloitte 2019; Grosshoff et al. 2018):

- Low security awareness among employees.
- Too much data to analyze.
- Lack of skilled personnel and failure to hire talent.
- Failure to prioritize security concerns.
- Low security awareness among employees.
- Weak third-party management.
- Lack of a security-aware culture.
- Operational stress leading to weak defense.

- Data management complexities.
- Rapid IT changes.
- Inadequate governance across the organization.
- Lack of funding and budget
- Lack of management support/awareness.
- Lack of contextual information from security tools
- Poor integration/Interoperability between security solutions
- Lack of effective solutions available in the market
- Inability to justify additional investment
- Too many false positives.

Meanwhile some recommendations for enterprise security management are (Dhingra et al. 2018; Goosen et al. 2018; Grasshoff et al. 2018; McLaughlin & Gogan 2018; Ponemon Institute 2014; Poppensieker & Riemenschnitter 2018; Telstra 2019; Westby 2012, p. 26):

- Establishing a board Risk Committee for managing enterprise risks and recruit directors with security, IT governance and cyber risk expertise.
- Appointing high level security leader and establishing senior positions such as Chief Risk Officer and Chief Security Office and having dedicated budget and team/unit (for example, some firms have more than 2,000 people working in the security/risk management areas).
- Prioritizing information assets and related risks and strengthening protection for key information assets.
- Establishing strategic information security governance.
- Recognizing the weakest links among employees and third-parties.
- Investing in appropriate tools and techniques and ensuring they are used.
- Committing to share, cooperate and collaborate.
- Actively seeking for latest information security best practices.
- Keeping on reviewing regulation updates and examining the associated impacts.
- Ensuring privacy and security roles are separated and their responsibilities are appropriately assigned.
- Establishing a cross-organizational team and discuss privacy and security issues at least once every moth.
- Creating a culture of security and respect for privacy and view security and privacy as a corporate social responsibility.
- Ensuring the quality of security program by regularly reviews and taking into consideration of best practices and industry standards.

- Ensuring the security and privacy requirements to third parties and vendors and preventing them from becoming the weakest link.
- Conducting annual audit of enterprise security program by relevant committees and act on identified gaps.
- Delivering regular security and privacy reports for board and senior executives.
- Assessing cyber risks and potential loss valuations and reviewing adequacy of cyber insurance coverage.
- Allocating sufficient resources for security and privacy programs
- Performing a comprehensive security health check/audit to see how strong is our information security detection and prevention systems.
- Developing information security incidents and best practices repositories.
- Continuously improving information security policies and processes.
- Providing substantial training and awareness activities.
- Hiring industry-certified/expert security personnel.
- Establishing metrics for security and closely monitoring its performance by referring to the established metrics.
- Predicting impending threats by applying artificial intelligence applications to predict and prevent security concerns even though they could also create security concerns.
- Planning and testing responses to security issues continuously.
- Building awareness campaigns and training programs.
- Paying close attention to security concerns arising from employees' own devices for work (i.e., BYOD), Internet of Things networks, and cloud computing.

Haag, Baltzan and Phillips (2008, pp. 330–339) suggest organisations can implement information security lines of defence through people first and technology second. They point out that most information security breaches result from people misusing an organisation's information either advertently or inadvertently. Their views are supported by Laseter and Johnson (2011), who believe the root causes of many security breaches are done by insiders. Bailey et al. (2017) point out that insiders are responsible for 50% of the cyberbreaches they studied while McLaughlin and Gogan (2018) suggest that employees are the weakest link. The first line of defence an organisation should follow is to create an information security plan detailing the various information security policies. Steps to creating an information security plan include (Haag, Baltzan & Phillips 2008, p. 333):

1. Developing the information security policies

2. Communicating the information security policies
3. Identifying critical information assets and risks
4. Testing and re-evaluating risks
5. Obtaining stakeholder support.

Information systems should be periodically examined, or audited, by a company's internal auditing staff or external auditors from professional accounting firms. Such audits should review and evaluate whether proper and adequate security measures and management policies have been developed and implemented (Laudon & Laudon 2018, p.355). However companies tend to focus too much on technology and not enough on organization, process, people (Deutshcer, Bohmayr & Asen 2017).

Many of the detrimental effects of information technology are caused by individuals or businesses that are not accepting ethical responsibility for their actions. Managers, business professionals, and information systems specialists as well as end users must accept their ethical responsibilities and practice ethically. Protecting private information is an increasingly challenging and critical issue in today's networked economy. For example, a personal e-health record could include such information as: (1) demographic information (including your name, date of birth, vital statistics such as height, weight, blood pressure, and pulse rate), (2) a list of emergency contacts as well as contacts for all of your health care providers, (3) information about your health insurance, (4) a brief history of your health, along with a list of illnesses and conditions your parents, grandparents, and siblings ever had, (5) information about allergies or sensitivities to medications, (6) a dated list of significant illnesses and hospitalizations, (7) your current health conditions and how they are being treated, (8) an inventory of the medication you take, including dosages and frequency, (9) a dated list of immunizations, and (10) copies of your living will and durable power of attorney for health care, if you have them (Halamak 2009). According to one survey of Harris Poll (cited in Sadauskas 2012) looking at how comfortable consumers are with the way of Facebook, Amazon and Google are handling their personal data, 66% of survey participants were comfortable with Amazon's use of previous visits for recommendations while only 41% and 33% of respondents agree with Google's use of prior website visits for displaying advertisements and Facebook's use of private data for advertising purposes.

Ethics are 'the principles and standards that guide our behavior toward other people' (Haag, Baltzan & Phillips 2008, p. 344). O'Brien and Marakas (2011, p. 531) suggest that when making ethical decisions in business issues, managers can look at several important ethical dimensions, such as equity, rights, honesty and exercise of corporate power. Even though there are some related laws and regulations, organisations often face the dilemma of being ethical versus being legal.

Organisations strive to build a corporate culture based on ethical principles that employees can understand and implement. Policies and procedures addressing the ethical issues of the use of information technology, including ethical computer use policy, information privacy policy, acceptable use policy, email privacy policy, Internet use policy, and anti-spam policy, should be established. Haag, Baltzan and Phillips (2008, p. 348) state 'These policies set employee expectations about the organization's practices and standards and protect the organization from misuse of computer systems and computing resources'. They also point out that 'Information has no ethics' (p. 346). Individuals form the only ethical component of an information system. How they use the system, how they are affected by the system and how their use of the system affects other people is largely determined by their ethics.

One of the greatest challenges of IS/IT on individuals is privacy (Schwab 2016). O'Brien and Marakas (2011, p. 547) express the view that while the Internet is notorious for giving its users a feeling of anonymity, they are actually highly visible and open to violations of their privacy. There is a lack of tough rules on what information is personal and private. Legislation has been developed to protect individuals' privacy. For example, the U.S. has put in place the Federal Privacy Act, which strictly regulates the collection and use of personal data by government agencies. Similar laws have been enacted in many countries around the world (including Australia) to protect the privacy and rights of individuals. One of the latest development is the implementation of The General Data Protection Regulation (GDPR) in Europe in 2018. GDPR has principles such as: Lawfulness (e.g., based on consent, contract, and legal obligation), Fairness (e.g., supplying sufficient information for data practices), Transparency (e.g., providing concise and easy-to-understand information), Purpose limitation (e.g., specific, explicit, and legitimate purposes), Data minimization (e.g., only collecting necessary data), Accuracy (e.g., accurate and current data), Storage limitation (e.g., not holding data permitting personal identification any longer than necessary), Security(e.g., ensuring protection against loss, damage, and unlawful processing), and Accountability (e.g., data controller's compliance responsibility)(Chinn, Hannigan & London 2019).

Other critical information systems management issues

On top of the above mentioned issues, some other critical information systems issues include:

• Digital Divide: Today more than 70% of the world's citizens live in the societies which are just in the beginning stage of digitization (Mainardi 2012). And we have still have about 4 billion Internet non-users worldwide (more than 50% of world population) (World Economic Forum 2016, p.10). The Networked Readiness Index reflects the degree of to which economies leverage ICT for enhanced competitiveness and is measured by four dimensions of environment (political and regulatory environment, business and innovation environment), readiness (infrastructure and digital content, affordability, skills), usage (individual usage, business usage, and government usage), and impact (economic impacts and social impacts) (Dutta, Bilbao-Osorio & Geiger 2012, pp.3-7). Most of advanced economies (e.g., Sweden, Singapore, Finland, Denmark, Switzerland, Netherlands, Norway, United States, Canda, and United Kingdom are top 10 NRI countries) have high Networked Readiness Index, and many sub-saharan African countries have very low ICT readiness with main reason of insufficient development of ICT infrastructure, which still remains very costly. In addition, for Baby Boomers, Generation Y, Generation X, Generation C, So called "Digital Natives", 21st Centuriers, and beyond, what are their relations with IS/IT?. As Kleiner (2012) argues for digital generation (those under 25 and are always-on), digital channel is definitely the preferred way of doing everything, and having to go offline is viewed as an annoyance.

• Internet Governance: Open access and infrastructure sharing are likely to be the foundation for future network (Biggs et al. 2012, p. 51). Open Internet could benefit consumers (e.g., they can get what they want efficiently and affordably), businesses (e.g., they can sell products & services with profit), and regulators (e.g., they are able to protect consumers, businesses and social institutions) (Meeker 2019, p.194). Some countries (e.g., Australia, Malaysia, Qatar, Singapore) have embarked on creating entirely new national broadband networks (deploying fibre optic technology throughout the core network), and investments in those networks are huge (e.g., Australia's NBN will cost AU$ 43 billion). Currently we are in a mixed mode policy environment where self-regulation, through a variety of Internet policy and technical bodies, co-exists with limited government regulation. As Eric Smith, Former Google Senior Executive argues (reported in Manyika 2008), there will not be easy to establish international agreement on Internet governance (for example, what is appropriate or legal in one country could be inappropriate and illegal in another country) since various legal and political challenges will be involved. It is not true that the Internet cannot be controlled, in fact, the Internet can be controlled, monitored, and regulated from a central location (such as done by China, Singapore, and others) Primary questions are: (1) who will control Internet and (2) what elements will be controlled and how.

• Internet Neutrality/Net Neutrality: Currently all Internet traffic treated equally (or neutrally)—all activities charged the same rate, no preferential assignment of bandwidth. However firms such as telecoms would like to be able to charge differentiated prices based on the amount of bandwidth consumed by the content-in other words, Internet usage should be charged as the usage of other utilities such as electricity, water, gas, especially for heavy users.

• Work-life balance: nowadays the line between leisure and work has become blurred. The technologies and the networks have made the work and the home life inseparable-for example, how often do you check your mobile phone? Your email accounts? Your social network pages? Surfing the net?

• Less-human: "Nobody knows you are a dog on the web": Have we become less human and more represented only by a series of the number of 0 and the number of 1?; have the technologies and the Internet made us stupid?; have we lost our ability of writing and thinking and over relied on computing devices and the Web?; how much do you believe statements/concepts such as the Internet is a brain?; the network is a computer?; the Web is the Internet?; and the hybrid human or machine-the mix of human flesh and IS/IT?.

• Digital referencing and monitoring: One CareerBuilder survey (reported in Ferguson 2012) indicated that employers have been searching information on job applicants and interview candidates online and using such information for hiring decision. Survey respondents (from HR departments/functions) suggested they have used online information for not hiring a candidate. And the information for not hiring decision includes: 49% shared provocative or in appropriate photos or information, 45% listed information about drinking or using drugs, 35% had poor communication skills, 33% had mouthed a previous employer, and 28% made discriminatory comments. In addition, applications (e.g., Digital Mirror) are now available for organizations to model people's digital communication style and monitor their digital behaviour at work (Ferguson 2012).

• Long Tail versus Power Law: as Eric Smith, Former Google Senior Executive argues (reported in Manyika 2008) while organizations need both tails (referring to long tail theory suggested by Chris Anderson in his book titled 'The Long Tail: why the Future of Business is Selling Less for More") and heads, the majority of revenue remains in the head (e.g., core products and services for a business). He also suggests the Internet will likely follow the power law and lead to more concentration (e.g., a few major players and brands). His views are supported by Elberse (2008), who reckons organizations should focus on their most popular products and services since most of the revenue will come from them, and the niche products (in the long tail) should not be the focus unless the organization wants to satisfy the appetite of its heavy and frequent customers, who are interested in products and services in both the head and then the tail.

1.5 Emerging Trends and Future Directions

In the 21st century, organisations are facing more uncertainty than ever. Technological change is one of the primary sources of this uncertainty. Haag, Baltzan and Phillips (2008, p. 430) state that good understanding of emerging trends and new technologies can provide organizations with valuable strategic advantages. Those organizations that can most effectively grasp the deep currents of technological evolution are in the better position to protect them against sudden and fatal technological obsolescence. Some trends that will have the greatest impact on future business include (Haag, Baltzan & Phillips 2008, pp. 431–435; 435-439):

- The world's population will double in the next 40 years' mostly in developing countries.
- The population in developed countries is living longer.
- The growth in information industries creates a knowledge-dependent global society.
- The global economy is becoming more integrated.
- The economy and society are dominated by technology.
- Pace of technological innovation is increasing.
- Time is becoming one of the most precious commodities.

Ten working forces in 2020

According to research into the workplace of the future, Fredette et al. (2012, pp. 116-117) suggest ten working forces in 2020:

- Demographics: there will be five generations working side by side
- The knowledge economy: except domain knowledge, a significant more complex set of interdisciplinary skills will be required.

- Globalization: by 2020, companies will rely on global marketplace rather than domestic or even international marketplace to fuel growth.
- The digital workplace: employees will find easier to create and access digital assets of the organization.
- Mobile technology: organizations could do more via mobile (smart) phones.
- Culture of connectivity: Hyper-connectivity will result in a connectivity culture in businesses and in our personal life.
- Participation: improved collaboration and knowledge/information sharing will foster a participating society.
- Social learning: Learning 3.0 (also called social learning), which incorporates social media, gaming, real-time feedback and simulation, would be used for teaching and learning purposes.
- Corporate social responsibilities: an increased cultural intelligence and a deeper appreciation of the relationship between business and society.
- The Millennial generation: This generation has grown up with hyper-connectivity and embracing it is an integral part of their life.

Technology-enabled threats and trends

According to a recent global survey of 864 executives from different industries and regions (reported in Roberts & Sikes 2011), some technology-enabled threats to organizations include (in the order):
- Rising customer expectations (for better or differentiated services).
- Significant changes in delivery costs (e.g., delivering for significantly less).
- Developing new offerings outside the business's traditional scope (e.g., mobile payment systems).
- Significantly improved products or services (including substitutes) from competitors with existing or lower prices.
- Emergence of new channels or points of purchase.
- Increased bargaining power for customers as a result of the easy access to the information.
- Increased use of third-party computing resources/infrastructure.

The survey results also indicate measures organizations have taken or plan to take in response to continuing economic uncertainty. Those measures include:
- Increasing infrastructure consolidation or virtualization.

• Looking to information systems as a lever to reduce costs in other areas of the business.

• Focusing on efficiency improvements in application development (e.g., lean approach and process streamlining).

• Renegotiating existing vendor contracts.

• Increasing outsourcing and/or offshoring.

• Reducing demand by cancelling or deferring projects/activities.

• Rationalizing or eliminating services or/and reducing service levels.

• Changing the scope of projects to reduce costs.

Bughin, Chui and Manyika (2010) present ten technology-enabled business trends executives need to understand and respond to:

• Wide adoption of distributed co-creation: organizations need to effectively use online communities to develop, market, and support products and services.

• Making the network the organization: networked organizations need to embrace open innovation and take full advantage of the opportunities of tapping into a world of talent (e.g., accessing expertise within and outside the organization). They also need to break down silos in the organization and focus on the orchestration of the tasks rather than existing organizational structure and the ownership of workers.

• Deeper collaboration: organizations need to leverage the productivity of knowledge workers by having technologies such as video conferencing, shared workspaces, virtual teams, and virtual organizations.

• The growing Internet of Things: organizations need to utilize the ability of capturing, computing, communicating, and collaborating information at large scale in real time provided by radio frequency identification tags, sensors and similar things embedded in the devices to gain improved capabilities of information collection & analysis and monitoring & responding.

• Using Big Data for experimenting and business intelligence: organizations need to effectively collect data from various sources (especially social data), analyse data, understand the implications of the results of data analysis, and use such information for improving operations, and enhancing business performance.

• Paying close attention to Green and Sustainable information systems: organizations need to actively work on reducing carbon emission from computing facilities (e.g., by adopting virtualization technologies to reduce the number of servers, using natural air for the cooling of data centers, using renewable energy (such as hydroelectric power, wind and solar energy) for powering data centers, only using environmental friendly components to build computing devices) and using information systems for reducing environmental stress (e.g., via smart meters to better allocate energy usage, smart grids to improve the efficiency of transmission and distribution of energy, smart buildings to monitor and optimize energy uses, powerful analytic software to improve logistics and routing for planes, trains, trucks to reduce the carbon footprint of transportation).

• Wide adoption of the service model of Paying only for what you use (as per usage): organizations (large and small) could actively pursue cloud computing and outsourcing options as a result of the global connectedness and technologies for effectively organizing, monitoring, measuring, customizing and billing for computing assets.

• The age of multisided business model (e.g., generating revenue from giving something free): organizations need to leverage on the network effects and learn to create value (e.g., developing additional revenue streams and customer insights from large amount of collected data) from large traffic and large customer base developed from free services.

• Creating opportunities from the bottom of pyramid: organizations need to have the skills to identify and prosper from extreme market conditions (e.g., customer demand for low prices, poor infrastructure, hard-to-access suppliers and low cost curve for talent) by developing technology-enabled solutions (e.g., deploying mobile payment systems for African countries in which Internet access is a luxury for many people; developing B2B online platforms like Alibaba.com for buyers to source cheap products and services from low cost suppliers; virtual research and service teams by tapping into low cost talent in some developing countries).

• Using technology for government services and community support: technology-enabled solutions such as e-government, smart community, e-learning, e-health, e-police, smart water grids should be provided to the public, but it should be a joint effort of government agencies, communities, organizations and individuals.

They further suggest that only understanding and adopting these technology-enabled trends is not sufficient, organizations need to strategically work on their organizational culture and structure as well as management practices to meet these new demands. In addition, the significance and approach for fostering unfamiliar collaboration with non-traditional partners should be clearly communicated to all the parties involved.

Brynjofsson and McAfee (2012) predict four emerging technologies having a large impact on the business in the coming decade:

•   Inexpensive industry robots: better and more affordable robots will be used for industrial and life purposes.

•   Voice recognition and translation software: full-ledged digital assistants translating for us while we travel will be a reality in the near future.

•   Sophisticated automated response systems: computing devices will be smarter by learning from Big Data and in the future more machines will perform better than IBM's supercomputer Watson who beat human champions in the show of Jeopardy! In 2011.

•   Autonomous vehicles: self-moving cars (more affordable and improved version of Google's expensive prototype of self-driving car) will be common phenomenon.

Some other trends

Meanwhile some other trends include:

•   The Speed of Growth: In recent years, young tech start-ups can grow at a dizzying pace, for example firms like Groupon grow to a multiple billion firm within three years. Ron Conway (cited in Conway 2012), special advisor to SV Angel reckons that in 2012, we may see a firm developing into a US$ one billion business within 12 months.

•   The Global Grid and Data Economy: Organizations need to think about opportunities arising from the global connectedness (of course associated impacts as well). On this global grid, every company is now a global company and have the potential to leverage the power of more than 4 billion connected minds (Bisson, Stephenson & Patrick Viguerie 2010). In addition, the massive amount of data collected from the global grid will provide organizations with opportunities to establish data marketplaces and create new revenue streams (e.g., from data-based products & services (Deichmann et al. 2016).

•   Machine versus Human intelligence: even though machines will be more self-aware through machine learning & other approaches and will be smarter in the future if we keep on feeding them with Big Data and continuously improve algorithms and methodologies, human being will still be in charge of the world, as Eric Smith, Former Google Senior Executive argues (reported in Manyika 2008). The former will be good at high volume analytical and replication work while the latter will always be excel at works requiring intuition, experiences, and insights. In the organization of the future, humans and machines will increasingly have to work together in a new and effective way (Bailey, Reeves & Whitaker 2019).

- SoLoMo (coined by John Doerr, Venture Capitalist and Partner of Kleiner Perkins Caufield & Byers, reported in Kleiner 2012): Social, Local and Mobile computing is the way to go. Smart phones could connect and locate people as well as recognizing whom they are connecting to; and businesses could have more targeted advertisements as well, providing more personalized and customized products and services through social, local and mobile computing capabilities.

- Cloud Computing & Agile Development: Organizations are embarking on cloud computing and agile development as well as other flexible delivery approaches and platforms to better utilize their information systems investments; have better flexibility, quicker responses to changes, enhanced ability for information systems to scale up, better ability of disaster recovery and business continuity; and focus on their core business (especially for small and medium firms). Meanwhile in a recent global study by Boston Consulting Group (reported in Bhalla, Dyrchs & Strack 2017, p.4), 90% of managers participating in the study said that agility is crucial to the execution of strategy.

- Big Data and Analytics: It is reported that 2.5 quintillion bytes of data are generated every day (Bhalla, Dyrchs & Strack 2017, p.4). Gathering and analysing large (or very large) volume data is quickly becoming popular in organizations for reasons such as large volume data from multiple channels and from traditional and non-traditional sources (e.g., machines-to-machines, machines-to-humans, humans-to-machines, humans-to-humans), the need for better understanding customers, the tangible benefits of gaining competitive advantages (e.g., the success of Amazon, Google), better tools, techniques & algorithms, more powerful computers, more talent, and rapidly declining data storage costs (Bughin, Livingston & Marwaha 2011; The Author's Own Knowledge).

- Searchable Content Business: In today's digital economy, almost every firm is in the business of content creation, and the content (whether it is in the format of text, voice, image and video) should be searchable (e.g., users should be able to search the required information in required format(s) easily and quickly) (Berman & Bell 2011; The Author's Own Knowledge).

- Changing Concept of Mobility and Emerging Virtual Workforce: consumers' understanding of mobility has been changing from 'having a car' to 'getting from A to B' as a result of advanced digital technologies & great connectivity (e.g., making car-sharing and booking a virtual chauffeur become much easier) and the rising cost and losing time & productivity associated with road congestion (Dhawan et al. 2019). As a result of the advance in digital technologies and great global connectedness, working virtually and remotely as well as working on-demand have provided good opportunities for both employees and organizations with efficiency (Eckhardt et al. 2019; Meeker 2019).

•   Social Computing/Social Commerce: According to one study by McKinsey Global Institute (reported in Chui et al. 2012, p. 142), one third of global consumer spending could be influenced by social media. According to IBM Institute for Business Value (cited in Berman & Bell 2011), 89% of millennial generation and 72% of baby boomers use social networking sites, and the gap is closing.

•   Hyper-connectivity: By 2020, the world's 7.6 billion population will use 11.6 billion mobile devices. On top of mobile devices, the exponential growth of data from social media platforms, and Internet of Things networks are all drivers of hyper-connectivity, which has key attributes of always on, readily accessible, information rich interactive, not just about people, always recording (Fredette et al. 2012, p. 113).

•   Automation and Human Skills Remained in Demand: Automation will have huge impact on us in the future (Heltzel 2017; Manyika 2017). It is predicted nearly half of all jobs in the U.S. could be automated by 2050 (Bhalla, Dyrchs & Strack 2017, p.4). On the other hand, even though computers are getting better, more powerful and smarter, they are only good at certain things (e.g., pattern recognition, processing of large volume data, complex communications), they are still not good at many things requiring intuition, judgment, experience, and insight. Some examples include: applied math & statistics (computers can't decide what analyses to carry out and how to interpret the results), negotiation & group dynamics, good writing, framing problems & solving open-ended problems, persuasion, and human interaction & nurturing (Brynjofsson & McAfee 2012). Leading management researcher Tom Peters argues that "… for the next 20 years, we're still safe believing in the importance of face-to-face contact…" (reported in Heywood, Smet, & Webb 2014, p.7). In addition, automation will lead to jobs lost, jobs gained (e.g., via increased spending & investment on healthcare, infrastructure, energy transition and technology development and deployment), and jobs changed (e.g., changing occupations, different skills, changing workplace) (Manyika et al. 2018).

•   Responsible Computing and Green Information Systems: Responding to ever increasing challenges from artificial intelligence (AI), we are now paying more and closer attention to Responsible computing by looking at perspectives such as strengthening consumer data; privacy & security protection and establishing framework & principles for beneficial, ethical and safe use of AI & other computing technologies; and sharing best practices & keeping on innovating the way of responsibly use and deploying AI and other computing technologies (Manyika et al. 2018). A good example of responsible computing is the newly established MIT Stephen A. Schwarzman College of Computing. Green information systems are also an emerging trend. Do you know 'performing two Google searches can generate a similar amount of carbon dioxide to boiling the kettle for a cup of tea'? (Leake & Woods 2009). According to IDC (cited in Trepant, Chow & Baker 2008), U.S. firms spend close to US$ 6 billion on the power needed to run data centers and another 3.5 billion to air-condition them. Trepant, Chow and Baker (2008) suggest organizations (such as Google notably) have used alternative sources of energy (e.g., wind, hydraulic) to power their data centres and have adopted technologies (such as virtualization) to better and more utilize servers to achieve savings in energy and reduce carbon emissions. They further argue organizations should adopt an EIP (environmental impact planning) system to monitor the environmental impacts of their business activities. Green information systems (Eco-information systems) solution/approach not only reduces the costs for the organization, but also shift IT from a cost player to revenue player when more and more consumers are considering the environmental impact of the products they purchase. According to Babcock (2010, p.10), it is estimated Google could have 500,000 to 600,000 servers across its 12 international data centers; and Microsoft is building a largest data center on earth with 300, 000 servers. He also suggests energy could make up 20% of the running cost of a data center (p. xii). On a related note, it is estimated that by 2040 emissions from PCs, Laptops, monitors, smartphones, and tablets will reach 14% of total emissions, and worldwide e-waste will increase to 120 million tonnes in 2050 from 50 million tonnes in 2018 (World Economic Forum 2019).

• Mobile Computing/Mobile Commerce/Location and The Emerging Digital Finance: El-Darwiche, Singh & Genediwalla (2012) suggest that more people today have access to a mobile phone than to electricity. With more than 6 billion connections worldwide and US$ 1.3 trillion in revenue, mobile telephony has become the largest ICT industry in history and surpassed the landline Internet by more than 3.5 billion users (Dutta & Bilbao-Osorio 2012). One significant element of mobile commerce is mobile payment systems (e.g., Google's Google Wallet, Amazon's Amazon Checkout, Paypal's mobile payment systems). For factors such as the wide adoption of mobile phones and devices (especially iPads), technologies such as NFC (near field communication), QR Codes, GPS applications, Augment reality (e.g., Google Goggles, Layar, and Wikitude), the popularity of mobile applications (e.g., i-tunes and games), and the convenience of paying anytime and anywhere without waiting in the checkout line, mobile payments have become an essential part of today's networked economy. There are more than 500 million mobile phone subscribers in Africa (Mainardi 2012). According to ABI Research (reported in Van Dyk 2012), while comparing with developed economies it has much fewer banks and ever fewer ATMS, Africa is a leader in mobile commerce. Mobile banking and mobile transactions is a standard there. Kenya only started its mobile commerce program in 2007, but 20% of country's GDP are transacted via simple text messages from mobile phones. Digital finance has been having big impact on the developing world: by 2025, it will (1) create 95 million new jobs; (2) increase GPD of emerging economies by 6% (i.e., $3.7 trillion); (3) provide banking access to 1.6 billion unbanked people; (4) generate $4.2 trillion new deposits and $ 2.1 trillion new credit, and (5) deliver $110 billion annual reduction in government leakage in public spending and taxation collection (Manyika et al. 2016). Meanwhile tablet-computers are getting popular among individual and business users. According to JP Morgan (cited in The Economist 2012), driven by the popularity of iPads, the table-computer market will reach US$ 35 billion in 2012 (from virtually nothing in 2009).

• Smart City: in recent years, many smart city initiatives have been emerging and will become more and more popular in the coming years. Smart city applications cover such perspectives as: Smart water (e.g., water consumer tracking, leakage detection and control, smart irrigation, water quality monitoring), Smart waster (e.g., digital tracking and payment for waste disposal, waste collection routine optimization), Smart engagement and community (e.g., local civic engagement applications, local connection platforms, digital services), Smart healthcare (e.g., telemedicine, remote monitoring, first-aid alert, infectious disease monitoring), Smart energy (e.g., building automation systems, smart streetlights, dynamic electricity pricing), Smart security (e.g., predictive policing, real-time crime mapping, smart surveillance, disaster early warning systems), Smart economic development and housing (e.g., digital business tax filling and business registration, digital building application, digital platforms and marketplaces for sharing economy), Smart mobility (e.g., real-time public transit information, self-driving cars, smart parking, predicative maintenance of transportation infrastructure), Smart living (e.g., smart home appliances, auto-temperature control, auto-moisture control), and Smart learning (e.g., digital learning, online university, learning platforms) (The Author's Own Knowledge; Woetzel et al. 2018).

Some other emerging technologies and trends, such as Quantum Computing, Internet of Things, 5G, Artificial Intelligence, Blockchain, Digital Platforms, Business Ecosystems, will be discussed in various topics of the book.

1.6 Summary

In this Chapter, some important concepts of information systems were examined. The key distinctions between information resources and traditional tangible resources were discussed. The required information systems competence for managers was explored as well. With the increasing role of information systems in business, government, and daily life, organisations have to address critical issues of information systems (e.g., security and privacy concerns) when they develop and implement their information system solutions. Information systems can be a double-edged sword. While it can bring us many benefits (especially the Internet-enabled capabilities), it also create new opportunities for unethical and immoral behaviours. Organisations have to take steps to protect the accuracy, reliability, security and accessibility of their information resources. Finally, emerging technologies and future directions of IS/IT, which are important for the organization's sustainable growth in the 21st century, were looked at. In the next chapter, how information systems can help organisations gain competitive advantages will be disucssed.

References

Babcock, C. 2010, *Management Strategies for the Cloud Revolution: How Could Computing Is Transforming Business and Why You Can't Afford to Be Left Behind*, McGraw-Hill, USA.

Bailey, T., Kaplan, J. & Weinberg, A. 2012, 'Playing war games to prepare for a cyberattack', *McKinsey Quarterly*, July 2012, pp.1-6.

Bailey, A., Reeves, M. & Whitaker, K. 2019, 'The company of the future', The Boston Consulting Group, 05 April 2019, Online, Available at: https://www.bcg.com/en-au/publications/2019/company-of-the-future.aspx (accessed on 2 June 2019).

Bailey, T., Kolo, B., Rajapolan, K. & Ware, D. 2018, 'Insider threat: The human element of cyberrisk', *Risk*, McKinsey & Company, September 2018, pp. 1-8.

Bauer, H., Scherf, G., Tann, V. V. D. & Klinkhammer, L. 2017, 'How CEOs can tackle the challenge of cybersecurity in the age of the Internet of Things', *Advanced Industries*, June 2017, pp. 1-10.

Berman, SJ & Bell, R 2011, 'Digital Transformation: Creating New Business Models Where Digital Meets Physical', *IBM Global Business Service Executive Report*, IBM Institute for Business Value, pp. 1-17.

Biggs, P., Johnson, T., Lozanova, Y. & Sundberg, N. 2012, 'Emerging issues for our hyperconnected world', in *The Global Information Technology Report 2012: Living in a Hyper-connected World*, Dutta, S. & Bilbao-Osorio, B. eds, INSEAD & World Economic Forum, pp. 47-56.

Bisson, P., Stephenson, E. & Patrick Viguerie, S. 2010, 'The global grid', *McKinsey Quarterly*, June 2010, pp. 1-7.

Bold, W. & Davidson, W. 2012, 'Mobile Broadband: Redefining Internet access and empowering individuals', in *The Global Information Technology Report 2012: Living in a Hyper-connected World*, Dutta, S. & Bilbao-Osorio, B. eds, INSEAD & World Economic Forum, pp. 67-77.

Brown, B. & Sikes, J. 2012, 'Minding your digital business', *McKinsey Global Survey Results*, McKinsey & Company 2012, pp. 1-9.

Brynjofsson, E. & McAfee, A. 2012, 'Winning the race with ever-smarter machines', *MIT Sloan Management Review*, Vol. 53, No. 2, pp. 53-60.

Bughin, J. Chui, M. & Manyika, J. 2010, 'Ten tech-enabled business trends executives need to watch to succeed', *McKinsey on Business Technology*, Number 20, Summer 2010, pp. 4-17.

Bhalla, V., Dyrchs, S. & Strack, R. 2017, 'Twelve Forces that Will Radically Change How Organizations Work', *The Boston Consulting Group*, March 2017, Online, Available at: http://image-src.bcg.com/Images/BCG-Twelve-Forces-that-Will-Radically-Change-the-Future-of-Work-Mar-2017_tcm87-152681.pdf (accessed on 20 May 2017).

Cheng, J.Y. & Groysberg, B. 2017, 'Why Boards Aren't Dealing with Cyberthreats', *Harvard Business Review*, February 22, 2107, Online, Available at: https://hbr.org/2017/02/why-boards-arent-dealing-with-cyberthreats (accessed on 30 April 2017).

Chinn, D., Hannigan, R. & London, S. 2019, 'Defense of the cyberrealm: How organizations can thwart cyberattacks', *Podcast*, McKinsey & Company, January 2019, pp. 1-13.

Choi, J., Kaplan, J., Krishnamurthy, C. & Lung, H. 2017, 'Hit or myth? Understanding the true costs and impact of cybersecurity programs', *Digital McKinsey*, July 2017, pp. 1-10.

Chui, M., Manyika, J., Bughin, J., Dobbs, R., Roxburgh, C., Sarrazin, H., Sands G. & Westergren, M. 2012, *The Social Economy: Unlocking Value and Productivity through Social Technologies*, McKinsey Global Institute, July 2012, pp. 1-170.

Conway, R. 2012, 'Where angels will tread', The World in 2012, *The Economist*, January 2012, p. 123.

CyberEdge Group 2016, *2016 Cyberthreat Defense Report*, pp. 1-36.

Deichmann, J., Heineke, K., Reinbacher, T. & Wee, D. 2016, 'Creating a successful Internet of Things data marketplace', *FinTechnicolor: The New Picture in Finance*, McKinsey & Company, pp. 35-37.

Deloitte 2019, 'The Future of cyber survey 2019', *Perspectives*, Deloitte 2019, Online, Available at: https://www2.deloitte.com/us/en/pages/advisory/articles/future-of-cyber-survey.html (accessed on 2 July 2019).

Deutscher, S., Bohmayr, W. & Asen, A. 2017, 'Building a Cyberresilient Organization', *BCG Perspective*, The Boston Consulting Group, 9 January 2017, Online, Available at: https://www.bcg.com/en-au/publications/2017/technology-digital-building-a-cyberresilient-organization.aspx (accessed on 10 December 2017).

Dhawan, R., Hensley, R., Padhi, A. & Tschiesner, A. 2019, 'Mobility's second great inflection point', *McKinsey Quarterly*, February 2019, pp. 1-11.

Dhingra, A., Gryseels, M., Kaplan, J. & Lung, H. 2018, 'Digital resilience: Seven practices in cybersecurity', *McKinsey Digital Blog*, June 20, 2018, Online, Available at: https://www.mckinsey.com/business-functions/digital-mckinsey/our-insights/digital-blog/digital-resilience-seven-practices-in-cybersecurity (10 January 2019).

Dutta, S. & Bilbao-Osorio, B. 2012, 'Executive Summary', in *The Global Information Technology Report 2012: Living in a Hyper-connected World*, Dutta, S. & Bilbao-Osorio, B. eds, INSEAD & World Economic Forum, pp. xi-xix.

Dutta, S., Bilbao-Osorio, B. & Geiger, T. 2012, 'The networked readiness index 2012: Benchmarking ICT progress and impacts for the next decade', In *The Global Information Technology Report 2012: Living in a Hyper-connected World*, Dutta, S. & Bilbao-Osorio, B. eds, INSEAD & World Economic Forum, pp. 3-34.

Eaton, J.J. & Bawden, D. 1991, 'What Kind of Resource Is Information', *International Journal of Information Management*, Vol. 11, No. 2, pp. 156–165.

Eckhardt, A., Giordano, A., Endter, F. & Somers, P. 2019, 'Three stages to a virtual workforce', MIS Quarterly Executive, Vol. 18, No. 1, pp. 19-35.

Economist Intelligence Unit 2005, Business 2010: Embracing the Challenge of Change, Economist Intelligence Unit Ltd, February 2005, pp. 32.

El-Darwiche, B., Singh, M. & Genediwalla, S. 2012, 'Digitization and Prosperity', *Strategy + Business,* Issue 68, Autumn 2012, pp. 1-10.

Elberse, A. 2008, 'Should you invest in the long tail', *Harvard Business Review*, July-August 2008, pp. 88-96.

Enterprise Management Associates 2012, *The Industrialization of Fraud Demands a Dynamic Intelligence-Driven Response, Enterprise Management Associates White Paper*, March 2012, pp. 1-12.

Ferguson, R. B. 2012, 'The digital you at work: what to consider", *MIT Sloan Management Review*, 09/09/2012, Online Available at: http://sloanreview.mit.edu/improvisations/2012/09/09/the-digital-you-at-work-what-to-consider/ (accessed Sep 21, 2012).

Fredette, J., Marom, R., Setinert, K. & Witters, L. 2012, 'The promise and peril of hyperconnectivity for organizations and societies', in *The Global Information Technology Report 2012: Living in a Hyper-connected World*, Dutta, S. & Bilbao-Osorio, B. eds, INSEAD & World Economic Forum, pp. 113-119.

Goosen, Rontojannis, A., Deutcher, S., Rogg, J., Bohmayr, W. & Mkrtchian, D. 2018, 'Artificial intelligence is a threat to cybersecurity. It is also a solution', The Boston Consulting Group, 13 November 2018, Online, Available at: https://www.bcg.com/en-au/publications/2018/artificial-intelligence-threat-cybersecurity-solution.aspx (accessed on 10 March 2019).

Grasshoff, G., Bohmayr, W., Papritz, M., Leiendecker, J., Dombard, F. & Bizimis, I. 2018, 'Banking's Cybersecurity blind spot-and how to fix it', The Boston Consulting Group, 1August 2018, Online, Available at: https://www.bcg.com/en-au/publications/2018/banking-cybersecurity-blind-spot-how-to-fix-it.aspx (accessed on 10 March 2019).

Haag, S., Baltzan, P. & Phillips, A. 2008, *Business Driven Technology*, 2nd edn, McGraw-Hill Irwin, Boston, USA.

Halamak, J. D. 2009, 'Your medical information in the digital age', *Harvard Business Review*, July-August 2009, pp. 22-23.

Heltzel, P. 2017, '9 Forces shaping the future of IT', *CIO*, July 11, 2017, Online, Available at: https://www.cio.com/article/3206770/it-strategy/9-forces-shaping-the-future-of-it.html (accessed on August 15, 2017).

Heywood, S., Smet, A.D., Webb, A. 2014, 'Tom Peters on leading the 21st-centrury organization', *McKinsey Quarterly*, September 2014, pp. 1-9.

IDG 2015, 'The Mobile Enterprise: Is Ease of Use Overriding Security?', *IDG QuickPulse*, pp. 1-4.

Kappelman, L., Johnson, V., Maurer, C., McLean, E., Torres, R., David, A. & Nguyen, Q. 2108, 'The 2017 SIM IT Issues and Trends Study', *MIS Quarterly Executive*, Vol. 17, No. 1, pp. 53-88.

Kleiner, A. 2012, 'Brand transformation on the Internet', *Strategy + Business*, June 25, 2012, Online Available at: http://www.strategy-business.com/article/00117?pg=all (accessed July 20, 2012).

Kleiner, A. 2012, 'The thought leader interview: Bob Carrigan (CEO IDG Communications)', *Strategy + Business*, Issue 66, Spring 2012, pp. 1-8.

Laseter, T. & Johnson, E. 2011, 'A better way to battle Malware', *Strategy + Business*, Issue 65, Winter 2011, pp. 1-6.

Laudon, K.C. & Laudon, J.P. 2012, *Management Information Systems: Managing the Digital Firm*, 12th edn, Prentice Hall.

Laudon, K.C. & Laudon, J.P. 2018, *Essentials of Management Information Systems: Managing the Dgital Firm*, 15th edn, Prentice Hall.

Mainardi, C. 2012, 'Forward', in *The Global Information Technology Report 2012: Living in a Hyper-connected World*, Dutta, S. & Bilbao-Osorio, B. eds, INSEAD & World Economic Forum, p. vii.

Manyika, J. 2008, 'Google's views on the future of business: An Interview with CEO Eric Schmidt', *McKinsey Quarterly*, September 2008, Online available at: https://www.mckinseyquarterly.com/Googles_view_on_the_future_of_business_An_intervie w_with_CEO_Eric_Schmidt_2229 (accessed Aug 2, 2012).

Manyika, J., Lund, S., Singer, M., White, O. & Berr, C. 2016, 'How digital finance could boost growth in emerging economies', *FinTechnicolor: The New Picture in Finance*, McKinsey & Company, pp. 26-27.

Manyika, J., Bughin, J. Chui, M., Silberg, J. & Gumbel, P. 2018, 'The promise and challenge of the age of artificial intelligence', *Briefing Note*, October 2018 McKinsey & Company, pp.1-8.

Manyika, J. 2017, 'What is Now and Next in Analytics, AI, and Automation', *Briefing Note*, May 2017, McKinsey & Company, pp.1-12.

McLaughlin, M. D. & Gogan, J. 2018, 'Challenges and best practices in information security management', *MIS Quarterly Executive*, Vol. 17, No. 2, pp. 237-262.

Meeker, M. 2019, *Internet Trends 2019*, June 11 2019, Online, Available at: https://www.bondcap.com/report/itr19/#view/title (accessed on 18 July 2019).

O'Brien, J. A. & Marakas, G. M. 2011, *Management Information Systems*, 10th Edition, McGraw-Hill, New York, USA.

Pearlson, K.E. & Saunders, C.S. 2016, *Managing and Using Information Systems: A Strategic Approach*, 6th edn, Wiley, Danvers.

Ponemon Institute 2014, *2014 Global Report on the Cost of Cyber Crime*, October 2014, pp. 1-30.

Poppensieker, T. & Riemenschnitter, R. 2018, 'A new posture for cybersecurity in a networked world', *Risk Practice*, McKinsey & Company, March 2018, pp. 1-9.

Ramakrishna, H.V., Vijayaraman, B.S. & Quarstein, V.A. 1995, 'Executives Speak out on MBA's Competency in Information Technology', *Journal of Systems Development*, Vol. 46, No. 2, pp. 14–17.

Roberts, R. & Sikes, J. 2011, 'How IT is managing new demands: McKinsey Global Survey results', McKinsey on Business Technology, Number 22, Spring 2011, pp. 24-33.

Sadauskas, A. 2012, 'No faith in Facebook: US consumer confidence in social network plummets', *Smartompamy.com.au*, July 26, 2012, Online Available at: http://www.smartcompany.com.au/information-technology/050900-no-faith-in-facebook-us-consumer-confidence-in-facebook-plummets.html (accessed July 26, 2012).

Schwab, K. 2016, 'The Fourth Industrial Revolution: What it means, how to respond', *World Economic Forum*, 14 January 2016, Online, Available at: https://www.weforum.org/agenda/2016/01/the-fourth-industrial-revolution-what-it-means-and-how-to-respond/ (accessed on August 10, 2017).

Silver, M.S., Markus, M.L. & Beath, C.M. 1995, 'The Information Technology Interaction Model: A Foundation for the MBA Core Course', MIS Quarterly, September 1995, pp. 361–390.

Telstra 2019, *Telstra Security Report 2019*, Telstra Corporation 2019, Australia.

The Economist (2012), 'The world in figures: industries', The World in 2012, *The Economist*, January 2012, pp. 117-118.

Trepant, H., Chow, G. & Baker, E. H. 2008, 'The Eco IT Solution', *Strategy + Business*, Issue 53, Winter 2008, pp. 1-3.

Turban, E, Lee, J.K., King, D., Liang, T.P. & Turban, D 2010, *Electronic Commerce: A Managerial Perspective 2010*, International edn, Prentice Hall, Upper Saddle River, USA.

Turban, E., King, D., Lee, J. Liang, T.P. & Turban, D. 2012, *Electronic Commerce: A Managerial and Social Networks Perspective 2012*, International edn, Prentice Hall, Upper Saddle River, NJ, USA.

Van Dyk, D. 2012, 'The end of Cash', *Time*, Vol. 179, No. 1, pp. 34-35.

Westby, J. R. (2012), 'How boards & senior executives are managing cyber risks', *Governance of Enterprise Security: CyLab 2012 Report*, Carnegie Mellon University CyLab, pp. 1-28.

Woetzel, J., Remes, J., Boland, B., Lv, K., Sinha, S., Strube, G., Means, J., Law, J., Cadena, A. & Tann, V. V. D, 2018, *Smart Cities: Digital Solutions for a More Livable Future*, McKinsey Global Institute, June 2018, pp. 1-140.

World Economic Forum 2016, Internet for All A Framework for Accelerating Internet Access and Adoption, White Paper, April 2016, Online, Available at: http://www3.weforum.org/docs/WEF_Internet_for_All_Framework_Accelerating_Internet_Access_Adoption_report_2016.pdf (accessed on 20 July 2018).

World Economic Forum 2019, A New Circular Vision for Electronics: Time for a Global Reboot, Report, 24 January 2019, Online, Available at: https://www.weforum.org/reports/a-new-circular-vision-for-electronics-time-for-a-global-reboot (accessed on 1 March 2019).

Chapter 2

Information Systems for Competitive Advantages

This chapter will review competitive forces and competitive information systems strategies for gaining competitive advantages, explain concepts of value chain, co-opetition, business eco-system, and digital platforms, and discuss innovation strategy and agile organization.

2.1 Competitive Strategies

Gaining competitive advantage is critical for organisations. Baltzan and Phillips (2010, p. 16) define competitive advantage as 'a product or service that an organization's customers value more highly than similar offerings from its competitors' (in other words, you have something useful (e.g., products, services, capabilities) that your competitors do not have). Competitive advantages are typically temporary as competitors often seek ways to duplicate the competitive advantage (Baltzan & Phillips 2010, p.16). In order to stay ahead of competition, organisations have to continually develop new competitive advantages. This section discusses how an organisation can analyse, identify, and develop competitive advantages using tools such as Porter's Five Forces, three generic strategies, and value chains.

Michael Porter's Five Forces Model is a useful tool to assist in assessing the competition in an industry and determining the relative attractiveness of that industry. Porter states that in order to do an industry analysis a firm must analyse five competitive forces (Baltzan & Phillips 2010, p.17):

- Rivalry of competitors within its industry
- Threat of new entrants into an industry and its markets
- Threat posed by substitute products which might capture market share
- Bargaining power of customers
- Bargaining power of suppliers.

To survive and succeed, a business must develop and implement strategies to effectively counter the above mentioned competitive forces. Some competitive strategies include: cost leadership, differentiation, innovation, growth, strategic alliance & partnership, and speed. Meanwhile, information systems could be a critical enabler of these competitive strategies (see Table 2-1).

Table 2.1. Competitive Strategies & Roles of Information Systems

Competitive Strategy	Roles of Information Systems
Cost Leadership	Organizations can use information systems to fundamentally shift the cost of doing business (Booth, Roberts &Sikes 2011) and/or reduce the costs of business processes and/or to lower the costs of customers or suppliers (e.g., using online business to consumer & business to business models, e-procurement systems to reduce operating costs).
Differentiation	Organizations can use information systems to develop differentiated features and/or to reduce competitors' differentiation advantages (e.g., using online live chatting systems and social networks to better understand and serve customers; using technology to create informediaries to offer value-added service and improve customers' stickiness to your web site/business (Booth, Roberts & Sikes 2011); applying advanced and established measures for online operations (e.g., more accurate and systematic ways of measuring efficiency and effectiveness of online advertising) (Manyika 2009).
Innovation	Organizations can use information systems to identify and create (or assist in creating) new products & services, business models and new revenue streams and/or to develop new/niche markets or/and to radically change business processes via such initiatives as design practices (Edson, Kouyoumjlan & Sheppard 2017), lean process (Bollard et al. 2017), automation (e.g., using digital modelling and simulation of product design to reduce the time and cost to the market (Chui & Fleming 2011), and advanced technologies (e.g., artificial intelligence, blockchain, Internet of Things, cloud computing, quantum computing, big data & data analytics, virtual reality, augmented reality, 3D printing). They also can work on new initiatives of establishing pure online businesses/operations. At the same time, the Internet and telecommunications networks provide better capabilities and opportunities for innovation. "Combinational innovation" and Open innovation are two good examples. There are a large number of component parts on the networks that are very expensive or difficult to source previously, organizations could combine or recombine components/parts on the networks to create new products and services (Manyika 2009). Meanwhile everyone is connected digitally via global grid, there are plenty of opportunities to co-create with customers, external partners and internal people. In addition, in recent years, using data to create new business models and additional revenue streams has become popular. It is suggested that by 2025, the total value of the data economy will exceed

	$400 billion (Grone, Peladeau & Samad 2019), and "data is new oil' and is the fuel oil for the digital economy (Pollard et al. 2017, p. 19).
Growth (including mergers and acquisitions)	Organizations can use information systems to expand domestic and international operations and/or to diversify and integrate into other products and services (e.g., establishing global intranet and global operation platform; establishing omni-channel strategy to gain growth (omni-channel strategy looks at leveraging advantages of both online (or digital) and offline (or non-digital) channels) (Rigby 2011).
Strategic Alliance & Partnership	Organizations can use information systems to create innovation networks and enhance relations with partners via applications, such as developing virtual organizations and inter-organizational information systems. The emerging trends are establishing digital platforms and business ecosystems for collaborating and co-creating with customers, employees, suppliers and partners for growth and new revenue streams.
Speed	Organizations could utilize technology-enabled organizational models (e.g., agile organization enabled by cloud computing, big data & data analytics, artificial intelligence, drones, self-driving vehicles, robotics) to respond to the changes (e.g., stringent regulations, security concerns, economic concerns) quickly.

(Source: Developed from Barsh, Capozzi & Davidson 2008; Bollard et al. 2017; Booth, Roberts & Sikes 2011; Edson, Kouyoumjlan & Sheppard 2017; Fisher 2019; Geissbauer, Vedeo & Schrauf 2016; Grone, Peladeau & Samad 2019; O'Brien & Marakas 2011, pp.49-51; Manyika 2009; Marinoya 2019; Chui & Fleming 2011; Kimura, Reeves & Whitaker 2019; Marcante 2017; Marcante 2018; Pollard et al. 2017, p.19; Rigby 2011; Sapin & Styliandes 2019; Schwieters & Moritz 2017; Smet 2018; Sukumar et al. 2018; The Author's Own Knowledge; Xu 2014, p.131; Zipser 2019)

On top of these strategies presented in Table 2.1, companies can also adopt other competitive strategies facilitated by information systems to shape their competitive advantage. Some examples include (Chui & Fleming 2011; Geissbauer, Vedeo & Schrauf 2016; O'Brien & Marakas 2011, p. 50-52; The Author's Own Knowledge) are:

• Locking in customers or suppliers by enhancing relations and building valuable new relationships via customer/partner relationship management systems/ applications (e.g., providing a bank's customers with multiple touch points via telephones, Internet, fax machines, videos, mobile devices, ATMs, branches, the bank's agents; providing comprehensive services via digital platforms).

• Building switching costs via extranets and proprietary software applications (e.g., Amazon's user-friendly and useful B2C website and Alibaba's B2B platform) so that a firm's customers or suppliers are reluctant to pay the costs in time, money, effort, and bear the inconvenience of switching to a company's competitors.

• Raising barriers to entry through improving operations and/or optimizing/ flattening organizational structure by increasing the amount or the complexity of the technology required (e.g., Google's search engine and P & G's digitization strategy/efforts-P & G is working on digitizing almost every aspect of its operation to make it the world's most technologically enabled firm).

Co-opetition (Competition & Cooperation)

In order to succeed in today's highly competitive market, firms also should practice 'co-opetition' since not all strategic alliances are formed with suppliers or customers. Co-opetition is a strategy whereby companies cooperate and compete at the same time with their competitors, complementors (e.g., hardware and software businesses), customers, and suppliers (Pearlson & Saunders 2014, p. 65). Through co-opetition, the best possible outcome for a business can be achieved by optimally combining competition and cooperation. A good example is Covisint (before it was purchased by Canadian firm OpenText in 2017), which was the auto industry's e-marketplace and was backed up by competitors of GM, Ford, Daimler Chryslers and others. Benefits of Covisint include speed in decision-making, reduced supply chain costs, and greater responsiveness in serving customers. The downside to co-opetition is that it may be viewed as collusion. Many countries have legislation in force to deter anti-competitive or price-fixing practices. The Australian Competition & Consumer Commission (ACCC) in Australia has imposed huge monetary fines on companies and the directors of those companies found guilty of anti-competitive or price-fixing practices.

2.2 Value Chain

Another important concept and tool that can help a business identify competitive advantage and opportunities for strategic use of information systems is Porter's value chain model. The value chain approach views an organisation as a chain, or series, of processes, and it classified an organization's activities into two categories: primary activities (e.g., inbound logistics, operations, sales & marketing, customer service, outbound logistics) and secondary/support activities (e.g., administration, human resources, technology, procurement) (O'Brien & Marakas 2011, p.56; Laudon & Laudon 2012, p. 135).

The value chain helps an organisation determine the 'value' of its business processes for its customers. The model highlights specific activities in the business where competitive strategies can be best applied and where information systems are most likely to have a strategic impact. By creating/adding value and thus creating competitive advantages, information systems could contribute to each part of an organization's value chain and extended value chain (including interactions/ties with external partners and strategic alliances). By leveraging on the Internet technologies, organizations could also create a value web (Laudon & Laudon 2012, p. 137) or a hub structure, both of them look at improving the efficiency and the effectiveness of value chain and supply chain by digitally connecting customers, suppliers, and partners; by reducing the information gaps/errors along the chain (especially demand and supply); and by bettering communication, cooperation and collaboration.

Latest digital technologies provide organizations with additional ways to enhance their value chain by (Schuster, Nath & Mitjavila 2018; The Author's Own Knowledge):

• Integrating data and data analytics throughout the value chain to develop consistent and unified view.

• Effectively utilizing collected large amount of data to have deep understanding of the issues the organization is facing.

• Enhancing planning effectiveness via predictive analytics and simulations.

• Understanding the full impact of decisions on various part of value chain.

• Making data accessible to generate insights for value-added services along the value chain.

• Developing new capabilities (e.g., digital skills, data analytics expertise, agile knowledge).

• Establishing support organizational structure.

• Developing required (or new) processes.

2.3 Business Eco-systems and Digital Platforms

In today's digital era, firms need to have a more dynamic view of the boundaries among firms, customers, and suppliers, with both competition and cooperation occurring with members of the industry set (more than one industry) (Laudon & Laudon 2012, p.140). For example, car, plane, bus, train are in the same industry set of transportation. Another example is the way that traditional universities are now competing with online learning and other (traditional and non-traditional) training and development firms.

Business eco-systems refer to "loosely coupled but independent network of suppliers, distributors, partners and strategic alliances (Laudon & Laudon 2012, p. 139). They typically provide such values as: acting as gateways for comprehensive services, harnessing network effects, and integrating data across various functions and services (Catlin et al. 2018). An excellent example of business eco-systems is the mobile Internet platform; industries such as mobile device manufacturers, software vendors, online services firms, Internet services providers are working together.

Meanwhile in order to stay ahead of the competition, organizations need to actively establish their business ecosystems. For example, looking at the competition between Apple and Sumsung, it can be said that Samsung is still very much a hardware player while Apple has been developing its ecosystem and venturing into areas of hardware, software, service, content and customer support in recent years (Wagstaff 2012). So who is doing better now? In addition, the world is too big and too much complicated for any one organization to have sufficient resources to deal with and to provide comprehensive services on its own, co-creating and working with others is an effective option if not a necessary solution for any organizations (Fisher 2019; Geissbauer, Vedeo & Schrauf 2016; Ringel et al. 2019; The Author's Own Knowledge).

Business ecosystems such as Alibaba's e-commerce ecosystem, Google's Android ecosystem, Apple's iOS ecosystem have been very successful (e.g., are able to rapidly adaptive to consumers' needs and are very scalable) by decentralizing business activities across large groups of firms and individuals (Kimura, Reeves & Whitaker 2019). Some considerations when organizations are embarking on business ecosystems include: having a clear ecosystem strategy, linking your ecosystem with innovation strategy, choosing a right type of ecosystem, having monetization strategy, ensuring mutual value creation, maintaining fluidity & flexibility, building trust among partners, developing community among partners, setting up governance model, identifying suitable players, examining how the ecosystem can generate value and what value it can generate, determining the relations in the ecosystem, setting clear goals and reviewing performance regularly, and making necessary adjustments to your ecosystem strategy as per the collected data, feedback and outcomes (Lang, Szczepanski & Wurzer 2019; Ringel et al. 2019).

The latest trend is the rise of hybrid ecosystems (e.g., combining digital and non-digital ecosystems via cloud computing and Internet of Things networks) (Reeves, Ueda & Chittaro 2017).

Another concept related to the business ecosystems is digital platform. Digital platform, which provides the interface and gateway connecting with suppliers, customers and third parties, could reduce costs (e.g., transaction and search costs) and improve the efficiency & value creation of the supply chain via bringing various parts of the supply chain together, aggregating different players in fragmented industries and unlocking new value from spare resources (Xu 2014, p.131). Digital platforms could be owned by companies (typically large ones) or set up by independent third-parties (e.g., Amazon as an example for the former and Alibaba as an example for the latter). Content, community and commerce are three important attributes of successful and sustainable digital platforms (Marinoya 2019). Meanwhile many considerations for business ecosystems discussed above could apply to digital platforms as well.

Both business ecosystems and digital platforms have blurred the boundary of the organization (e.g., working with internal and external parties) and the distinction between collaborators and competitors (e.g., collaborators could become competitors while competitors could be become collaborators) (Kimura, Reeves & Whitaker 2019).

2.4   Innovation Strategy

Open innovation strategy

Open innovation emphasizes an organization's efforts of engaging and collaborating with external sources and its partners in its innovation process (Lichtenthaler, Hoegl & Muethel 2011). The telecommunication networks and Internet technologies have made the open innovation more appealing to organizations. Open innovation strategy has been adopted by many most innovative companies in the world. For example, 3M has been very successful in developing smart products via its open innovation approach: 10,000 research & development people in 73 locations from 63 full-scale operating businesses across dozens of industries work together as well as working with large number of external partners via 300 joint programs and customers via 30 customer technology centers around the world (Jaruzelski, Holman & Baker 2011).

One of the biggest barriers to promote open innovation in the organization is to do with employees' attitudes of not-invented here and not-sold-here, some strategies to deal with such attitudinal tendencies include (Lichtenthaler, Hoegl & Muethel 2011):

• Clearly communicating open innovation strategy across the organization, especially the benefits of opening up the innovation process to outside expertise.

• Demonstrating top management support: senior executives have to be champions and role models of open innovation strategy, and simply providing lip services is not going to work.

• Establishing incentive/reward systems: need to reduce the traditional emphasis on internal-only innovation process and develop both monetary and non-monetary reward mechanism (e.g., granting open innovation award, providing opportunities to work in the partner organization for some time (especially in a different location/country) for open innovation practice.

• Fostering pro-open innovation environment by working on organizational culture and structure.

One of the excellent/prominent examples or leaders of successfully implementing open innovation strategy is Mozilla Corporation, which has developed an open-source and free web browser: Firefox. It has extensively relied on external people (a broader group of volunteers) outside the firm for creative ideas, development of products, and decision making (in fact the number of outside contributors is much larger than that of internal people). What are some recipes for Mozilla's success of open innovation strategy? Michelle Baker, Chairperson and former CEO of Mozilla Corporation provide with some answers (reported in Mendonca & Sutton 2008):

• Effectively managing the mode of participation: setting up frameworks where people can get involved in a very relaxed/decentralised way; having discipline in certain areas (e.g., programming codes going into the Firefox); putting quality control process in place; clearly specifying where input is needed; giving people the feeling of ownership thus inspiring their desire for creating an open, participatory and safe Internet.

• Balancing internal people and outside volunteers: you need both groups. Without the former Firefox won't be an established force while without the latter the Firefox project won't last for long.

• Having transparent and distributed decision-making process: decision-making process is unrelated to employment status (non-employees can also take part in the decision-making process).

• Having the confidence that giving people control or voice in an elegant manner can create innovations and generate good opportunities (even revenue).

• Practising open management style: giving up some control and turning people loose (of course you need to figure out appropriate space and range) could bring in great results beyond expectation. Leaders of the organization also need to have the courage to acknowledge they are not perfect and admit when they are wrong!

At the same time, by drawing on the experiences of successful open-source innovation initiatives (e.g., Wikipedia, ATLAS particle detector, Firefox web browser, Sun Microsystems' Solaris operating systems, and others), Bughin, Chui & Johnson (2008) present suggestions for effective open innovation management:

• Attracting and motivating co-creators/contributors: organizations need to effectively understand motivations of contributors and provide the right incentives to the right people. Participants are largely interested in making a contribution and seeing it become a reality. And many contributors do enjoy non-financial rewards, such as fun, fame/recognition, and altruism. Trust and brand affinity are also important influencing factors. People generally don't want to work with brands/firms they don't trust or like.

• Establishing appropriate structure for participation: projects/problems need to be broken down into smaller ones and let contributors work parallel on different pieces.

• Having governance mechanism to facilitate co-creation: clear rules, leadership, and transparent processes for setting goals and resolving conflicts should be put in place and clearly communicated.

• Assuring quality: a quality assurance process should be implemented.

In addition, managing risks of open innovation is another critical issue. One typical risk is intellectual property (IP). Organizations need to clearly understand potential IP risks and the investments/costs associated with identified risks, and could take measures such as establishing IP sharing agreement and/or rewards/risks sharing arrangement to deal with IP issues (Alexy & Reitzig 2012; Bughin, Chui & Johnson 2008). Updating & maintaining open source codes and providing technical support to users are also important (Pearlson & Saunders 2010, p. 340). Some other factors influencing open innovation initiatives include: understanding the industry context, examining the legal and regulartory environment, implementing support processes early, establishing pro-open innovation mind-set and processes, and knowing all the contributors well (Briel & Recker 2017).

Google's way of innovation management

Google is one of the leaders in innovation management. What are some of its best practices? Google's Former Senior Executive Eric Schmidt provides us with some insights (reported in Manyika 2008):

• Believing in the notion of the wisdom of the crowd: groups make better decisions than individuals, especially when the group are selected to be among the smartest and most interesting people.

• Having different views and always questioning/challenging established ways of doing thing: how can we do in different and better ways?

• Imposing a deadline: a good combination of flexibility and discipline is required, and both of them are essential.

• Perfecting the art of encouragement: we believe "the best ideas don't come from executives".

• Providing people with time for new ideas: we allocate 20% time for people to pursue their ideas.

• Having small and undirected teams for innovation and giving people space and time for thinking and reflection: we believe "innovation always has been driven by a person or a small team that has the luxury of thinking of a new idea and pursuing it……Innovation is something that comes when you are not under the gun….".

Amazon's way of innovation management

Amazon, which developed the innovated and most successful B2C e-commerce model, is another great example of innovation management. Some things organizations can learn from Amazon regarding innovation management include (Dumont, Kaura & Subramanian 2012: The Author's Own Knowledge):

• Having business systems (that can be easily broken into simpler sub-systems) and architecture (could be organized by simply plugging in modules and components) designed for rapid product development and quick responding to changes: Amazon has been successful in venturing into different areas and dealing with huge number of customers without diminishing service quality.

• Having customer-centric mind-set: Amazon and its Zappos.com are examples of customer centric business. They provide what customers want and even beyond that.

• Having a good balance between control & speed and between vertical & horizontal integration to achieve differentiation and accelerate product cycles as well as venturing into new areas (especially adjacent markets).

Apple's way of innovation management

It could be argued that Apple's way of innovation management centres on two perspectives:
- Steve Job's innovation leadership
- User experience innovation developed through innovative product designs.

When does it make sense to be an early IS/IT adopter?

Another important and highly debated topic in innovation strategy management is when organizations should be an early adopter of new technologies. Companies like eBay (online auction) and Apple computer (software/hardware) 'got there first' and leveraged their first-mover/early adopter competitive advantage. Companies such as Citibank (ATM), Sony (video tape), Chemdex (B2B digital exchange), Netscape (Internet browser), lost their first-mover advantages to late movers. Intel (microchip) and Google (online search engine) are some good examples of companies who were later movers but gained success over earlier adopters by being the best (Turban et al. 2006, p. 592).

The first mover in an industry has the advantage of being the first to offer a product or service to the market. This can help create an impression that the firm is the pioneer or the initiator in the customer's mind. In addition this firm will be able to capitalise on the demand for the product or service until another firm enters the market (Turban et al. 2006, p. 591). However, first movers take the risk that new goods and services may not be accepted by the market. Some suggested factors that determine the success or failure of the first mover strategy include (Turban et al. 2006, p.591):
- Size of the opportunity: big enough opportunity and the company is big enough for the opportunity
- Commodity products: simple enough to offer but hard to differentiate (e.g., books and airline seats). Products such as clothes and restaurants are more easily differentiated by later movers with better features and services encouraging a switch to late movers.
- Be the best: in the long run, best-mover advantage not first-mover advantage determines the market leader, such as Apple's iPhone, Google's search engine, Amazon's e-commerce platform.

In the long term, organisations have to keep on being innovative and investing in research and development (R & D) to stay ahead of the competition or even survive in the market. And innovation is the effective way to deal with network effects and winners-takes-all phenomenon imposed by existing large players in the market (especially those large players on the Internet) (Evan & Schmalensee 2016). In fact, firms who are very active in innovation and seriously invest into their R &D are top performers. Some top spenders on R & D include: Toyota, General Motors, Ford, Volkswagan in the Auto industry; Pfizer, Johnson & Johnson, Roche Holding, Novartis, AstraZeneca, Merck in the Health Care industry; Apple, Samsung, Intel, Cisco in the Computing and Electronics industry; Amazon, Alphabet, Oracle, Microsoft in the Software and Internet industry, and Siemens in the Industrials sector (Jaruzelski & Dehoff 2008, 2010, 2011; Jaruzelski, Loehr & Holman 2012; Jaruzelski, Staack & Shinozaki 2016; Jaruzelski, Chwalk & Goehle 2018). On the other hand, it is argued the success in innovation isn't really about how much money you spend but about how you spend (you need to spend wisely so you do better with less). For example the most innovative firms identified in the 2010 & 2011 Global Innovation 1000 study (reported in Jaruzelski & Dehoff 2011; Jaruzelski, Loehr & Holman 2012 respectively) (such as in 2010 Apple (invested US$ 1,782 million/ 2.7% sales revenue into R & D activities), Google (3,762 million/12.8%), 3M (1,434 million/5.4%), and GE (3,939 million/2.6%); and in 2011 Apple (US$ 2.4 billion/2.2%), Google (5.2 billion/13.6%), 3M (1.6 billion/5.3%), Samsung (9.0 billion/6.0%) are serious about investing into R & D but they are not top spenders on R & D (such as in 2010 Roche Holding (9,466 million/21.1%), Pfizer (9,413 million/13.9%), Novartis (9,070 million/17.9%), Microsoft (8,714 million/14.0%; in 2011 Toyota (9.9 billion/4.2%), Novartis (9.6 billion/16.4%), Roche Holding (9.4 billion/19.6%), Pfizer (9.1 billion/13.5%)). Other factors influencing the success of innovation management include (Barsh, Capozzi & Davidson 2008; Jaruzelski & Dehoff 2010, 2011; Jaruzelski, Loehr & Holman 2012; Jaruzelski, Chwalk & Goehle 2018; The Author's Knowledge; Ziper 2019): innovation vision championed by senior management and supported by the people, top management's innovation skills, having innovation process (including effective management of ideas generation and the process of from idea generation to product development), alignment between innovation strategy and business strategy, pro-innovation culture, strong customer focus & customer experience orientation,, good understanding of customers via data-driving decision making, rapid investment in new technology, keeping on bringing the most innovative products to the customers, establishing innovation networks, and having an effective innovation process (including ideation, project selection, product development, and commercialization). Among these factors, top management's innovation skills and attitude are very critical one. If top leaders are not willing to and not good at innovation, then the chance of the success of organizational innovation efforts will be very slim, and they will not take the lead or do a good in developing innovation culture, establishing innovation process, and pushing the alignment between innovation strategy and business strategy.

While established brands do help organizations in the marketplace, it is the continuous innovation efforts have provided them with sustainable growth and competitive advantage. It is particularly true in some industries, such as media and publishing- many examples of failed traditional news and referencing materials publishers as a result of emerging digital content providers (e.g., Wikipedia, Google, Youtube and many others online players). Meanwhile when we are talking about innovation, we are referring not only to research & development for new products but also to changes and new things in the various parts of the business, such as business processes, customer services, marketing & sales, training & learning, talent management, knowledge management, data collection & decision-making, design of organizational structure, intra-organizational & inter-organizational communications, procurement, payment systems, logistics management, among many others.

Furthermore organizational learning (especially open learning) could be viewed as an important element of innovation, without effective and continuous learning and quick responses to market changes, organizations won't be able to have the skills and knowledge for creative ideas. It can be said that even though the success and failure of the business is a result of multiple factors including management issues (such as leadership, management experiences and skills, decision making process, investment strategies), organizational factors (such as culture, structure, processes, people's skills), changes in the industry & in the marketplace, economic conditions, the ability & commitment to continuous innovation are definitely critical to sustainable competitive advantages and long-term growth of the organization.

In fact, innovation is the source of the added-values and profits, for example Chinese manufacturers working on OEM orders typically make very slim margin while the owner of the intellectual property owner does much better. If an organization is able to make its innovation accepted as industry standard, then competitive advantages and good financial outcomes will be flowing in easily-just looking at the competition between Google's Android operation system and Apple's iOS (iPhone operating system) for mobile devices.

Furthermore when we are talking about using IS/IT for innovation, IS/IT alone won't be enough for successful innovation, and it is a joint effort of IS/IT and business (Roberts & Sikes 2011). On a related note, Kleiner (2012) argues that only a few firms (e.g., Amazon, Apple) have successfully locked down their intellectual capital (technological information), and most companies hope that the speed of innovation beats the risk of leaking information to competitors. Continuous innovation could be used for dealing with intellectual property issues.

Having an innovation culture is critical to the organization's innovation initiatives. To establish a pro-innovation culture, organizations should (Shelton 2016):

• Build Internal and external collaborations: Innovation is a team game and need the support, resources and capabilities inside and outside your organization. Is your firm ready for open innovation?

• Develop and encourage entrepreneurship within your organization: Measure and motive intrapreneurship;

• Emphasize speed and agility: Look at the speed and agility of start-ups, can large organizations do the same regarding accelerating innovation?

• Think like a venture capitalist: Need to be good at understanding the benefits and risks of the new idea, and be able to realize the expected benefits and deal with identified risks;

• Balance operational excellence with innovations: Need to be excel in both existing operations and new things.

According to The CIO Executive 2016 IT Innovation Survey (reported in McGowan 2016), some innovation barriers are (in the order): not having enough time for innovation, insufficient allocated funds for innovation efforts, scattered and not formalized innovation activities, being slow to the change, lack of vision and focus on innovation from senior management, lack of innovation activities (e.g., brainstorming new ideas), office politics, silos in the organization, and too many management restrictions & hurdles. Meanwhile some practices encouraging innovation identified from the same survey include: leadership providing & advancing innovation vision, leadership driving change, creative brainstorming sessions, specific dedicated time for brainstorming, innovation labs, innovation being part of job requirement, speeches on innovation by outside experts, innovation days, creative thinking training, and hackathon events. Other success factors include: dedicating time for innovation opportunities, partnering with other organizations, allocated innovation funds, holding innovation contests, and having a Chief Innovation Officer (Heneghan, Snyder & Symons 2017).

2.5 Agile Organization

In recent years, agile organization, which is "dawning as a new dominant organizational paradigm… the agile organization is a living organism", is becoming popular (Smet 2018, p.5). Agile organization focuses on agility, flexibility and fast response. Some characteristics of agile organization include: a network of empowered teams, rapid decision & learning cycles, effective leadership motivating people to take full ownership and perform, technology & infrastructure (e.g., cloud computing, big data & data analytics, artificial intelligence) being integrated throughout the organization to unlock value and enable quick reactions to business and stakeholder needs, and emphasis on co-creating value with and for all stakeholders (Marcante 2017; Marcante 2018; Smet 2018).

Some activities and steps of embarking on agile organization include (Aghina et al. 2019; Bossert, Kretzberg & Laartz 2018; Brosseau et al. 2019; Dias et al. 2017; Ritter & Chim 2019; Schuster, Nath & Mitjavila 2018; The Author's Own Knowledge):

• Aligning and committing to the vision and scope of agile transformation, informed by close examination of the current situations.

• Articulating agile strategy clearly and linking agile strategy with business strategy.

• Identifying how agile approach can assist in unlocking the value and designing more efficient operating model and processes (e.g., dividing the blocks of work and assigning components to small independent teams and then coordinating among teams).

• Developing roadmap for implementation.

• Conducting pilots to test the agile approach and operating model.

• Working on requirements on the core processes, people and technology to enable agility and required changes in culture and mind-sets.

• Correcting course according to data collected and feedback.

• Scaling up and rolling out agile initiatives throughout the organization.

• Deploying flexible and modular architecture, infrastructure, and software delivery.

• Enabling agile decision making (i.e., using data to inform changes).

• Establishing agile and customer-centric culture.

• Paying close attention to select and develop individuals for agile teams (e.g., looking at their motivation, their expectation of others, attitude towards customer-centric approach, and job satisfaction).

• Focusing on establishing and fostering independent teams: establishing cross-functional and autonomous teams with required experiences and expertise; providing teams with required information, technology, and resources; fostering team work by reduced unnecessary bureaucracy and red tape; defining roles and expected outcomes clearly, and providing sufficient coaching and learning time & opportunities.

Agile transformation touches on every part of the organization (including people, process, strategy, structure, and technology) (Brosseau et al. 2019; The Author's Own Knowledge):

• Workforce size and work location: Taking a mission-oriented approach to workforce sizing and location.

• Reporting structure: Simplifying the reporting structure.

• Roles and responsibilities: Limiting the interference from the central to the minimum.

• Governance: Streamlining decision-making.

• Supporting systems and tools: Ensuring the right technology to support agile approach.

• Supporting architecture: Designing the architecture based on agile requirements.

• Testing and Delivery pipeline: Automating testing to enable fast and continuous delivery.

• IT infrastructure and operations: Having the appropriate infrastructure and operations to deal with rapid changes.

• Leadership: Ensuring leaders provide vision, inspire, model and mentor rather than direct.

• Talent management: Ensuring recruiting and retaining the required talent.

• Organizational culture: Having pro-agile culture.

• Community: Developing cross-organization community and communication.

• Team: Identfying suitable teams and better team-working practices.

• Resource utilization: Developing mechanism for sharing resources for collaboration.

• Business planning and decision-making processes: Adopting continuous planning approach and data-driven flexible decision-making process to rapidly test and learn.

• Performance management: Adopting outcome-oriented and responding performance management mechanism.

2.6 Summary

In this chapter an important dimension of information systems, identifying competitive advantages and enhancing competitive strategies through information systems, was discussed. Organisations can apply tools such as Porter's five forces and value chain to analyse their competitive position, examine their competitive advantages, and identify relevant competitive strategies. Information systems can play a very important role in the success of organisation's competitive strategies. However competitive strategies alone cannot create magic. In order to meet the 'IS/IT's unmet potential', both IS/IT and non-IS/IT executives need to work hard together to have better understanding each other's areas (Roberts & Sikes 2008). The transparency in the planning and execution of information systems projects should be visible to business leaders. Accountability of information systems projects should be applied to both information systems and business parts in the organisation. In the next chapter, planning and evaluating information systems will be discussed.

References

Aghina, W., Handscomb, C., Ludolph, J., West, D. & Yip, A. 2019, 'How to select and develop individuals for successful agile teams: A practical guide', *Organization*, McKinsey & Company, January 2019, pp. 1-12.

Alexy, O. & Reitzig, M. 2012, 'Managing the business risks of open innovation', *McKinsey Quarterly*, January 2012, pp. 1-5.

Baltzan, P. & Phillips, A. 2010, *Business Driven Technology*, 4th edn, McGraw-Hill Irwin, Boston, USA.

Barsh, J., Capozzi, M.M. & Davidson, J. 2008, 'Leadership and innovation', *The McKinsey Quarterly*, Number 1, 2018, pp. 37-47.

Dias, J., Khanna, S., Paquette, C., Sood, R. 2017, 'The next-generation operating model for the digital world', *Digital McKinsey*, McKinsey & Company, January 2017, pp. 8-15.

Booth, A., Roberts, R. & Sikes, J. 2011, 'How strong is your IT strategy?', *McKinsey on Business Technology*, Number 23, Summer 2011, pp. 2-7.

Bossert, O., Kretberg, A. & Laartz, J. 2018, 'Unleashing the power of small, independent teams', *McKinsey Quarterly*, July 2018, pp.1-9.

Briel, F. V. & Recker, J. 2017, 'Lessons from a failed implementation of an online open innovation community in an innovative organization', *MIS Quarterly Executive*, Vol. 16, No. 1, pp. 35-46.

Brosseau, D., Ebrahim, S., Handscomb, C. & Thaker, S. 2019, 'The journey to an agile organization', *Organizational Practice*, McKinsey & Company, May 2019, pp.1-10.

Bughin, J., Chui, M. & Johnson, B. 2012, 'The next step in open innovation', *McKinsey Quarterly*, June 2008, pp. 1-8.

Catlin, T., Lorenz, J. T., Nandan, J., Sharma, S. & Wascho, A. 2018, 'Insurance beyond digital: The rise of ecosystems and platforms', *Insurance Practice*, McKinsey & Company, January 2018, pp. 1-13.

Chui, M. & Fleming, T. 2011, 'Inside P & G's digital revolution', *McKinsey Quarterly*, November 2011, pp. 1 11.

Dias, J., Khanna, S., Paquette, C., Sood, R. 2017, 'How to start building your next-generation operating model', *Digital McKinsey*, McKinsey & Company, January 2017, pp. 27-33.

Dumont, C., Kaura, A. & Sunramanian, S. 2012, 'The Faster New World of Health Care', *Strategy+Business*, iss. 66, Spring 2012, pp. 1-3.

Edson, J., Kouyoumjlan, G. & Sheppard, B. 2017, 'More than feeling: Ten design practices to deliver business value', *McKinsey Design*, McKinsey & Company, December 2017, pp. 1-8.

Evans, D.S. & Schmalensee, R. 2016, 'Why Winner-Takes-All Thinking Doesn't Apply to the Platform Economy', *Harvard Business Review*, May 4, 2016, Online, Available at: https://hbr.org/2016/05/why-winner-takes-all-thinking-doesnt-apply-to-silicon-valley (Accessed on November 10, 2016).

Fisher, B. 2019, 'Innovation's changing mindset: Where are you', *Forbes*, June 9, 2019, Online, Available at: https://www.forbes.com/sites/billfischer/2019/06/09/innovations-changing-mindset-where-are-you/ (accessed on 2 July 2019).

Gregersen, H. & Dyer, J. 2012, 'How innovative leaders maintain their edge', Forbes, Sep 5, 2012, Online Available: http://www.forbes.com/sites/innovatorsdna/2012/09/05/how-innovative-leaders-maintain-their-edge/?utm_source=INSEAD+List&utm_campaign=3f5cd84337-News_Alert_Most_Innovative_Companies&utm_medium=email (accessed Sep 12, 2012).

Grone, F., Peladeau, P. & Samad, R. A. 2019, 'Tomorrow's data heroes', *Strategy+Business*, February 2019, pp. 1-13.

Heneghan, L., Snyder, M. & Symons, C. 2017, 'The route to digital business leadership', *Insight*, KPMG, 7 September 2017, Online, Available at: https://assets.kpmg/content/dam/kpmg/xx/pdf/2017/09/the-route-to-digital-business-leadership.pdf (accessed on 1 May 2019).

Jaruzelski, B. & Dehoff, K. 2008, 'Beyond the borders: the global innovation 1000', *Strategy+Business*, iss. 53, Winter 2008, pp. 1–16.

Jaruzelski, B. & Dehoff, K. 2010, 'The global Innovation 1000: How the top innovators keep winning', *Strategy+Business*, iss. 61, Winter 2010, pp. 1–14.

Jaruzelski, B. & Dehoff, K. 2011, 'The global innovation 1000: Why culture is the key', *Strategy+Business*, iss. 65, Winter 2011, pp. 1–16.

Jaruzelski, B., Holman, R. & Baker, E. 2011, '3M's Open Innovation', *Strategy+Business*, May 30, 2011, Online Available at: http://www.strategy-business.com/article/00078?gko=121c3 (accessed July 12, 2012).

Jaruzelski, B., Loehr, J. & Holman, R. 2012, 'The global innovation 1000: Making ideas work', *Strategy+Business*, iss. 69, Winter 2012, pp. 1–14.

Jaruzelski, B., Staack, V. & Shinozaki, A. 2016, 'Global Innovation 1000: Software-as-a-Catalyst', *Strategy +Business*, Issues 85, Winter 2016, pp. 1-16.

Jaruzelski, B., Chwalk, R. & Goehle, B. 2018, 'Global Innovation 1000: What the Top Innovators Get Right', *Strategy +Business*, Issues 93, Winter 2018, pp. 1-24.

Kimura, R., Reeves, M. & Whitaker, K. 2019, 'The new logic of competition', *The Boston Consulting Group*, 22 March 2019, Online, Available at: https://www.bcg.com/en-au/publications/2019/new-logic-of-competition.aspx (accessed on 1 May 2019).

Kleiner, A. 2012, 'Brand transformation on the Internet', *Strategy + Business*, June 25, 2012, Online Available at: http://www.strategy-business.com/article/00117?pg=all (accessed July 20, 2012).

Lang, N., Szczepanski, K. V. & Wurzer,C. 2019, 'The Emerging Art of Ecosystems Management', The Boston Consulting Group, 16 January 2019, Online, Available at: https://www.bcg.com/en-au/publications/2019/emerging-art-ecosystem-management.aspx (accessed on 1 March 2019).

Laudon, K.C. & Laudon, J.P. 2012, *Management information systems: Managing the digital firm*, 12th edn, Prentice Hall.

Lichtenthaler, U., Hoegl, M. & Muethel, M. 2011, 'Is your company ready for open innovation', *MIT Sloan Management Review*, Vol. 53, No. 1, pp. 45-48.

McGowan, B. 2016, 'How IT Leaders can define and drive IT innovation?', *CIO*, Nov 17, 2016, Online, Available at: https://www.cio.com/article/3142322/leadership-management/how-it-leaders-can-define-and-drive-it-innovation.html (accessed on 2 November 2017).

Manyika, J. 2008, 'Google's views on the future of business: An Interview with CEO Eric Schmidt', *McKinsey Quarterly*, September 2008, Online available at: https://www.mckinseyquarterly.com/Googles_view_on_the_future_of_business_An_interview_with_CEO_Eric_Schmidt_2229 (accessed Aug 2, 2012).

Manyika, J. 2009, 'Hal Varian on how the Web challenges managers", *McKinsey Quarterly*, January 2009, Online available at: https://www.mckinseyquarterly.com/Strategy/Innovation/Hal_Varian_on_how_the_Web_challenges_managers_2286 (accessed July 23, 2012).

Marcante, J. 2017, 'This transformation model enables Vanguard IT to increase speed and innovation', *The Enterprise Project*, January 12, 2017, Online, Available at: https://enterprisersproject.com/article/2016/11/transformation-model-enables-vanguard-it-increase-speed-and-innovation (accessed on 10 June 2018).

Marcante, J. 2018, 'Is what you're doing "true" agile?', *The Enterprise Project*, November 27, 2018, Online, Available at: https://enterprisersproject.com/article/2018/11/what-youre-doing-true-agile (accessed on 2 February 2019).

Marinoya, P. 2019, 'Mary Meeker makes first investment out of bond capital', *Fortune*, May 21, 2019, Online, Available at: https://fortune.com/2019/05/21/mary-meeker-canva-bond/ (accessed on 2 July 2019).

Mendonca, L. T. & Sutton, R. 2008, 'Succeeding at open-source innovation: An interview with Mozilla's Mitchell Baker', *McKinsey Quarterly*, January 2008, pp. 1-8.

O'Brien, J. A. & Marakas, G. M.2011, *Management Information Systems*, 10th Edition, McGraw-Hill, New York, USA.

Pearlson, K. E. & Saunders, C. S. 2010, *Managing and Using Information Systems: A Strategic Approach*, Fourth Edition, John Wiley & Sons, USA.

Pearlson, K.E. & Saunders, C.S. 2013, *Managing and using information systems: A strategic approach*, Fifth Edition, John Wiley & Sons, USA. Pollard, S., Rajwanshi, V., Murphy, M. R., Auty, S., Huang, T. T., Anmuth, D., Yao, A., Hariharan, G., Willi, A. & Coster, P. 2017,

An Investor's Guide to Artificial Intelligence, Global Equity Research, J.P. Morgan, 27 December 2017, pp. 1-112.

Reeves, M., Ueda, D. & Chittaro, C. 2017, 'Getting physical: The rise of hybrid ecosystems", The Boston Consulting Group, 15 September 2017, Online, Available at: https://www.bcg.com/en-au/publications/2017/business-model-innovation-technology-digital-getting-physical-rise-hybrid-ecosystems.aspx (accessed on 10 December 2018).

Rigby, D. 2011, 'The Future of Shopping", *Harvard Business Review*, December 2011, pp. 65-76.

Ringel, M., Grassl, F., Baeza, R., Kennedy, D., Spira, M. & Manly, J. 2019, 'The Rise of AI, Platforms, and Ecosystems', *The Most Innovative Companies in 2019*, The Boston Consulting Company, pp. 1-18.

Ritter, D. & Chim, L. 2019, 'Why Agile Works', *The Boston Consulting Group*, 29 April 2019, Online, Available at: https://www.bcg.com/en-au/publications/2019/why-agile-works.aspx (accessed on 2 June 2019).

Robert, R & Sikes, J 2008, 'McKinsey global survey results: IT's Unmet potential', *McKinsey Quarterly*, November 2008, pp. 1–9.

Roberts, R. & Sikes, J. 2011, 'How IT is managing new demands: McKinsey Global Survey results', *McKinsey on Business Technology*, Number 22, Spring 2011, pp. 24-33.

Sapin, D. & Stylianides, G. 2019, 'Innovation at a crossroads: Restoring trust in technology', *Risk Insights, PwC Blogs*, 01 March 2019, Online, Available at: https://pwc.blogs.com/resilience/2019/03/innovation-at-a-crossroads-restoring-trust-in-technology-.html (accessed on 10 June 2019).

Schuster, R., Nath, G. & Mitjavila, L. 2018, 'Transforming value chains in process industries with digital and AI', *The Boston Consulting Group*, 23 October 2018, Online, Available at: https://www.bcg.com/en-au/publications/2018/transforming-value-chains-in-process-industries-with-digital-and-ai.aspx (accessed on 1 February 2019).

Schwieters, N. & Moritz, B. 2017, '10 principles for leading the next industrial revolution', *Strategy+Business*, Issue 88, Autumn 2017, pp.1-12.

Smet, A. D., 2018, 'The agile manager', *McKinsey Quarterly*, July 2018, pp.1-6.

Shelton, R. 2016, 'These Five Behaviours Can Create an Innovation Culture', *Strategy+ Business*, S+B Blogs, June30, 2016, Online Available at: http://www.strategy-business.com/blog/These-Five-Behaviors-Can-Create-an-Innovation-Culture?gko=85549 (accessed on October 20, 2016).

Sukumar, N., Cleary, S., Voelkel, M., Rohrig, M., Rouhana, R. & Schaette, C. 2018, 'FINTECH DECODED: Capturing the opportunity in capital markets infrastructure', *Global Banking Practice*, McKinsey & Company, March 2018, pp. 1-28.

Turban, E., King, D., Viehland, D. & Lee, J. 2006, *Electronic Commerce 2006: A Managerial Perspective*, International edn, Prentice Hall, Upper Saddle River, NJ.

Wagstaff, J. 2012, 'Samsung challenge: sold the phone, how to keep the customer', *Reuters*, Online Available at: http://www.reuters.com/article/2012/09/06/us-samsung-ecosystem-idUSBRE8841J520120906?feedType=RSS&feedName=technologyNews&utm_source=feedburner&utm_medium=feed&utm_campaign=Feed%3A+reuters%2FtechnologyNews+%28Reuters+Technology+News%29 (accessed on Sep 12, 2012).

Xu, J. 2014, *Managing Digital Enterprise: Ten Essential Topics*, Atlantis Press & Springer.
Zipser, D. 2019, 'How China's largest online travel agency connects with the world: An interview with Ctrip CEO Jane Sun', *Consumer Package Goods & Retail Practices*, McKinsey & Company, *February 2019*, pp. 1-6.

Chapter 3

Information Systems Strategy and Investment

This chapter will discuss the importance of alignment between information systems strategy and business strategy, argue the importance of evaluating the performance of information systems initiatives/investments, describe metrics for measuring performance of information systems initiatives/investments, present methods for information systems investment justification, discuss difficulties associated with justifying information systems investments, and look at digital transformation.

3.1 Information Systems Strategy

Business goals and information systems plans need to be aligned. Information systems plans need to align with business goals and support those goals, especially in the environment where technologies are changing rapidly and uncertainty is common phenomenon in the market. Some benefits of doing so are (McNurlin & Sprague 2004, pp. 116–117):

• A good planning process helps organisations learn about themselves and promote organisational change and renewal.

• Managing information systems requires planning for changes in business goals, processes, structures, and technologies.

• Good information systems planning can greatly assist organisations' efforts in strategic use of information systems for competitive advantage

• Many information systems projects in organisations have not been successful. One of the important reasons is the lack of proper planning for them.

However IS/IT planning is not an easy task. Some reasons are (Judah et al. 2016; McNurlin & Sprague 2004, pp. 116-117; Overbuy 2017; Zetlin 2018):

• Technologies are rapidly changing: Generally speaking, strategic planning practices tend to evolve slowly while technology is changing rapidly. How should you plan when information technologies are changing so rapidly? The fast pace of technological change makes the alignment between IT and Business difficult as well.

- There are confusions between strategic planning and budgeting.
- Strategic planning is only done by the senior management without the input from people on the front line interacting with customers directly.
- Companies need portfolios rather than projects: How can they fit into other projects? How can they balance the portfolio of projects?
- Responsibility needs to be joint: Business planning could be business plan mainly, but it should be IT-informed Business Strategy.
- A balanced approach is needed: a balance is needed between (1) top down approach and bottom-up approach and (2) between radical change and continuous improvement.
- CIO needs to part of senior management and ideally reports directly to the CEO, and he/she has significant involvement and influence in business strategy.
- CIOs need to communicate more effectively. Some IT leaders lack the communication skills.
- Business managers may not recognize the importance of technology in the ever changing environment (i.e., business is running on top of the technology).
- Organizations traditionally are not effective at Business and IS/IT strategy and planning. According to Gartner's 2017 CIO Survey, 23% of respondents indicated that their organizations are effective or very effective in business strategy and planning while 29% suggested that their organizations are effective or very effective in IS/IT strategy and planning. The biggest challenge is how IS/IT leaders can feel comfortable with business strategy and can develop IS/IT strategy around business strategy.

McNurlin and Sprague (2004, p. 118) state that traditionally strategy formulation has followed a linear process, where (1) business executives created a business plan that described the directions of the business;(2) information systems executives could then develop an information systems strategic plan responding to how information systems would support the business plan; and (3) following that an implementation plan was created to address the details of implementation.

McNurlin and Sprague (2004, p. 118) further point out that nowadays the Internet and other technological advances require changing some assumptions that were made about information systems strategy formulation:

- The future cannot be predicted: who predicted the Internet, Amazon, eBay, and Google?

- Information systems do not just support the business anymore: they are an essential platform for and an integral part of the business.
- Top management may not know best: need to look at both internal and external expertise.
- An organisation is not like an army: the industrial era metaphor is not relevant any more.

The new information systems strategic planning process should be a two-way street where, on the one hand, information systems align with business strategies and support planned business operations, while on the other hand information systems also have impacts (or inject input) on the making of business strategy (e.g., by demonstrating information systems-based capabilities and predicting emerging technologies and trends before business strategy is made) (McNurlin & Sprague 2004, p.119). Information systems and the business should stay together rather than the conventional practice of business first and information systems second.

Information systems strategy development should involve business managers while corporate strategy planning should have the input from information systems operation/function. Managers should be educated and be keen in understanding capabilities of new technologies/systems and emerging trends and future directions of information systems, and information systems staff should step into the role of "Business Strategist" (Copper & Nocket 2009). In addition, another critical point for information systems success in the organizations (especially large organizations) is head of information systems operation/function (e.g., chief information officer) should be a member of senior executive team of the organization and most importantly he/she should have a say to the development of business strategies of the organization. Furthermore, organizations need to distinguish strategic and non-strategic dimensions of information systems (Boochever, Park & Weinberg 2002): information systems infrastructure (e.g., telecommunication networks, network management) are essential but non-strategic information systems while applications such as enterprise resource planning systems, customer relationship management systems, knowledge management systems and supply chain management systems are strategic information systems.

Furthermore, traditional planning at 'start of year' is not good enough anymore. In response to the rapid changes in the market and dramatic advancement in technology, McNurlin and Sprague (2004, p. 116) suggest that there is a need for continuous planning, where a best-available vision of the future upon which to base current decision making is first developed. In other words, a rolling plan you make changes to as needed, should be adopted (Bradley, Hirt & Smit 2018). They also point out advanced technology groups should be formed to monitor technology trends and recommend suitable new technology to the organization. In large organisations there is also a trend for Chief Information Officers (CIOs) to be part of senior management. Meanwhile the traditional top-down approach of making information systems strategy is becoming more and more irrelevant in the current business context, and both top-down and bottom-up (elements are essential in achieving effectiveness of IS/IT planning.

Some other suggested considerations when organization are working on their strategic planning include (Barrows 2009; Dye & Sibony 2007; Judah et al. 2016; Perkin 2019; The Author's Own Knowledge):

• Starting with the issues: Identifying the key issues with rigorous analysis and research.

• Allowing time for big picture & planning and going through appropriate process.

• Securing full commitment from senior management.

• Engaging with the right people and allowing open communication: Involving most knowledgeable and influential people across the organization and encouraging open and honest communication regardless of their positions in the organization.

• Ensuring the input from people on the front line is sought and seriously considered.

• Designing tailored planning approach to suit the needs of each business.

• Linking strategic planning with strategic execution.

• Documenting strategic planning activities and outcomes properly.

• Implementing a strategic performance management system to track and monitor the execution of strategic initiatives.

• Integrating human resources systems into the strategic plan to evaluate and compensate people's performance accordingly.

O'Brien and Marakas (2011, p. 584) suggest a business/information systems planning process, which emphasises a customer and business value focus for developing business strategies and models before information systems strategies and an information systems architecture are developed. They also suggest that components of Business/Information Systems Planning include:

(1) Strategy development: establishing business strategies that support business vision.

(2) Resource management: designing strategic plans for managing or outsourcing information systems resources.

(3) Information Technology Architecture: making strategic information systems choices that reflect a computing architecture designed to support business/information systems initiatives. Architecture includes:

' Technology platform. including networks, computer systems, system software and integrated enterprise application software.

• Data resources: consisting of operational and specialised databases.

• Applications architecture: integrated architecture of enterprise-wide systems.

• Information systems organization: organisational structure and management of the IS function.

Assessing the quality of information systems strategy

That following a good approach to develop information systems strategy is not sufficient to ensure the ultimate success of well-planned information systems strategy. Good execution is another critical factor, and in fact it can be argued (at least to some extent) sometimes a good execution of third-grade strategy is better than poor execution of first-grade strategy. Another important dimension, which has not been well exposed and practiced, is how to assess the quality of information systems strategy-in other words, many executives have no clear idea of how they can know whether their organizations have a good/strong information systems strategy. Booth, Roberts and Sikes (2011) has contributed in this area by proposing a set of ten tests/questions to help executives (information systems and non-information systems) to judge the quality and rigor of their information systems strategy and plans. Their recommended tests/questions are:

1. Are information systems focusing on beating the competition OR just keeping the lights on (for immediate operational needs and meeting the near-term demands of business units)?

2. Do information systems take a systematic and granular view of required capabilities across the whole organization (e.g., understanding critical business processes and delivery demands for different business units and working on synergies across the firm) OR simply assume every part of the business has the same needs?

3. Does information systems strategy take into consideration of potential technology disruptions and emerging trends Or simply stick to the old assumptions?

4. Does information systems strategy factor in flexibility in staffing and budgeting to meet unforeseen situations/changes Or is simply developed from false precision and overcommits to existing programs?

5. Does information systems strategy take a long term view and look at establishing a portfolio including both near-term, well understood projects and larger efforts with potential future value Or is locked into a fixed plan with limited ability to responding changes?

6. Can information systems strategy be effectively translated into clear actions and required resources Or simply sets on vague and non-actionable statements?

7. Does information systems strategy clearly involves non-information systems investments (e.g., process redesign, training, system deployment, change management) Or Does it take an "information systems only" stance?

8. Does information systems strategy win the support of all major stakeholders (internal and external) Or Is it simply pushed by information systems function and/or top management (If information systems strategy has not been discussed and shared with internal (e.g., different business units) and external stakeholders (e.g., partners and customers))?

9. Does information systems strategy pay sufficient close attention to soft factors influencing the success of information systems (e.g., people, relations, structure, culture, management support) Or Does it simply focus on technical issues?

10. Does information systems strategy aim at actively reducing complexity and moving to a simpler and more flexible architecture Or Does it allow the complexity to looks after itself (hope it can fade away automatically)?

3.2 Measuring the Success of Information Systems Initiatives/Investments

When organisations can gain benefits from investing in information technology (Stiroh 2001), there is also a need for organisations to routinely analyse efficiency and effectiveness metrics to measure the performance of information systems projects and justify their information systems investments. The costs of information systems projects have been climbing, many expensive information systems projects have not been completed successfully (typically over the budget and behind the schedule), and many business leaders have perceived information systems as a "blackbox" for investment (Cooper & Nocket 2009) and/or as a pure cost center: a necessary evil for running the business (Alvarez & Raghavan 2010). The worries of business leaders for information systems investments are reasonable, especially given the large scale of annual information systems investments (for example, according to Gartner (cited in Alvarez and Raghavan 2010), in 2009 the worldwide corporate information systems investments were more than US$ 1.3 trillion).

There is an old saying that: 'If you cannot measure it, you cannot manage it'. According to Turban et al. (2006, p. 603) through systematic assessment of their strategic initiatives, organisations can:

(1) Ensure their strategic initiatives are delivering what they are supposed to deliver and apply corrective actions,

(2) Determine if their strategic initiatives are still viable in the current environment,

(3) Reassess the initial strategy and projects and improve future strategic planning,

(4) Identify failing initiatives and projects and causes as soon as possible and avoid the same mistakes/problems for future initiatives/projects.

Meanwhile through effectively managing IS/IT investment benefits, organizations can also achieve such benefits as: (1) better planning, (2) improved relationship between IS/IT and business, (3) better IS/IT investment decisions, and (4) increased realized benefits from IS/IT investments (Peppard, Ward & Daniel 2007). Haag, Baltzan and Phillips (2006, p. 486) point out that by quickly confirming success or immediately identifying corrective actions needed, metrics provide feedback to the firm and can assist senior managers in making better strategic decisions. In the meantime, companies also need to assess the success of information systems projects after they have been completed.

In order to measure the performance of information systems, organisations need to create a set of metrics. Efficiency metrics and Effectiveness metrics are two primary types of information systems measurement metrics. Efficiency metrics focus on technology (e.g., throughput, speed, availability, accuracy, Web traffic, and response time) while effectiveness metrics deal with the impact technology has on business processes and activities, concentrate on an organisation's goals, strategies, and objectives (e.g., usability, customer satisfaction, conversation rates and financial metrics) (Haag, Baltzan & Phillips 2006, pp. 30–31). Equipped with effectiveness and efficiency metrics, organizations could constantly review information systems projects and take actions accordingly (including terminating a project if it does not meet the established/agreed metrics).

3.3 Justifying Information Systems Investments

There is an increased demand for financial justification of investing in information systems projects. In many businesses, information systems are a significant part of the annual budget (Pearlson & Saunders 2004, p. 223; Pearlson & Saunders 2010, p. 292). Organisations also don't want to be pushed into buying information systems by the vendors, and they want to spend on information systems projects which can actually produce value. Furthermore, the majority of the businesses will ask their information systems executives to demonstrate the potential value, payback or budget impact of their information systems projects (Pearlson & Saunders 2010, p. 292; Pearlson & Saunders 2004, p. 223). As a result, there exists a clear need to understand and demonstrate the true return of information systems projects.

However measuring and addressing accountability is difficult. Some reasons identified by Pisello (2004) reported in Turban et al. 2006 (p. 621) include: (1) many company executives lack the knowledge or tools to do return of investment (ROI) calculations; (2) there is a lack of formal processes or budgets in place for measuring ROI; and (3) many company executives do not measure how projects coincide with promised benefits in a timely manner. In addition, very often companies have to make tough decisions on selecting appropriate information systems projects due to funding and resources constraints. Analysis is needed to determine whether funding for information systems investments is appropriate. And in some large companies, and in many public organisations, a formal evaluation of requests for funding of information systems projects is mandated (Turban et al. 2006, p. 621).

The five financial metrics of (1) Net present value (NPV- the present value of the stream of net (operating) cash flows from the project minus the project's net investment); (2) Internal rate of return (IRR-the rate at which the NPV of an investment equals zero); (3) Return on investment (ROI–indicates the earning power of a project and is measured by dividing the benefits of a project by the investment); (4) Payback period (PB–the period of time required for the cumulative cash inflows from a project to equal the initial cash outlay; and (5)Total cost of ownership (TCO–including direct and indirect costs, incurred throughout the life cycle of an asset, including acquisition, deployment, operation, support, and retirement)(Haag, Baltzan and Phillips (2006, pp. 487–492), can be used to justify the information systems investments. Gunasekaran et al. (2001) propose that when organisations are deciding on information systems projects, five areas should be addressed:

• Strategic considerations: including strategic objectives of information systems investments, support for corporate strategy, top management support, competitive performance objectives, long term costs and benefits.

• Tactical considerations: including performance indicators, data generation, evaluation methods, security, and senior managers' involvement.

• Operational considerations: including existing information systems, data migration, software, users' attitude, servers, system integration.

• Intangibles: including competitive advantages, services to society, job enrichment, quality improvement, enhanced relations, happier customers, teamwork, and good image.

• Tangibles: including financial dimension such as budgets, ROI, revenue, profit, margin and non-financial dimensions such as lead-time, inventory, labour absence, product, defective rates, set-up time.

Alvarez and Raghavan (2010) suggest a very useful roadmap/process/ framework of managing information systems investments, which consists of four steps:

• Identifying required information systems capabilities for supporting organizational strategic priorities/objectives.

• Prioritizing information systems projects as per two criteria of strategic importance and value potential for the investment (e.g., improved performance, reduced costs). By applying these two criteria (we can depict them in two dimensions), there are four types of information systems investments: (1) invest to keep the lights on (low strategic importance and low value potential); (2) invest to sustain high strategic importance and low value potential); (3) invest to refine (low strategic importance and high value potential); and (4) invest to grow (high strategic importance and high value potential). Even though invest to grow is the desirable situation, in reality organizations need to have a balanced portfolio including different types of IS/IT investments to achieve a balance between survival and sustainable growth. The emphasis of matching IS/IT projects with strategic direction and objectives can be seen as taking the approach of demand (for IS/IT) management approach (Cooper and Nocket 2009).

• Deciding the sequence of investment and associated activities (and the flow/plan of the associated activities).

• Working out required support for the approved investment (e.g., cultural & structural fit, top management support).

Zhu (2013) recommends a set of evaluation methods:

• IT Cost Breakdown: IT savings (IT work positively impacting the bottom line); Expenses as % of sales; IT spend per employee; IT employees as % of total employees; Uptime% for business critical system; Customer service% of positive responses; Utilization of key IT managed resources; Total cost of IT; IT ROI Ratio (net operating revenue-(total expenses-total cost of IT))/total cost of IT); and Return on IT investment (net operating profit/total cost of IT).

•   IT Performance Quadrants: Customers (e.g., Customer's advocacy of IT function, Customer satisfaction of service desk, Lead time to ship an order, %of Support customer called fixed at the first call or before a call(self-healing), %of order returns, Time to make a new offering, %of business suppliers linked to your IT); IT Service/Project Performance (e.g., Projects delivered on time, Projects developed on time and budget, Adherence/defects in controls and compliance (e.g., SOX, PCI)); Fiscal Health (e.g., Average cost, Balanced Budget, effective and measurable IT Service Chargeback system); and Organizational Capacity (e.g., Turn-over, Absenteeism, Engagement, Learning & Development).

•   PMO (Project Management Office) KPIs: Every IT project is a business project. Question 1: If I own this company, what do I like to see from my IT department?; Question 2: How much IT budget is spent on (1) keeping the current situation, (2) doing business better, and (3) growing business? Some measures include: ROI of PMO (the influence of the PMO on the business performance); Time to market of PMO (the speed at which projects are delivered); and Resource Utilization of PMO (e.g., IT Spend per employee, Employee customer satisfaction, % of Projects in IT Budget versus Run, IT Maturity Level, and IT R & D spending).

•   Business/IT Capabilities: IT Capabilities to enable business growth (e.g., Improving speed/agility, Improving revenue, Reducing risk, and Reducing cost); Change Capability (e.g., Effectiveness and efficiency of People Change, Process Change, and Technology Change); Value-added Capabilities (e.g., Transparency, Efficiency, Effectiveness, Agility, Digital Capability, Innovation Capability, Flexibility, Scalability, and Monitoring & Control); and Business Capabilities from Multiple Perspectives (e.g., People, Process, IT Investment and longevity of Investment, Technology (e.g., usefulness and user friendliness), Governance (e.g., looking at both Evaluation, Scope and Monitoring at the governance level) and Run, Build, Deploy & Monitor at the tactical management level)).

Another important aspect of managing information systems investments is benefit realization management for reasons such as clearer and better information systems planning, improved relations between business and information systems, wiser information systems investments, and increasing the benefits realized from information systems investments (Peppard, Ward & Daniel 2007). One essential element of benefit realization of information systems investments is developing an effective benefit realization strategy and successfully implementing benefit realization process (Blick & Quaddus 2003).

Reasons suggested by Turban et al. (2006, pp. 624–627) for the difficulties in measuring and justifying information systems investments include:

1. Difficulties in measuring productivity and performance gains:

•   Data and data analysis may hide the productivity gains. It is more difficult to measure (e.g., defining input and products) the gains in service industry than in manufacturing industry. And most of the time, the benefits of information systems projects are less tangible than manufacturing products or building plants.

•   Productivity gains may be offset by losses in other areas, such as online sales gains may be offset by losses of offline sales.

•   What should be measured is incorrectly defined, for example, productivity gains may not be the same as profit gains.

•   Information systems projects may take a few years to show results but many studies do not allow for such a time frame.

2. Difficulties in relating information systems expenditures to organisational performance: Soh and Markus (1995) present a process to examine the relationship between information systems investment and its impact on organisation:

•   The relationship between investment and performance is indirect and follow the direction of Information Systems Expenditure>>Information Systems Assets>>Information Systems Impacts>>Organizational Performance.

•   Factors such as shared information systems assets and how they are used can impact organisational performance and make it difficult to assess the value of information systems investments.

3. Difficulties in measuring costs and benefits:

•   Many costs and benefits of information systems projects are difficult to quantify, especially those intangible costs and benefits. At the same time, information systems are too deeply embedded in most business processes. It is very hard to isolate and measure information systems as a separate element. Meanwhile nowadays many systems are very complex with multiple layers of hardware, software and networks across various functions and different geographic locations.

Another potential difficulty is the mismatch between company timelines. Strategic planning generally spans one to five years whilst financial planning (working on budgets) just looks at the next financial year. The benefits of information systems projects can be expected over several years or even the entire life of the project. A further difficulty in justifying information systems investments is the knowledge that within a few years of the implementation, new systems will make present information systems investments outdated.

Organizations thus need to pay close attention to market changes and emerging trends and technologies. Turban et al. (2006, p. 622) also point out that justification may not be necessary when (1) the value of the investment is relatively small for the organisation; (2) the relevant data are not available, inaccurate, or too volatile; and (3) the project is mandated – it must be done regardless of the costs and benefits involved (e.g., requested by regulations and laws).

3.4 Digital Transformation

Digitization and its impact

We are in the digital economy in which digitization is essential part of the way we live, work and conduct the business. In line with the potential opportunities and the rapid development of digitization, many organizations have set up designated position for their digitization efforts, such as Head of Strategy & Programs for Digital Innovation, Philips; EVP, Digital Strategy & Emerging Business, Discovery Communications; VP, Digital Banking Strategy, Wells Fargo; EVP, Digital Media, BET Networks; VP, Digital Strategy, BAE Systems; VP, Digital Marketing & Media, GSN; Director, Digital Marketing & Communication, PBS; VP, Innovation, Deutsche Telelkom; VP, Digital, Technology R & D, UFC; VP, Digital Strategy, Dell; CTO, Digital Operations, Education Week; VP, Audience Insights, TiVO; Director, Digital Strategy, Rodale Grow; Director, Online Strategy & Media, The Story Stuff Project; Global Head of Social Media, Bloomberg; among many others.

According to a research conducted by consulting firm McKinsey (cited in Hazan, Manyika & Pelissie du Rausas 2011), from 2005 to 2009, the Internet is accounted for 21% of combined GDP growth of nine developed economies (including Sweden, Germany, United Kingdom, France, South Korea, United States, Italy, Canada, and Japan). Organizations need to actively look for opportunities unlocked by the Internet and digital technologies, such as reinventing business models to leverage the global connectedness, exploring emerging Internet-related trends and technologies (e.g., the Internet of Things, Cloud Computing, Big Data & Data Analytics, Artificial Intelligence) to improve the efficiency of business operations, and embrace new and flexible organizational structure via linking with employees, customers, suppliers and business partners (Hazan, Manyika & Pelissie du Rausas 2011).

The IBM 2010 Global CEO study (cited in Berman & Bell 2011, p.1) identified technology was second only to market factors as a force for change. According to IBM Institute for Business Value (cited in Berman & Bell 2011, p. 2), evolution of digital transformation has so far gone through three stages:

• Stage 1 (from late 1990s): digital products (e.g., music, entertainment) and infrastructure (e.g., telecommunications, software, information systems).

• Stage-2 (around 2000s): digital distribution and web strategy (e.g., e-commerce, online services).

• Stage-3 (around 2010s): mobile revolution, social media, hyper digitization, and power of analytics.

They also suggest nowadays people are using mobile devices and interactive tools to decide who to trust, where to go and what to buy. They have been increasingly empowered by the capability and convenience of accessing information anytime and anywhere, their expectations have risen dramatically, and they have now become the primary force behind digital transformation across industries.

Reported in El-Darwiche, Singh & Genediwalla (2012), in 1990, there were 100 million PCs worldwide, 10 million mobile phone users, and less than 3 million Internet users; but by 2010 there were 1.4 billion personal computers, 5 billion mobile phone users, and 2 billion Internet users.

El-Darwiche, Singh and Genediwalla (2012) argue that the national economic growth is associated with the adoption of information and communications technology, and they suggest countries that have achieved mass adoption of digital technologies and ICT applications by individuals, businesses, and governments (in other words, advanced level of digitization) have realized significant economic, social, and political benefits. They further point out that countries with most advanced digitization development which is measured by such factors as ubiquity (the level of access to digital services and applications), affordability (pricing), reliability (the quality of connection), speed (the rate of data throughput), usability (how easy is to get online and use online applications and services), and skills (the ability of users to incorporate digital applications and services into their lives and businesses), could derive 20% or more in economic benefits than those who are in the beginning stage.

According to Sabbagh et al. 2012 (p. 122), digitization can be measured across six key attributes:

• Ubiquity (the extent to which consumers and enterprises have universal access to digital services and applications): it could be measured by fixed broadband penetration, mobile phone penetration, mobile broadband penetration, personal computers, population penetration, and 3G mobile connection penetration.

• Affordability (the extent to which digital services are priced in a range that makes them available to as many people as possible): it could be measured by fixed line installation cost, fixed cost per minute, mobile connection fee, mobile prepaid tariff, and fixed broadband Internet access tariff.

• Reliability (the quality of available digital services): it could be measured by investment per subscriber (mobile broadband and fixed line).

• Speed (the extent to which digital services can be accessed in real time): it could be measured by international Internet bandwidth and broadband speeds

• Usability (the ease of use of digital services and the ability of local ecosystems to boost adoption of these services): it could be measured by Internet retail as % of total retail, E-government web measure index, % of individuals using the Internet, Data as % of wireless ARPU (average revenue per user), domains by country per 100 inhabitants, IP addresses per 100 inhabitants, social network unique visitors per month, and average SMS usage per customer.

• Skills (the ability of users to incorporate digital services into their lives and businesses): it could be measured by the number of engineers per 100 inhabitants, % of labour force with more than secondary education.

Meanwhile they suggest the impact of digitization could be looked at from three perspectives:

• Economy (the impact of digitization on the growth of economy): it is measured by GDP growth, job creation, and innovation.

• Society (the impact of digitization on the society well-being of a country): it is measured by quality of life and access to basic services.

• Governance (the impact of digitization on public sector): it is measured by transparency of government operations and business activities, E-government, and education.

Digital Transformation

How do you assess your organization's readiness for digital transformation? Berman and Bell (2011, p.10) suggest the following questions from two perspectives of reshaping customer value proposition and optimizing operation to be looked at:

• How are you engaging with customers to understand their needs and expectations? And how they are changing in the digital environment?

- How will you drive the digital agenda in your industry rather than having it imposed on you by competitors?
- How do you integrate online and social media touch points, customer information and insights across your entire enterprise?
- What are you doing to make sure you are putting the customer at the center of your supply chain planning and execution every time?
- How are you realizing the benefits of open collaboration-within your enterprise, with customers and with partners?
- How are you optimizing your digital and physical (non-digital) components across all aspects of your operating model?

IBM Institute for Business Value (cited in Berman & Bell 2011, p.11) suggests six capabilities of digital transformation:
- Business model innovation: building customer value as a core competency.
- Customer and community collaboration: engaging with customers fully via various channels and touch points.
- Cross-channel integration: integrating digital and non-digital channels.
- Insights from analytics: taking advantage of the predicative power of Big Data and Data Analytics.
- Digitally enabled supply chain: optimizing and integrating all components of supply chain.
- Networked workforce: getting the right skills around the right business opportunities.

   Meanwhile some factors influencing the implementation of digital transformation include (Boomi 2018; Boutetiere, Montagner & Reich 2018; Burkacky et al. 2018; Capgemini Consulting 2011; Catlin et al. 2016; Catlin et al. 2017; Deakin, LaBerge & O'Beirne 2019; Ducro et al. 2019; Gerbert, Mohr & Spira 2019; Harle, Soussan & Tour 2017; Sebastian et al. 2017; Samoun et al. 2019; Sia, Soh & Weill 2016; Singh & Hess 2017; The Author's Own Knowledge; Tynan 2018):
- Developing clear & distinctive digital strategy and road map (e.g., from vision>>evaluation>>selection of strategy>>roadmap>>portfolio>> project>> pilot>>scale-up &transformation>>performance assessment >>adjustment & update and making hard decision (e.g., keep or kill)>>overall performance evaluation>>continuous improvement and execution >>new initiatives>>....).
- Clearly explaining the chosen digital strategy and associated targets and key performance indicators (KPIs) to the people.
- Allocating sufficient resources for digital transformation initiatives.

- Cultivating digital leadership and appoints a Chief Digital Officer or Chief Digital Transformation Officer.
- Establish a corporate/central digital transformation office/function.
- Ensuring transformation is a top business priority of senior leaders.
- Updating the transformation progress regularly by senior management.
- Exploring innovation opportunities (e.g., new products & services, new business models, new operating models) and providing people with framework and tools for digital innovation.
- Encouraging and fostering team work and agile approach.
- Focusing on value creation for all the stakeholders arising from digital transformation and strong governance.
- Establishing or reinforcing customer-centric and service-oriented mindset in the organization.
- Managing data effectively.
- Managing speed and scope effectively.
- Managing change effectively.
- Winning people's trust.
- Gaining critical senior management's support (e.g., their fostering of sense of urgency).
- Establishing a cross-functional digital transformation team (e.g. IT and business need to speak the same language, the team members have required skills).
- Ensuring your people are on board.
- Defining people's roles and responsibilities clearly.
- Laying out incentive mechanism and performance goals clearly.
- Encouraging people to challenge old ways of working and experiment with new ideas.
- Selecting appropriate organizational structure.
- Digitizing business processes and customer interfaces and channels when possible and reasonable.
- Encourage intra-organizational (as well as inter-organizational) collaboration and resource-sharing across the organization and between organizations.
- Conducting pilot test and improving based on the feedback.
- Scaling up successful pilot-tested initiatives.
- Acquiring and/or developing required talent and capabilities.
- Building required ecosystem involving the right partners.
- Committing to establish supporting organizational culture.

• Providing people with sufficient training and opportunities for learning new practices and systems.

• Ensuring digital integration and interoperability with global units and partners.

• Actively embarking and deploying advanced technologies, platforms and digital tools.

3.5 Summary

In this chapter, the importance of information systems planning and measuring the performance of information systems initiatives/investments was discussed. Different measurement metrics were reviewed. And some methods for justifying information systems investment and associated difficulties with justifying information systems investments were presented. In addition, perspectives of digitization and digital transformation were discussed. In the next chapter, we will look at developing and implementing information systems.

References

Alvarez, E. & Raghavan, S. 2010, 'Road Map to Relevance: How a capabilities-driven information technology strategy can help differentiate your company', *Strategy + Business*, Iss. 61, pp. 1-6.

Barrows, E. 2009, 'Four fatal flaws of strategic planning', *Harvard Business Review*, March 13, 2009, Online, Available at: https://hbr.org/2009/03/four-fatal-flaws-of-strategic.html (accessed on 2 July 2019).

Berman, SJ & Bell, R 2011, 'Digital Transformation: Creating New Business Models Where Digital Meets Physical', *IBM Global Business Service Executive Report*, IBM Institute for Business Value, pp. 1-17. Blick, G. & Quaddus, M. 2003, *Benefit Realization with SAP: A Case Study*, Graduate School of Business, Curtin University of Technology, Australia, pp. 1-16.

Boochever, J. O., Park, T. & Weinberg, J. C. 2002, 'CEO vs CIO: Can this marriage be saved', *Strategy + Business*, Iss.28, pp. 1-10.

Boomi 2018, 'Why digital transformation projects fail: Three winning steps for every CIO', *Boomi.com*, Online, Available at: https://boomi.com/wp-content/uploads/why-dx-projects-fail.pdf (accessed on 8 January 2019).

Booth, A., Roberts, R. & Sikes, J. 2011, 'How strong is your IT strategy?', *McKinsey on Business Technology*, Number 23, Summer 2011, pp. 2-7.

Boutetiere, H. D.E., Mintagner, A. & Reich, A. 2018, 'Unlocking success in digital transformation', *Organization*, October 2018, McKinsey & Company, pp. 1-14.

Bradley, C., Hirt, M. & Smit, S. 2018, 'Eight shifts that will take your strategy into high gear', *McKinsey Quarterly*, April 2018, pp. 1-11.

Burkacky, O., Deichmann, J., Hepp, D. & Muhlreiter, B. 2018, 'A blueprint for successful digital transformations for automotive suppliers', *Digital McKinsey*, pp. 1-9.

Capgemini Consulting 2011, *Digital Transformation: A Roadmap for Billion-dollar Organizations*, pp. 1-67.

Catlin, T., Khanna, S., Lorenz, J. T. & Sancier-Sultan, S. 2016, 'Making digital strategy a reality in insurance', *Digital McKinsey*, September 2016, pp. 1-7.

Catlin, T., Lorenz, J. T., Sternfels, B. & Willmott, P. 2017, 'A roadmap for a digital transformation', *Financial Services*, March 2017, McKinsey & Company, pp. 1-11.

Copper, B. & Nocket, K. 2009, 'Toyota's IT Transformation', *Strategy + Business*, Iss.55, pp. 1-3.

Deakin, J., LaBerge, L. & O'Beirne, B. 2019, 'Five moves to make during a digital transformation', *McKinsey Digital*, April 2019, pp. 1-10.

Ducro, D., Noterdaeme, O., Sliczna, M., Somers, K. & Niel, J. V. 2019, 'A guidebook for heavy industry's digital journey', *Operations Practice*, McKinsey & Company, June 2019, pp. 1-6.

Dye, R. & Sibony, O. 2007, 'How to improve strategic planning', *McKinsey Quarterly*, Number 3, 2007, pp. 40-48.

El-Darwiche, B., Singh, M. & Genediwalla, S. 2012, 'Digitization and Prosperity', *Strategy + Business,* Issue 68, Autumn 2012, pp. 1-10.

Gerbert, P., Mohr, J. H. & Spira, M. 2019, 'The next frontier in digital and AI transformations', The Boston Consulting Group, pp. 1-16.

Gunasekaran, A., Love, P.E.D., Rahimi, F. & Miele, R. 2001, 'A Model for Investment Justification in Information Technology Projects', International Journal of Information Management, Vol. 21, pp. 349–364.

Haag, S., Baltzan, P. & Phillips, A. 2006, *Business Driven Technology*, 1st edition, McGraw-Hill Irwin, Boston, U.S.A.

Harle, N., Soussan, P. & Tour, A. D.L. 2017, 'What deep-tech startups want from corporate partners', *BCG Perspectives*, The Boston Consulting Group, pp. 1-7.

Hazan, E., Manyika, J. & Pelissie du Rausas, M. 2011, 'Sizing the Internet's economic impact', *McKinsey on Business Technology*, Number 24, Autumn 2011, pp. 18-21.Judah, M., O'Keeffe, D., Zehner, D. & Cummings, L. 2016, 'Strategic planning that produces real strategy', *Brief*, Bain & Company, February 10, 2016, Online, Available at: https://www.bain.com/insights/strategic-planning-that-produces-real-strategy/ (accessed on 31 July 2018).

McNurlin, B.C. & Sprague, R.H. 2004, *Information Systems Management in Practice*, 6th edn, Pearson Education, New Jersey.

O'Brien, J. A. & Marakas , G. M. 2011, *Management Information Systems*, 10th Edition, McGraw-Hill, New York, USA.

Overby, S. 2017, Anatomy of an IT Strategic Plan in the era of Digital Disruption, *CIO*, Oct 27, 2017, Online, Available at: https://www.cio.com.au/article/629233/anatomy-an-it-strategic-plan-era-digital-disruption/ (accessed on 30 October 2017).

Pearlson, K.E. & Saunders, C.S. 2004, *Managing and Using Information Systems: A Strategic Approach*, 2nd edn, Wiley, Danvers.

Pearlson, K. E. & Saunders, C. S. 2010, *Managing and Using Information Systems: A Strategic Approach,* Fourth Edition, John Wiley & Sons, USA.

Peppard, J., Ward, J. & Daniel, E. 2007, 'Managing the realization of benefits from IT investment', *MIS Quarterly Executive*, Vol. 6, No. 1, pp. 1-11.

Perkin, K. 2019, 'The Top 10 Strategic Planning Best Practices', *OnStrategy*, Online, Available at: https://onstrategyhq.com/resources/the-top-10-strategic-planning-best-practices/ (accessed on 24 July 2019).

Sabbagh, K., Friedrich, R., El-Darwiche, B., Singh, M. & Ganediwalla, S. & Katz, R. 2012, 'Maximizing the impact of digitization', in *The Global Information Technology Report 2012: Living in a Hyper-connected World*, Dutta, S. & Bilbao-Osorio, B. eds, INSEAD & World Economic Forum, pp. 121-133.

Samoun, M. H. B., Holmas, H., Santamarta, S., Forbes, P., Clark, J. T. & Huges, W. 2019, 'Going digital is hard for oil and gas companies-But the payoff is worth it', The Boston Consulting Group, pp. 1-7.

Sebastian, I. M., Ross, J. W., Beath, C., Mocker, M., Moloney, K.G., & Fonstad, N. O., 2017,'How big old companies navigate digital transformation', *MIS Quarterly Executive*, Vol. 16, No. 3, pp. 197-213.

Sia, S. K., Soh, C. & Weill, P. 2107, 'How DBS bank pursued a digital business strategy', *MIS Quarterly Executive*, Vol. 15, No. 2, pp. 105-121.

Singh, A. & Hess, T. 2017, 'How Chief Digital Officers promotes the digital transformation of their companies', *MIS Quarterly Executive*, Vol. 16, No. 1, pp. 1-17.

Soh. C. & Markus, L.M. (1995). 'How IT Creates Business Values: A Process Theory Synthesis', *Proceedings of the 16th International Conference on Information Systems*, Amsterdam, Netherlands, pp. 29–41.

Tynan, D. 2018, '8 digital transformation mistakes (and how to fix them)', *CIO*, October 8, 2018, Online, Available at: https://www.cio.com/article/3310944/8-digital-transformation-mistakes-and-how-to-fix-them.html (accessed on 10 December 2018).

Turban, E., King, D., Viehland, D. & Lee, J. 2006, *Electronic Commerce 2006: A Managerial Perspective*, International edn, Prentice Hall, Upper Saddle River, NJ.

Zetlin, M. 2018, 'Why IT-Business alignment still fails', *CIO*, 26 September 2018, Online, Available at: https://www.cio.com/article/3307873/why-it-business-alignment-still-fails.html (accessed on 10 January 2019).

Zhu, P. 2013, The CIO's Four Views on IT KPIs, *Future of CIO*, March 31, 2017, Online, Available at: http://futureofcio.blogspot.com.au/2013/03/four-views-of-it-kpis.html (accessed on 31 October 2017).

Chapter 4

Developing and Implementing Information Systems

This chapter will describe the system approach to problem solving, explain the steps of the systems development life cycle, point out the need for successful project management, change management and risk management, and compare different development approaches organisations can apply.

4.1 Information Systems Development Processes

The need for system development

Developing and implementing information systems is critical to the success of the business. Haag, Baltzan and Phillips (2008, p. 202) stress properly developed an deployed information systems can make an organization more flexible and agile. On the other hand, poorly developed and implemented information systems can have damaging effects on business performance (e.g., decreased revenue, increased liabilities, losses in productivity, damage to brand reputation, vulnerability to the technological disruption, poor user experience and customer retention (Gnanasambandam et al. 2017)) and can even cause a business to fail. McKeown (2000, p. 221) states that systems development is needed when:

• potential competition and developments in technology lead to the development of a new system to carry out an existing function.

• existing systems are modified to carry out additional functions.

• a system has to run through its full life cycle (i.e. from Phase 1 of Development to Phase 2 of Effective operational use to Phase 3 of Decline in usefulness).

• In addition, organisations may need to initiate system development to comply with regulations and policies.

The system approach

The system approach can be regarded as a special type of problem solving method based on the scientific method where problems and opportunities are examined in a system context. O'Brien and Marakas (2011, p. 482) suggest that the system approach, which focuses on 'seeing both the forest and the trees' (system orientation), has the following characteristics:

• Seeing interrelationships among systems rather than linear cause-and-effect chains when events occur

• Seeing process of change among systems rather than discrete snapshots of change whenever change occurs

• Applying a system context: identifying systems, sub-systems, and components of systems.

There are five broad stages in the system approach. These five stages are (O'Brien & Marakas 2011, p. 482):

1.   Defining a problem/opportunity using system thinking
2.   Developing and evaluating alternative system solutions
3.   Selecting the system solution that best meets your requirements
4.   Designing the selected system solutions to meet your requirements
5.   Implementing and evaluating the success of the designed system.

Systems development approaches

When the system approach to problem solving is applied to the development of information systems solutions to business problems, it can be viewed as a multiple process called information systems development cycle, also known as the systems development life cycle (SDLC). A number of different software development methodologies are available.

Waterfall methodology/SDLC

Waterfall method is sequential in nature. It is typically executed in specific order, and is most commonly used in software/system development. It allows for increased control throughout each phase, provides a more formal planning stage that may enhance the chances of capturing all project requirements up front, and could reduce the loss of any key information and requirements in the initial stages; on the other hand, it can be quite inflexible, slow and difficult if scope changes may be anticipated later or other changes are needed later. Newer methods, focusing on flexibility, productivity & efficiency, faster responses and easier to accommodate changes through agile and iterative as well as user-centered approaches, have been developed (Baltzan, Lynch & Blakey 2013; Pearlson & Saunders 2013, p. 308; Pearlson, Saunders & Galletta, 2016, p.242). Some examples of such newer methods include Agile method, Rapid application development methodology (RAD), Extreme programming, Prototyping, Object-oriented programming, DevOps, Microservices, The Lean Start-up approach, End-user development, and Open-source approach.

Rapid application development methodology (RAD)

It is an iterative construction approach and involve the user heavily, and it typically adopts the prototyping method and have tools for developing the system (e.g., RAD systems to allow the user to simply "drag and drop" many objects on graphical user interface) (Pearlson, Saunders & Galletta, 2016, p.243). One method, which is very closely related to the RAD, is joint application development (JAD). JAD basically looks at engaging a group of users for system development purposes (e.g., soliciting requirements in details via group discussions and interviews).

Extreme programming (XP) methodology

This approach breaks a project into tiny phases and developers can't continue on to the next phase until the first phase is completed. And within each phase, iteration will be done until satisfaction is achieved. Very often, the XP approach is done in pairs (e.g., one reviews another's work and provides feedback) and the best practices are adopted in the project (Satzinger, Jackson & Burd 2016, p.312; Wallace 2013, p.361).

Agile methodology

A form of XP with less focus on team coding and more on limiting the scope (i.e., setting a minimum number of requirements and turns them into a deliverable product faster and more flexible). It is suitable for projects requiring less control and real-time communication, and it typically works in self-motivating teams. Agile software development is getting popular among IS/IT programmers and functions. It pushes for fast and iterative development through closely working with end users and allowing continual feedback and refinement. Instead of years of development time for large software development projects, small-scale and more user-focused systems and capabilities can be deployed in a matter of weeks and months (Alexander 2017; Roberts, Sarrazin & Sikes 2010). Agile software development approach provides more flexible IS/IT capabilities for organizations to deal with changes in the business needs.

However agile methodology isn't the answer to every problem. Once the project gets to a certain size, then agile approach won't work. On a related note, SCRUM is a part/kind of agile method and it is executed in even shorter periods (e.g., 30-day Sessions/Sprints). In addition, not being clearly articulating system deliverables in the beginning, underestimating designing and documentation, and being easy to get off the track resulting from not clear about the final outcome as well as the chance of not being able to work with large-scope projects or large quantities of data or a large number of customers are some common issues for approaches like agile method (Laudon & Laudon 2018, p.535; Pearlson, Saunders & Galletta 2016, p.244).

An important part of agile method is to build a strong agile team, which focuses on flexibility, adaption and collaboration (Poepsel 2019). A team with balanced skills in line with the objectives and scope of the project needs to be organized. Risk taking and learning from mistakes should be encouraged with supporting rules and practices in place. Transparent, clear and collaborative communication also has to be in the equation for a strong agile team as well. On the other hand, discipline and structured approaches are still needed for the agile method (i.e., otherwise it will be off the track easily); and cultural adjustments & training could help address these issues (Wallace 2013, pp.362-363).

DevOps

DevOps is an extension of agile method, addressing both development and operations and working on a fully automated, continuous, holistic and integrated workflow to develop and deploy software & systems (Casey 2019; Rudder 2018). It could be argued that Agile method primarily focuses on development (e.g., once the coding/development is done, the system is handled over to others to deploy and look after) while the DevOps approach is more holistic and will address all the environment factors and ensure the developed system is performing its functions as per users' needs. Benefits of DevOps consist of agility, better collaboration across the organization, ownership of the product, automation of workflow, continuous learning & improvement, and effective communication in the organization (Pagerduty 2019). Some measures of DevOps project could include: Mean time to recovery, First-time success rate of deployments to production, Number of production deployments, and Lead time (e.g., from coding to system/product implementation/deployment) (Casey 2018).

Microservices & Component-based approach

Microservices represent a method which allows individual teams to develop and deploy certain services/functions/components with a specific purpose and such individually developed services/functions/components could be put together to serve the customers' needs (Casey 2017; Rudder 2015). This approach provides organizations with benefits such as: faster development and deployment, focusing on certain services/functions (good for both functions and risk management), providing team with more autonomy (and ownership), and being easier to scale up (Marcante 2017; Posta 2017; Wright 2018). This concept of Microservices is very close to the previously known concept of Service-oriented Architecture (SOA), and the difference is the former is expected to be able to provide more integrated digital experiences as a result of technological advancement and the shift to more customer-focused approach (Red Hat 2019a). This method is very close/similar to component-based approach.

Prototyping

This method is about building an experimental system rapidly and inexpensively for end users to evaluate. Benefits of such approach includes: improved communications with the users, better engagement with and ownership by users, better understanding users' requirements, quicker development process, and laying good foundation for final system development (Pearlson, Saunders & Galletta, 2016, p.244).

Object-oriented development

Using the object (e.g., putting data and processes for using the data together) as the basis unit of information systems development. System development could be viewed as a collection of different objects; such approach makes reusing components (or building blocks) and implementing changes much easier, and thus improve the productivity and efficiency of system development (Laudon & Laudon 2014, p.534-536; Pearlson, Saunders & Galletta, 2016, p.246).

The Lean Startup Approach

This approach is popular among technology start-ups, which usually have limited budget and face fierce competition. Such approach tends to focus on developing solutions for identified significant opportunities or the problems worth working on and do only as much as required or perceived to be essential (Ward 2017).

End-user development

Some types of information systems/applications could be developed by end users with little or no formal technical assistance, especially by using some software packages and tools (e.g. PC software tools, query language, report generator, graphics language, application generator, application software package, very high-level programming language) (Laudon & Laudon 2018, pp.535-536).

Open source approach

Open source approach looks at utilizing the expertise and skills of a large community (e.g., online community) to build and improve "free" software. Some principles of open source community include: (1) shared problems are solved faster; (2) transparency forces authenticity and honesty; (3) participative communities are more open to change; and (4) open standards provide business agility (Walker 2017, p.21). Some benefits of open source include: agility, cost saving & better resource utilization, flexible & fast development and deployment, attracting better talent, access to the latest innovators, high quality, customization, learning via making contribution, and emerging large-scale adoption (Congdon 2015; Red Hat 2019b; Senz 2018). Some good practices of open source approach include: actively engaging with open-source community, building pro-open source culture, breaking down silos, encouraging sharing and transparency, improving communication & collaboration, enforcing compliance of open source policies, and addressing security and risk concerns associated with open source (GitHub 2019). On the other hand, some concerns are: security, level of support, and compatibility issues (Red Hat 2019b).

Design thinking

Design thinking focuses on having deep understanding of customers' needs of the customer first before developing product/system to meet their needs, and it reflects the shift from product-centric thinking to customer-centric approach across the organization (Overby 2018a). It provides organizations with significant opportunities to examine the current processes and systems, improve their value chains, and foster innovative activities in the organization (Overby 2018b). It can be viewed as a more of a culture and mindset changing approach, therefore the top management's support and the implementation of pro-design thinking culture, structure and processes are critical to the success of the design thinking method.

All software development methodologies use the systems development life cycle (SDLC) even though the way that they use it differs (Haag, Baltzan & Phillips 2008, p. 460). For example, all projects must have planning and testing phases, however one project might use the waterfall approach and have the planning occur at the beginning of the project and the testing occur at the end. Another project might use the XP method and have small planning and testing phases occurring all the time. Another example is SDLC can typically be used for large projects (especially in the large firms), but within large projects, agile development to produce some parts by smaller project teams of the overall master project.

Methods such as RAD, XP and Agile approach are more suitable for smaller and more end-user focuses projects or some parts of the overall master project by smaller project teams. The key success factors for these methods is to ensure the required organizational/cultural change is in place (Rudder 2015). On a related note, other approaches such as purchasing the available packages, using third-party services and outsourcing are also available options for organizations.

Systems development life cycle (SDLC) models

Haag, Baltzan and Phillips (2008, pp. 203–204) present a seven-stage system development life cycle, which includes planning phase, analysis phase, design phase, development phase, testing phase, implementation phase, and maintenance phase. Each phase consists of several activities (see Table 4.1).

Table 4.1. Haag, Baltzan & Phillips' (2008) SDLC

Phase of SDLC	Primary Activities
Planning	1.Identify and select the system for development 2.Assess project feasibility 3.Develop the project plan
Analysis	1.Gather business requirements 2.Create process diagrams 3.Perform a buy vs. build analysis
Design	1.Design the IT infrastructure 2.Design system models
Development	1.Develop the IT infrastructure 2.Develop the database and programs
Testing	1.Write the test conditions 2.Perform the system testing
Implementation	1.Write detailed user documentation 2.Determine implementation method 3.Provide training for the system users
Maintenance	1.Build a help desk to support the system users 2.Perform system maintenance 3.Provide an environment to support system changes

(Source: Developed from Haag, Baltzan & Phillips 2008)

O'Brien and Marakas (2011) classify SDLC into five phases of Investigation, Analysis, Design, Implementation, and Maintenance (see Table 4.2). The Implementation stage of O'Brien and Marakas (2011) includes the three phases of development, testing and implementation stated in Haag, Baltzan and Phillips (2008).

Table 4.2. O'Brien and Marakas's (2011) SDLC

Phase of SDLC	Primary Activities
Systems Investigation	1. Identify and select system for development 2. Assess feasibility 3. Develop a project management plan
Systems Analysis	1. Understand current organization and its current systems 2. Analyze information needs of stakeholders 3. Gather functional requirements to meet the information needs
Systems Design	1. Develop specification for hardware, software, people, network, data resources, and associated information products for new system 2. Design logical models of new system
Systems Implementation	1. Acquire (or develop) hardware and software 2. Test the new system and convert to the new system 3. Train the users and manage associated change management
Systems Maintenance	1. Conduct post-implementation review 2. Make adjustments to the new systems as needed

(Source: Developed from O'Brien & Marakas 2011)

On a related note, after system analysis phase/stage, organizations need to decide whether they are going to buy or build the system. If the decision is to buy the system, a process, including such activities of request for proposal (RFP), vendor evaluation & selection, contract negotiation & signing, customization, implementation and maintenance, should be followed (Wallace 2013, pp. 363-364). One important aspect associated with implementing the new system is the conversion process, which is very critical to the success of new system in the organization. There are four conversion approaches and each has its advantages and disadvantages (see Table 4.3). Organizations need to select a conversion approach carefully by weighing its pros and cons, and could adopt the combined approach, such as having pilot approach within phased approach; adopting parallel approach (i.e. keeping the option of going back to the old system until the new system is running smoothly).

Table 4.3 Conversion approaches

Conversion Approach	Characteristics	Advantages	Disadvantages	Risk
Direct	Simultaneously shutdown old systems and commence new systems	Fast, lower cost and could be used for small or less critical systems or the systems that were not available previously	New systems may not work and the cost could be very high if the systems do not work	High
Parallel	Run old & new systems at the same time	Able to fix problems with new system while old system is in operation	Slower than direct approach, Expensive to run both versions, Performance problems due to running two systems, Additional resources required.	Low
Pilot	Install & test in one part of organisation before installing everywhere	Find and fix problems without affecting entire organisation	Problems with high volumes of transactions may not be found	Moderate
Phased	System installed sequentially at different locations	Requires less installation staff, Problems at one location can be fixed before installing elsewhere.	Different locations are not using the same version of the system	Moderate
Hybrid Approach	Have more than one conversion approaches (e.g., phased approach combined with pilot approach)	Have less disruption to the existing systems and current operation than any single conversation approach (e.g., phased or pilot approach)	Have different versions of the system coexisting in the chosen department/function area of the organization	Low

(Source: Developed from Laudon & Laudon 2018; McKeown 2000; Marakas & O'Brien 2011; Pearlson, Saunders & Galletta 2016; The Author's Own Knowledge)

4.2 Project Management

A successful system development is backed up by effective project management, which is 'the application of knowledge, skills, tools and techniques to project activities in order to meet or exceed stakeholder needs and expectations from a project" (Haag, Baltzan & Phillips 2008, p.478). The previously discussed SDLC can be viewed as a specific project management approach, which is a tailored project management approach toward the development and implementation of information systems (O'Brien & Marakas 2011, p. 507). In many circumstances, a project team, consisting of both insiders from different departments and outsiders (e.g., vendors and consultants), will be formed, especially for large and complex systems development and implementations. A project manager is needed for the project management team. Haag, Baltzan and Phillips (2008, pp. 479–480) argue while a project manager could be responsible for many tasks, the three primary activities performed by a project manager include choosing strategic projects, setting the project scope, and managing resources and maintaining the project plan.

Some reported factors for IS/IT project failures include: Unclear or missing/overlooked business requirements, Skipping SDLC phases, Failure to manage project scope, Failure to manage project plan, Overly aggressive timelines, Underestimated costs, Unanticipated complications, Insufficient resources, Changing technology, Poor Governance, Human mistakes (e.g., bad coding, wrong configuration), Lack of collaboration between business and IT, Inflexible or slow processes, Lack of integration of new and existing technologies, Outdated technologies, Lack of properly skilled teams, Lack of clearly defined and/or achievable milestones & objectives, Poor communication, Lack of communication by senior management, Employee resistance, and Insufficient funding (Baltzan, Lynch & Blakey 2013, pp. 257-258; Haag, Baltzan & Philips 2008, pp.215-217; PwC and PMI Surveys reported in Pratt 2017; The Author's Own Knowledge).

Haag, Baltzan and Phillips (2008, p. 486) describe some successful project management strategies: (1) establishing project success criteria; (2) developing a solid project plan; (3) dividing large tasks into smaller manageable ones; (4) planning for change and having flexibility; and (5) effectively managing (negative) risks associated with the project. Similarly Nelson (2007) identifies some classic project management mistakes and proposes some relevant solutions. His identified mistakes include: (1) poor estimating and/or scheduling the delivery of the project; (2) ineffective stakeholder management; (3) insufficient risk management; (4)

insufficient planning; (5) poor quality assurance; (6) weak personnel (no sufficient skills and experiences for the project) and team issues (e.g., difficulties associated with making global teams work effectively as a result of the lack of face-to-face interaction, time-zone differences, cultural differences (including language barriers); and (7) insufficient project sponsorship.

He also suggests several solutions/measures to deal with these issues, including (1) adopting agile development; (2) developing effective communication plan; (3) applying estimate-convergence graph; (4) using joint application development: (5) having comprehensive project chart; (6) establishing project manage office; (7) working on retrospectives; (8) embarking on staged delivery; (9) managing stakeholder assessment; and (10) implementing work breakdown structure.

In addition, justifying IS/IT systems as capital investments and crafting and executing effective benefits realization strategy (especially for large-scale information systems projects such as ERP system implementations) as well as getting the wide user involvement & senior management support from the beginning, assigning non-IT executives to IS/IT projects, designing systems for growth and change (but with not too many essential requirements), establishing appropriate success metrics, closely evaluating the cost & progress of the project & making timely adjustments (including termination of the project), good & consistent standards and documentation, clearly clarifying roles & responsibilities, and frequent testing and revising are essential as well (Baltzan, Lynch & Blakey 2013, pp. 258-259; Blick & Quaddus 2003; McKeen & Smith 2015, pp.324-330; The Author's Own Knowledge).

Large-scale information systems projects (i.e., more than US$ 15 million) have a tendency to complete behind the schedule, blow the planned budget, and fail to deliver the expected results. A joint study by McKinsey & University of Oxford, which surveyed 5,400 large information systems projects, found that on average large projects run 45% over budget and 7% over time, while 56% delivering less value than expected (cited in Bloch, Blumberg & Laartz 2012). The joint study also identified major issues resulting in most project failures: missing focus (e.g., unclear objectives, lack of business focus); content issues (e.g., shifting requirements, technical complexity); skill issues (unaligned team, lack of skills); and execution issues (unrealistic schedule, reactive planning). In addition, the joint study further provided suggestions for project success: managing strategy and stakeholders (looking at such factors as: clear objectives, well-defined business case, alignment of major project scope, minimized & stable project scope, robust vendor contracts with clear responsibilities, executive support); mastering technology and content (looking at such factors as standardized & proven software technology, user involvement to shape solution); building team & capabilities (looking at such factors as experienced project manager, qualified & motivated project team, sustainable mix or internal & external resources); and excelling at project management practices (looking at such factors as reliable estimates & plans, appropriate transparency about project status, proven methodologies & tools).

4.3 Change Management

Introducing new systems into organisations will inevitably result in resistance from the users of the systems. This is quite normal since it is human nature to look at anything new with suspicion. Very often people will ask the question: What is in it for me? As a result, change management, which is defined as 'a set of techniques that aid in evolution, composition, and policy management of the design and implementation of a system' (Haag, Baltzan & Phillips 2008, p. 483), is essential. Good change management can help organisations reduce risks and costs of change and optimise the benefits. The most difficult aspect to handle in change management is dealing with people (in both communication and in culture aspects).

Some guiding principles for change management include (Fæste, Reeves & Whitaker 2019; Jones, Aguirre and Calderone 2004; O'Brien and Marakas 2011, p. 472; The Authors' Own Knowledge; Wang 2010):
• Emphasizing the importance of addressing "human side" side systematically and effectively answering the question of "What is in it for me": The most difficult aspect to handle in change is to do with people. Resisting to changes is human being's nature. Organizations need to make sure people understand the benefits of changes to the organization as well as to them and the risks of not making changes. At the same time, people's needs have to be looked after.
• Focusing on top management and developing leadership: Leaders should be initiators of the change, lead the change management, take responsibilities for the change management, and set good examples for people to follow.

- Creating change vision: understanding strategic vision, creating compelling story, and making vision comprehensive and operational.
- Defining change strategy: assessing change readiness, choosing best change configuration, and putting change governance into place.
- Involving people from different parts and different levels of the organization: better understanding and better education will make the change management easier.
- Building and sustaining commitment: forming teams, managing stakeholders, communicating effectively and sufficiently, dealing with resistance, disseminating best practices and knowledge/skills, and acknowledging achievements in every possible public opportunity.
- Managing individual's performance: organizations need to clearly and honestly communicate to individuals regarding what is expected of them and how they will be measured. And once success and failure metrics and incentives/penalties are established they should be properly followed. Organizations also need to realign certain roles to ensure people stick to the change and new approach/process.
- Taking evidence-based approach and Realizing business benefits: building business case and constantly quantifying/tangiblizing benefits by utilizing data analytics capabilities.
- Developing required culture: identifying the culture gap and implementing required cultural changes.
- Adjusting structure: identifying and implementing necessary changes to organizational structure to embrace the change.
- Preparing for the unexpected and embracing uncertainty & complexity in change management: it is very rare that a change management program goes completely according to the plan. Organizations need to continually assess the progress and performance of their change management programs and deal with the unexpected effectively in a timely manner. Resilience and preparedness for the unknown should be an integral part of the change management process. In addition, they need to have risk mitigation measures in place to ensure minimum disruption to the business during the change management process. New metrics and analytical approaches (including artificial intelligence) could be used to optimize & enhance the change process and detect & respond the early warning-signals in the process.

4.4 Risk Management

Another important factor having impact on the success of proposed systems development is project risk, which is 'an uncertain event or condition that, if it occurs, has a positive or negative effect (in Chinese the risk (described in two Chinese characters of 危机) means both danger/thread and opportunity) on a project (Haag, Baltzan & Phillips 2008, p.484). However in reality, while we talk about the (project) risk, we normally refer to negative side of the risk. Risks could come from inside (e.g., the withdrawal of support by the top management, the insufficient allocated resources, key people leaving the project suddenly) outside (e.g., changes in the industry standards, new regulations, and competitors' move/advantages in the similar/same projects) of the organization. Just like dealing with any other types of risks, an effective process/framework should be put into place. A simple framework of project risk management can be viewed as: identifying the risk>>quantifying the risks (probably and the impact)>>developing and implementing risk management solutions>>constantly assessing the performance of implemented solutions and making required adjustments/changes.

Some factors affecting the project risk include: complexity (e.g., highly complex projects could be more risky than simpler ones), size (e.g., large projects could have more risky than smaller ones), and clarity (e.g., unclear system/user requirements would be more risky than projects with clear understanding of deliverables and requirements) (Pearlson, Saunders & Galletta 2016, p.249). Some key success factors of effective risk management practices are: establishing cross-functional project management with good experiences (including risk management experiences), utilizing both internal and external expertise (e.g., external consultants and vendors), and maintaining effective communications and good relationships with all project stakeholders Pearlson, Saunders & Galletta 2016, p.250). Meanwhile effective risk management practices are not common phenomenon for many organizations, and it has only been in the last decade that risk management has been seriously considered as part of managerial responsibilities.

4.5 Information Systems Development Approaches

When organisations are developing new systems, they face several choices:
• Internal development.

- Outsourcing.
- Acquisition – purchase off the shelf.
- Use of application service providers (ASP).

Each of them has its own advantages and disadvantages (See Table 4.4).

Table 4.4. Comparison of Development Options

Development Options	Advantages	Disadvantages
Internal Development	Competitive advantage, Complete control over final system, Building technical skill and functional knowledge of developers.	Requires dedicated effort of in-house staff, Development can be slow, Costs may be higher than working with other approaches, System may not work when completed or may not provide desired functionality.
Outsourcing	Cost savings, Ease of transition to new technologies, Better strategic and business focus, Better management of information systems staff – vendor has the knowledge and skills in effectively managing information systems staff, Handling peaks with greater capacity of vendor, Consolidating data centers is a very difficult task to be done by an internal group, Infusing cash via selling equipment to the outsourcing vendor.	Loss of control, Loss of confidentiality, High switching cost, Selection difficulties (e.g., compatibility, cultural fit in addition to the price and location concerns), Contracting and execution of agreed contract issues (e.g., contract length, getting out of the contract), outsourcing scope struggles (e.g., full vs selective outsources), Lack of technological innovation, Loss of strategic advantage, Reliance on outsourcer, Security and reliability, Evaporation of cost saving (e.g., perceived costs may never be realised due to factors such as out-of-date processes, costs arising from software upgrades, unspecified growth and new technologies not anticipated in the contract. And some savings may be hard to measure).

Acquisition	Purchasing of a complete system from a vendor, Packages ranging from office suite to functional information systems to enterprise systems (e.g., ERP systems), Fastest approach of all.	Little competitive advantage, Must accept functionality of the purchased system, May not integrate well with existing systems, May require modification to meet needs.
Use of Application Service Providers (ASPs)	The benefit of less need for dedicated internal information systems staff (especially for SMEs), Saving money on internal infrastructure and initial capital layouts, Could be easier to 'rent' software from an ASP and avoid the problems associated with installing, operating and maintaining complex systems like ERP, Easier to walk away from unsatisfactory systems solutions, Quicker to respond to market with applications available from ASP.	Less control over the applications (e.g., when application is upgraded or how access to it is facilitated), Tend to address routine problems and no enough attention in how particular problems the organisation is facing are addressed, Tend to be rather generic (e.g., only have minor customisation (i.e., less than 20)).

(Source: developed from Baltzan, Lynch & Blakey 2013, pp. 259-262; Hoffer et al. 2005, pp. 32–33, 38–39, 40–41; Laudon & Laudon 2018, pp. 536-539; McKeown 2000, p. 251; Perlason & Saunders 2010, pp. 192-194; Pearlson, Saunders & Galletta 2016, p.250)

So how can an organisation choose the best system development approach? Organisations can choose any of the four development approaches (presented in Table 4.4) after evaluating advantages and disadvantages of different development approaches and taking into consideration of their organisational circumstances and requirements. Alternatively a combined system development approach also can be pursued (e.g., using a prototype as part of the traditional life cycle, using a small application package as a prototype, adopting aspects of a traditional life cycle to purchasing an application package, and adding a user development component to the traditional life cycle). On a related note, for small and medium enterprises they also can try online outsourcing service providers such as freelancer.com, which aims to become the "the eBay of jobs". In the coming years, one of the bigger challenges for organizations is how to outsource their IT operations and services to the cloud.

4.6 Summary

In this chapter, an understanding of the system approach to problem solving and its application in developing information systems (i e , the systems development life cycle (SDLC)) was developed. Details of steps of the SDLC were reviewed. Project management, change management and risk management, which all play important roles in the success of systems development, were also covered. A comparison between different systems development approaches and discussion between various conversation approaches were presented. The discussion of information systems infrastructure management will be discussed in the next chapter.

References

Alexander. M. 2017, "How to pick the best project management methodology for success", *CIO*, July 20, 2017, Online, Available at: https://www.cio.com/article/2950579/methodology-frameworks/how-to-pick-a-project-management-methodology.html (accessed on August 10, 2017).

Baltzan, P., Lynch, K. & Blakey, P. 2013, *Business Driven Information Systems*, 2nd Edition, McGraw Hill, Australia.

Blick, G. & Quaddus, M. 2003, *Benefit Realization with SAP: A Case Study*, Graduate School of Business, Curtin University of Technology, Australia, pp. 1–16.

Bloch, M., Blumberg, S. & Laartz, J. 2012, "Delivering large-scale IT projects on time, on budget, and on vlaue', *McKinsey Technology Office*, October 2012, pp. 1-6.

Casey, K. 2017, "How to explain microservices in plain English", *The Enterprises Project*, August 16, 2017, Online Available at: https://enterprisersproject.com/article/2017/8/how-explain-microservices-plain-english (accessed on 28 June 2019).

Casey, K. 2018, "How not to kill your DevOps team", *The Enterprises Project*, June 04, 2018, Online Available at: https://enterprisersproject.com/article/2018/6/how-not-kill-your-devops-team (accessed on 25 June 2019).

Casey, K. 2019, "Agile vs. DevOPs: What is the difference", *The Enterprises Project*, January 03, 2019, Online Available at: https://enterprisersproject.com/article/2019/1/agile-vs-devops-whats-difference (accessed on 25 June 2019).

Congdon, L. 2015, "8 advantages of using open source in the enterprise", *The Enterprises Project*, February 03, 2015, Online Available at: https://enterprisersproject.com/article/2018/6/how-not-kill-your-devops-team (accessed on 28 June 2019).

Github 2019, *How to become an open source enterprise: Transform the way your team builds software with open source code, tools, and best practices*, Github 2019, pp.1012.

Gnanasambandam, C., Harryson, M., Mangla, R. & Srivastava, S. 2017, "An executive guide to software development", *High Tech*, Feb 2017, McKinsey & Company, pp.1-6.

Haag, S., Baltzan, P. & Phillips, A. 2008, *Business Driven Technology*, 2nd edn, McGraw-Hill Irwin, Boston, USA.

Hoffer, J.A., George, J.F. & Valacich, J.S. 2005, *Modern Systems Analysis and Design*, 4th edn, Prentice Hall.

Jones, J., Aguirre, D. & Calderone, M. 2004, "10 Principles of Change Management", *Strategy + Business*, April 2004, pp. 1-5.

Fæste, L., Reeves, M. & Whitaker, K. 2019, *The Science of Organizational Change*, Boston Consulting Group, pp.1-9.

Laudon, K.C. & Laudon, J.P. 2014, *Management Information Systems: Managing the Digital Firm*, 13th edn, Global Edition, Pearson, U. K.

Laudon, K.C. & Laudon, J.P. 2018, *Management Information Systems: Managing the Digital Firm*, 15th edn, Global Edition, Pearson, U. K.

Marcante, J. 2017, "Vanguard CIO: Why we're on a journey to evolve to a microservices architecture", *The Enterprises Project*, February 21, 2017, Online Available at: https://enterprisersproject.com/article/2017/2/vanguard-cio-why-we-re-journey-evolve-microservices-architecture (accessed on 28 June 2019).

McKeen, J.D. & Smith, H. A. 2015, *IT Strategy: Issues and Practices*, Third Edition, Pearson Education, United Kingdom.

McKeown, P. 2000, *Information Technology and the Networked Economy*, Thomson Learning, Boston. Nelson, R.R. 2007, "IT Project Management: Infamous Failures, Classic Mistakes, and Best Practices", *MIS Quarterly Executive*, Vol. 6, No. 2, pp. 67-78.

O'Brien, J. A. & Marakas, G. M. 2011, *Management Information Systems*, 10th Edition, McGraw-Hill, New York, USA.

Overby, S. 2018a, "*Design thinking: 7 questions to ask before you start*", *The Enterprises Project*, October 2, 2018, Online Available at: https://enterprisersproject.com/article/2018/10/design-thinking-7-questions-ask-you-start (accessed on 25 June 2019).

Overby, S. 2018b, "*Design thinking: 10 design thinking myths debunked*", *The Enterprises Project*, November 16, 2018, Online Available at: https://enterprisersproject.com/article/2018/11/10-design-thinking-myths-debunked (accessed on 25 June 2019).

Pagerduty 2019, *DevOps for the Enterprise: A Guide to Introducing DevOps to the Enterprise*, Online, Available at: https://www.pagerduty.com/resources/ebook/enterprise-devops/ (accessed on 22 June 2019).

Pearlson, K. E. & Saunders, C. S. 2010, *Managing and Using Information Systems: A Strategic Approach*, Fourth Edition, John Wiley & Sons, USA.

Pearlson, K.E. & Saunders, C.S. 2013, *Managing and using information systems: A strategic approach*, 5th edn, John Wiley & Sons Inc. USA.

Pearlson, K.E., Saunders, C.S. & Galletta, D. F. 2016, *Managing and using information systems: A strategic approach*, 6th edn, John Wiley & Sons Inc. USA.

Poepsel, M. 2019, "How to build a strong agile team", *The Enterprises Project*, June 14, 2019, Online Available at: ht https://enterprisersproject.com/article/2019/6/agile-team-how-to-build (accessed on 25 June 2019).

Posta, C. 2017, "About When Not to Do Microservices", *Red Hat Developer Blog*, October 19, 2017, Online, Available at: https://developers.redhat.com/blog/2017/10/19/about-when-not-to-do-microservices/?intcmp=701f2000000tjyaAAA (accessed on 28 June 2019).

Pratt, M. K., *"Why IT Projects Still Fail"*, CIO, Aug 1, 2017, Online, Available at: https://www.cio.com.au/article/625522/why-it-projects-still-fail/ (accessed on 31 October 2017).

Red Hat Inc. 2019a, *"What are microservices"*, *Opensources.com*, Online, Available at: https://opensource.com/resources/what-are-microservices?intcmp=701f2000000tjyaAAA (accessed on 28 June 2019).

Red Hat Inc. 2019b, *The State of Enterprise Open Source*, Online, Available at: https://www.redhat.com/en/enterprise-open-source-report/2019 (accessed on 26 June 2019).

Roberts, R. Sarrazin, H. & Sikes, J. 2010, 'Reshaping IT management for turbulent times', *McKinsey on Business Technology*, Number 21, pp. 2-9.

Rudder, C. 2015, "What CIOs need to know about microservices and DevOps", *The Enterprises Project*, October 05, 2015, Online Available at: https://enterprisersproject.com/article/2015/9/what-cios-need-know-about-microservices-and-devops (accessed on 25 June 2019). Rudder, C. 2018, "How to be a strong DevOPs leader: 9 tips", *The Enterprises Project*, July 31, 2018, Online Available at: h https://enterprisersproject.com/article/2018/7/how-be-stronger-devops-leader-9-tips (accessed on 28 June 2019).

Satzinger, J., Jackson, R. & Burd, S. 2016, *Systems Analysis and Design*: *In a Changing World*, 7th Edition, Cengage Learning, Australia.

Senz. K. 2018, "The hidden benefit of giving back to open source software", *Research & Ideas, Working Knowledge*, 05 Sep 2018, Online, Available at: https://hbswk.hbs.edu/item/the-hidden-benefit-of-giving-back-to-open-source-software (accessed on 26 June 2019).

Wang, K. W. 2010, 'Creating Competitive Advantage with IT Architecture', *McKinsey on Business Technology*, Number 18, Winter 2010, pp. 18-21.

Walker, M. 2017, "Introduction to Part 1", *The Open Organization Guide to IT Culture Change: Open principles and practices for more innovative IT department*, 2017, Red Hat Inc., pp. 19-22.

Wallace, P. 2013, *Information Systems in Organizations: People, Technology, and Processes*, Pearson Education, New Jersey, United States.

Ward, C. 2017, *Comparing Methodologies: Agile vs. DevOps vs. Lean Startup*, E-Guide, TechTarget 2017, pp. 1-16.

Wright, C. 2018, "Disrupt or to be disrupted: 3 trends enabling next-level IT agility", The Enterprises Project, June 13, 2018, Online Available at: https://enterprisersproject.com/ article/2018/6/disrupt-or-be-disrupted-3-trends-enabling-next-level-it-agility?page=1 (accessed on 28 June 2019).

Chapter 5

Managing Organization's Data & Knowledge Resources

This chapter will define data, information and knowledge; explain database, data warehouse, and data center; discuss the phenomenon of Big Data & Blockchain; and look at knowledge management and knowledge management systems.

5.1 Data, Information and Knowledge

Even though in reality we tend to use data, information and knowledge interchangeably for the purpose of convenience, it is essential to define and distinguish data, information and knowledge before discuss managing organization's data and knowledge assets. While there exist no universal definitions on these terms, data can be viewed as "raw figures and simple facts" (e.g., 180, 180cm) and information as "processed data and data with meaning" (e.g., height-180cm). And knowledge (e.g., Jun Xu's height is 180cm) can only be obtained through learning, practising and doing and is normally sitting on human's brains (yours' or others').

Meanwhile knowledge can be basically divided into two categories: tacit knowledge and explicit knowledge (Alavi & Leidner 2001; Leonard & Sensiper 1998; Nonaka & Takeuchi 1995; Polanyi 1962, 1967; Spender 1996). Some common applications of tacit knowledge are problem solving, problem finding, and prediction and anticipation (Leonard & Sensiper 1998). Tacit knowledge consists of two dimensions: cognitive and technical elements (Nonaka & Takeuchi 1995). The cognitive dimension of tacit knowledge refers to 'mental models', which assist human beings in interpreting and understanding the world around them; individuals' perspectives, beliefs, and opinions are some examples of tacit knowledge (Nonaka & Takeuchi 1995). The technical element of tacit knowledge includes things such as know-how, crafts, and skills (Nonaka & Takeuchi 1995).

Tacit knowledge is personal and context-specific; therefore, it is more difficult to formalize and communicate (Nonaka & Takeuchi, 1995). In contrast with tacit knowledge's subjective nature, explicit knowledge is more objective and generally can be codified or documented in a formal or systematic format (Nonaka & Takeuchi 1995), and other people's tacit knowledge is explicit knowledge for you when they are presented to you in the codified and documented formats. Information in databases, libraries, and the internet are some examples of explicit knowledge. Tacit knowledge has much higher value than explicit knowledge since people always know more than they can tell (Sveiby, 1997, p. 34; Moody & Shanks, 1999). Furthermore, in order to apply explicit knowledge in practice, it must be converted to tacit knowledge (Moody & Shanks, 1999). For example, students have to understand the knowledge (e.g., the concepts, definitions, theories, formulas) they learn in the classroom and books before they can apply them to interpret, understand, and solve the problem in reality.

5.2 Database, Data Warehouse and Data Center

Database and database related terms refer to technologies and applications for managing (including organizing, storing, and accessing) data, information (processed data and data with meaning), and knowledge (e.g., codified and documented version of lessons learned, past projects, experiences). In practice, we very often use data and information interchangeably while we are talking about data resources, data management, and Big Data. Effective management of data in today's Big Data Era where a massive volume of data and information is available is critical to the success and survival of the organisation. It is suggested that "the typical car contains about 2,000 components, 30,000 parts, and 10 million lines of software code" (MacDuffie & Fujimoto 2010).

Database

In the past, different functional areas and groups developed their own files independently. Traditional file environments create problems such as data redundancy and inconsistency, program-data dependence, inflexibility, poor security, and lack of data sharing availability (Laudon & Laudon 2012, p. 240).

Database technology can provide solutions to many of the problems of a traditional file processing and data organisation approach. A database is a collection of data organised to service many applications efficiently by storing and managing data (Laudon & Laudon 2005, p. 238). Haag, Baltzan and Phillips (2008, p. 68) point out that benefits of database technology for businesses include: increased flexibility, increased scalability, reduced information redundancy (duplication), increased information integrity (quality), and increased information security. A single database can serve multiple applications. A single database can serve multiple applications and allow an organisation to easily pull out all the information for different purposes. For example, instead of storing employee's data for personnel, payroll and benefits in separate files (or in different places or even in separate information systems), the organisation could establish a human resources database (Laudon & Laudon 2005, p. 238).

The database management system (e.g., Microsoft Access) is a special software, which permits an organization to centralize data, manage them efficiently, and provide access to the stored data by application programs. Through data management system users and application programs can interact with a database. There are many different database models of how to organise information in a database, including hierarchical, network, relational, multi-dimensional and object-oriented databases. The hierarchical database is used for structured, routine types of transaction processing and is organised in a treelike manner (e.g., looking like a family tree and an organisational chart) (Laudon & Laudon 2005, p. 238). Within each record, data elements are organised into pieces of records called segments. The top level of segment is called root. An upper segment is logically linked to a lower segment in a parent–child (children) relationship.

A hierarchical database is used to model one-to-many relationships, which must be specified in advance. It is complex, not flexible, difficult to modify and doesn't support ad hoc requests well (Laudon & Laudon 2005, p. 243). The network database structure is even more complex than the hierarchical model and depicts many to many relationships, which must be specified in advance as well. While the former is more flexible, it doesn't readily support ad hoc requests (Laudon & Laudon 2005, p. 243). Both of them are older logical database models. The relational model databases store data elements in simple tables and are able to link data elements from various tables. They are very supportive of ad hoc requests but slower at processing large amounts of data than hierarchical or network models. They are more flexible and easier to maintain than hierarchical and network models (Laudon & Laudon 2005, p. 257). The relational database model stores information in the form of logically related two-dimensional tables. Entities, entity classes, attributes, primary keys, and foreign keys are all fundamental concepts included in the relational database model (Laudon & Laudon 2005, p. 240).

The multi-dimensional database is a variation of the relational model. Compared to normal relational databases that store data in simple two-dimensional tables, the multidimensional database stores information in cubes and cubes within cubes and is used for online analytical processing (OLAP) applications (manipulating and analysing large volumes of data from multiple perspectives) (O'Brien & Marakas 2011, p. 185). The object-oriented database use objects, which can be automatically retrieved and shared, to store both data (e.g., customers' bank accounts) and the procedures acting on the data (e.g., actions such as checking balance, charging interests).

The object-oriented database also supports inheritance. Inheritance refers to new objects that can be automatically created by replicating some or all of the characteristics of one or more parent objects (O'Brien & Marakas 2011, pp. 185). Compared to conventional data base structures (including the relational model) that are not very good at dealing with multimedia or graphical data, the object-oriented data model is a key technology for storing multi-media or graphical based information, especially for web-based applications (Laudon & Laudon 2005, p. 257). It is good for complex, high-volume applications. Many computer-aided design (CAD) applications have adopted object-oriented databases. On the other hand, although object-oriented databases have the capacity to store more complex types of information than relational databases, they can be relatively slower compared to relational databases while dealing with large numbers of transactions. A hybrid object-relational database can combine the capabilities of both relational model for traditional information and object-oriented model for multimedia information (Laudon & Laudon 2012, p. 245; O'Brien & Marakas 2011, p.187).

Graph databases are becoming more popular in recent years. Given the large amount of structured and unstructured data from various sources and media, identifying relationships is the key to connect the dots to create a picture. Based on graph theory, graph databases are able to pull out relationships other database technologies can't do via employing nodes, edges, and properties (e.g., like a map with street interactions as nodes and roads as edges), and they are excel at managing widely connected data sets and complex queries (IBM 2013; Wikipedia 2019).

In the case of enterprise systems (e.g., enterprise resource planning systems), there is centralised database (also called backbone or central repository), which can be used by a single processor (e.g., mainframe computer) or by multiple processes (e.g., mini-computers/mid-range computers) in a client-server network. A database can be distributed, and there are alternative ways of distributing a database. For example, the database in the headquarter can be partitioned so that each remote processor has the necessary data to serve its own local needs, and it can also be replicated at all remote locations (Laudon & Laudon 2005, p. 246).

Organisations usually end up having several databases. Sharing and organising information sitting in multiple databases could be very time-consuming and inefficient if there is no integration across multiple databases in different information systems across various departments/functions. Haag, Baltzan and Phillips (2008, p. 71) introduce two primary methods of integrating information across multiple databases:

• Forward integration – takes information entered into a given system and sends it automatically to all downstream systems and processes.

• Backward integration – takes information entered into a given system and sends it automatically to all upstream systems and processes.

Meanwhile as an important part of online operations, organisations need to link their internal databases to the web. Fortunately, many middleware and other software products are available in the market to help access organisations' legacy systems through the web (e.g., searching product information online from your home computers).

Data warehouse

A data warehouse is a single, server-based data repository that allows centralised analysis, security, and control over the data while data mart is a small data warehouse designed for a strategic business unit (SBU) or a department – it is a lower-cost and scaled-down version. Data warehouses support reporting and query tools, store current and historical data, and consolidate data for management analysis and decision-making (Laudon & Laudon 2012, p. 252). A data warehouse extracts current and historical data from both internal (e.g., current data including operational data, customer data, manufacturing/production data, and historical data) and external data sources (e.g., competitor information, regulations, market changes, consumer insights, and other information from strategic alliances, partners and research agencies) and re-organises collected data/information into a centralised database for management reporting and analysis via various tools (i.e. queries & reports, online analytic processing (OLAP), data mining).

The primary purpose of data warehouses (and data marts) is to perform analytical processing via Data Mining and OLAP (Haag, Baltzan & Phillips2008, p.81). The insights into organisational information that can be gained from analytical processing are instrumental in making critical business decisions (e.g., setting strategic directions and goals) (Laudon & Laudon 2012, p.253).

Data mining is a major use/application of data warehouse. information in data warehouses is analysed to reveal hidden correlations, patterns, and trends, which involves sifting through an immense amount of data to discover previously unknown patterns (O'Brien & Marakas 2011, p. 200). Through data mining, firms can search for valuable business information and business opportunities. Online analytical processing (OLAP) is another important data analysis method, and it supports manipulation and real-time analysis of large volumes of data from multiple dimensions and perspectives (O'Brien & Marakas 2011, p. 201).

Databases normally contain information in a series of two-dimensional tables, which means that you can only ever view two dimensions of information at one time. In a data warehouse, information is multi-dimensional, and it contains layers of columns and rows (Haag, Baltzan & Phillips 2008, p. 83). Each layer in a data warehouse represents information according to an additional dimension. Dimensions could include such things as products, promotions, stores, category, region, stock price, date, time, and even the weather. The ability to look at information from various dimensions can add tremendous business insight (e.g., identifying trends in spending according to age, sex, marital status and postcode).

An organisation must maintain high-quality information in the data warehouse. It is very important to ensure the cleanliness of information. Without high-quality information the organisation will be unable to make good business decisions. A common catch-cry is GIGO – garbage in, garbage out. Organisations can adopt information cleansing and scrubbing, which is 'a process that weeds out and fixes or discards inconsistent, incorrect, or incomplete information' (Haag, Baltzan & Phillips 2008, p. 84) to enhance the quality of information. Meanwhile organizations need to effectively deal with sources of poor quality information, prevention is one of the most effective approaches for enhancing the quality of the information. Some sources of low quality information include: (1) customers intentionally entering inaccurate information to protect their privacy; (2) information from different systems that have different information entry standards and formats; (3) call centre operators entering abbreviated or erroneous information by accident or to save time; and (4) third party and external information containing inconsistencies, inaccuracies, and errors (Haag, Baltzan & Phillips 2008, p.388).

Data Center

As a result of the rapidly increasing global connectivity, exploding data volumes, and the shift to the cloud-based services, large organizations (especially very large technology and telecommunication firms such as Google, Microsoft, Facebook, Amazon, Facebook, China Telecom, China Mobile), who have the needs and the capital, have been building their data centers. Data centers can vary in size and the number of servers hosted. When a data center exceeds 5,000 hosted servers and 10,000 square feet in size, it can be considered as a "Hyperscale" data center, some hyperscale data centers can house hundreds of thousands, even millions, of servers (Kidd 2018). Hyperscale data centers are built on such concepts as: (1) the infrastructure and distributed systems are able to support the operations of the data center, (2) the scalability for computing tasks (usually involving a robust system with flexible memory, networking, and storage capabilities) can ensure efficient performance based on the demand, and (3) appropriate revenue can be generated from the operations of the data center (Barnett 2018).

On top of the computing needs, the hyperscale data centers provide benefits such as: maximizing cooling efficiency, allocating electrical power in discrete packages, making sure the availability of electricity, and ensuring balanced workload across servers (Fulton 2019). On a different note, a server farm is not same as a data center, it can viewed as bare-bones data center and it is typically amateur setup for specific tasks (e.g., mining Bitcoin) with little or no supporting infrastructure (Digital Realty 2019).

The largest data center in the world is China Telecom's $2.5 billion Inner Mongolia Information Park. It is 100 hectares in size and hosts more than 700,000 servers. It is estimated that by 2020 it will reach 3 million hosted servers and reach $11.5 billion industrial output with 20% of year-on-year growth (China Daily 2018). Meanwhile some large organizations have multiple data centers in various parts of the world (e.g., Google has 9 in the U.S., 2 in Asia, and 5 in Europe (Google 2019); Microsoft has 7 in the U.S., 4 in Asia, 3 in Ocenia, 2 in Europe and 1 in South America (Datacenters.com 2019a); Facebook has 10 in the U.S., 4 in Europe and 1 in Asia (Dataceners.com 2019b)). Other sources suggest that there were around 400 hyperscale data centers in the world (with companies such as Amazon/AWS, Microsoft, IBM and Google, each has 45 or more) and by the end of 2019, close to 500 will be in operation or planning stages; meanwhile leading countries in terms of the number of large data centers include (in the order): the U.S., China, Japan, U.K., Australia, and Germany (Kidd 2018; Synergy Research Group 2017).

Data centers are not cheap, initial capital and operating expenditures of a typical center consist of (Day & Pham 2017, p.3):

- Net renewable square feet (NRSF): 165,141.
- Capital expenditure per NRSF: $1,305.
- Initial capital expenditures: $215.5 million.
- Land acquisition: $13.4 million.
- Construction building: $45 million.
- IT equipment: 157.1 million.
- Annual operating expenditure: $18.5 million.
- Power: $7.4 million.
- Staffing: $2.8 million.
- Real estate taxes and insurance: 1 million
- Maintenance, administration, and others: $7.3 million.

Energy consumption and carbon emission are critical issues for data centers. One estimate says by 2030 data center electricity demand will be up to 8% of global demand, meanwhile it is reported that data centers account for 0.3% to overall global carbon emission while the whole ICT sector accounts for 2% global carbon emission (Jones 2018). Organizations could work on energy saving by looking at areas such as: IT equipment (e.g., server virtualization, decommissioning unused servers, consolidation of lightly utilized servers, better management of data storage, installing more energy-efficient servers and equipment), air management (e.g., hot aisle/cold aisle layout, variable speed fan drives, properly deployed airflow management devices), and heating, ventilation and air-conditioning configurations (e.g., server inlet temperature & humidity adjustments, air-side economizer, water-side economizer) (Energystar 2019).

Some very large data centers are purposely built near water for electricity generation and cooling purposes. The emerging quantum computing and computers could dramatically reduce the size and electricity consumption of large data centers (Technavio Blog 2018). On top of energy consumption and carbon emission issues, some other factors influencing data center performance include changing customer landscape, margin reduction, difficulties in demand forecasting, different levels of utilization, and high demand of customization

(Kannan & Thomas 2018). Some suggestions for enhancing data center performance include (Forbes Insights 2018; Kannan & Thomas 2018; The Author's Own Knowledge; Upsite Technologies 2019):

• Developing and implementing energy-efficient data center design and action plans.
• Having agile data infrastructure.
• Providing strong data protection and effectively dealing with & preventing security threats and ensuring continuous availability.
• Being active in exploring new and emerging technology.
• Achieving intelligent operations (e.g., by adopting AI applications).
• Investing in both R & D and operations.
• Actively preparing for the required talent for future growth.
• Continuously developing innovative new services.
• Focusing on creating value for customers.
• Fostering long-term relations with customers and becoming their strategic partners.

5.3 Big Data & Data Analytics

Gathering and analysing large scale (or very large scale) data is quickly becoming popular organizations for reasons such as large volume data from multiple channels and various sources, the need for better understanding customers, and the tangible benefits of gaining competitive advantages by doing this (e.g., the success of Amazon, Google) (Bughin, Livingston & Marwaha 2011). Big data can be defined as "data sets whose size is beyond the ability of typical database software tools to capture, store, manage and analyse" (Manyika et al. 2011, p.1). Big data is different with traditional concept of data in four perspective (Dijcks 2012; Brow, Chui and Manyika 2011):

• Bigger volume: in 2010 enterprises and consumers stored 13 exabytes (1exabytes=1,024 petabytes=1,024 X1,0124=1.049 million terabytes =1,024X1, 024X1,024=1.074 billion gigabytes) of new data on devices and the projected annual growth in global data generated is 40% (just imaging the information produced by more than 4 billion mobile phones, by 30 million network sensor nodes, social networks-do you know there are more than 30 billion piece of content (photos, notes, blogs, web links, and news stories) shared on Facebook every month and 2.9 billion hours of video are watched at Youtube every month?). Ericsson estimates (cited in Dutta, Bilbao-Osorio & Geiger (2012, p.3)) there will be more than 50 billion connected devices in the world by 2020. Have you imagined to live in a yotta world (1,000 trillion gigabytes data and your every move will be digitized and added to the data flow of the world) (Siegele 2012). According to EMC/IDC Digital Universe Study 2011 (cited in Siegele 2012), Global digital data will reach 2,720 exabytes by the end of 2012, and 7,920 exabytes by the end of 2015. It is said more data were created between 2008 and 2011 than in all history before 2008 (Biggs et al. 2012, p.48). IDC also predicts (reported in Pollard et al. 2017, p. 19) that global data volumes will reach 180 zettabytes by 2025. In the past, data storage was expensive and a lot of data have been thrown away. However the price of storage is dropping significantly, according to Forrest Research (cited in Siegele 2012), by 2020, storing a petabyte data will only cost US$ 4.

• Higher velocity: for example even at 140 characters per tweet, Twitter generated data volume is large than 8 terabytes per day as a result of high velocity or frequency. And it is reported (cited in Conway 2012) 90% of the world's data are generated in the last two years.

• More data variety: including traditional and non-traditional data and structured and unstructured data (e.g., social media data. It is estimated that 95% of the world data is unstructured data, which makes big data more meaningful and challenging (Oracle 2012). Gartner projects (cited in SAP AG 2012) in the future 80% of enterprise data (from both traditional and non-traditional sources) will be unstructured.

• Higher economic value: huge financial gains can be realized via Big Data via more powerful and accurate decision-making and thus significantly improving business operations and organizational performance.

Big Data could exist in various formats (including video, image, audio, text/numbers), and include various types of data, including (1) traditional enterprise data (e.g., customer, transaction, operation information), machine-generated/sensor data (e.g., call details records, weblogs, information from smart meters, manufacturing sensors, equipment logs), and social data (e.g., information from blogs (including micro-blogging sites such as Twitter, social networks). Start-up firms like Lexalytics and Klout have been established for understanding social data (Dijcks 2012).

Big Data could create value for organizations in several ways (Manyika et al. 2011, pp. 5-6) : (1) creating transparency and improving efficiency via much easier access to more data across the organization; (2) improving productivity and organizational performance through quicker, deeper and more accurate discovery, prediction and analysis; (3) better segmentation with more tailored customization actions; (4) better (automation) support in decision making; (5) enhancing existing products and services and creating new ones through better understanding customers' needs and stronger capabilities in identifying opportunities for new products and services; and (6) becoming a key basis of competition and growth through the use of Big Data for organizations. Meanwhile it has been said that "data is new oil' and is the fuel oil for the digital economy (Pollard et al. 2017, p.19). Specifically Big Data could bring huge financial value to various sectors, for example (Brown, Chui and Manyika 2011; Grone, Peladeau & Samad 2019; Manyika et al. 2011, p.8):

• By 2025, the total value of the data economy will exceed $400 billion.
• $300 billion value per year to US health care sector.
• More than 60% net margin increase to US retail sector.
• EUR€ 250 billion value per year to Europe public sector administration.
• Up to 50% decrease in product development and assembly costs to manufacturing sector.
• $100 billion and $700 billion for service providers and end users for the sector of global personal location data.
• Huge benefits to sports industry?!-have you watched the popular movie of Moneyball? (Stafford 2012; Lohr 2012), and many others.

On a related note, the capture and realization of the above mentioned value has been hindered by factors such as uneven penetration of GPS enabled smartphone globally, lack of analytical talent, silo data issues, acceptance issues, interoperability & data sharing concerns, and leaders' understanding of the impact & support (Henke et al. 2016, p.29).

Some notable examples of using Big Data for competitive advantages include: Google, Amazon, Apple, Zipcar, and Netflix. Hagström & Gill (2012, p.102) point out that the combination of hyper-connectivity, Big Data, and powerful analytics, has enhanced organizational ability to know dialogue, and innovate. In association with the big data phenomenon, there is a shortage of people who have required skills to deal with Big Data. For example, it is reported the U.S. alone faces a shortage of 140,000 to 190,000 people with deep analytical skills and 1.5 million data-savvy (being able to analyse Big Data and make decisions from Big Data) managers which are equivalent to 50 to 60% gap in supply of required talent (Brown, Chui & Manyika 2011; Manyika et al. 2011, p.3). Organizations need to work on attracting, developing and retaining data talent. While monetary incentives are useful, other factors such as common vision (e.g., working on meaningful projects, having impact on firm and society), pro-data & data analytics culture, and good training programs, and care advancement opportunities are also important (Buluswar et al. 2016; Court 2015; McAfee & Brynjolfsson 2012).

It can be assumed in the future titles/positions such as "data strategist", "data scientist", "chief data officer", "data expert", "data specialist", "data technology officer/expert/specialist", "data engineer", "data architect", "data translator", "data owner", "chief data governance officer", 'data quality director", "business intelligence specialist", and similar titles, will become common terms for organizations. Some core technical skills required for positions such as data scientist include: Python, R, SQL, Hadoop, Java, SAS, Spark, Matlab, Hive, and Tableau (Rayome 2017). On a related note, for data analytics to be successful in the organization, a combination of business skills, technology skills, and analytic skills is required (Diaz, Rowshankish & Saleh 2018).

A more general term of "digital workforce" (Chui & Fleming 2011) has been suggested in recent years, and it includes people with different skills (from programming, computing modelling simulation, data analysis to analytical thinking and many others) for the current digital economy (also called knowledge economy). In addition, for knowledge workers (coined by Peter Drucker) such skills as organizing, accessing, processing, visualizing, understanding, analysing & extracting the value from (large volume) information available in the organization, are essential for doing their tasks effectively in the 21st century (Manyika 2009). On a related note, according to a recent global survey among telecom, high-tech, media, cable, and Internet companies, top digital capabilities in short supply is Big Data Analytics (Caylar & Menard 2016).

Meanwhile some techniques for analysing big data include: A/B testing, Association rule learning, Classification, Cluster analysis, Crowdsourcing, Data fusion and data integration, Data mining, Ensemble learning, Genetic algorithms, Machine learning, Natural language processing, Neural networks, Network analysis, Optimization, Pattern recognition, Predictive modelling, Regression, Sentiment analysis, Signal processing, Spatial analysis, Supervised learning & unsupervised learning, Simulation, Time series analysis, Visualisation, and many others (Manyika et al. 2011, pp. 27-31). Some technologies and applications for Big Data are: Big table, Data warehouse, Cassandra, Cloud computing, Distribute system, Dynamo, Google file system, HBasem, Hadpoop, MapReduce, Metadata, Stream processing, Visualisation, and many others (Manyika et al. 2011, pp. 31-33).

On top of required techniques & technologies and talent to take advantage of the potential big data, organizations also need to (1) put appropriate data policies in place (especially addressing data sourcing, accessing and disseminating issues and critical but complex (as a result of the size and the sources of data) data security and privacy issues); (2) obtain top management support; (3) make necessary organizational adjustments (including structural and cultural changes, end user education, business process redesign, automate workflows); (4) ensure top management's skills and support for big data use in the organization; (5) address data security and data privacy issues carefully; (6) treat data legal issues seriously; (7) have a clear vision for data analytics and a data driven strategy (e.g., linking data and data analytics with business objectives, developing a data-driven culture, integrating data-generated insights to life, and developing & implementing appropriate technological infrastructure and architecture with purposes); (8) implement data governance; (9) ensure smooth data integration, (10) focus on data quality; (11) build trust; (12) focus on business value via measuring outcomes and demonstrating the quantitative impacts of data analytics; (13) experiment data before defining objectives; (14) communicate results and have analytics translators unlocking and translating the value of data analytics; and adopt open innovation approach (e.g., exploring open source solutions actively); (15) have clearly defined data analytics roles & effective governance model; (16) manage the costs of data-cleansing efforts that could be very expensive; (17) have roadmap and actions plans for data analytics implementation, (18) collect data from internal systems and external sources; and (19) build frontline and management capabilities ((Brocchi et al. 2018; Brown 2019; Court 2015; Buluswar et al. 2016; Fleming et al. 2018; Hapler 2017; Henke et al. 2016; Kumar, Sedra & Casanova 2019; Macias-Lizaso 2018; McAfee & Brynjolfsson 2012).

Data quality is one of the most critical factors (if not the most critical factor) for using Big Data for decision making, in order to avoid the problem of "Garbage in and Garbage out", organizations need to work hard on the sources of the data (sources/data partners must be reliable) and on the acquisition/collection of data (e.g., right questions and research design; good understanding of data constraints; and ensuring real-time or timely data) (Chui & Fleming 2011).

Another critical area is data privacy regulation compliance (especially after the implementation of GDPR in May 2018). Even though there are differences among various privacy regulations, they normally cover areas such as: accountability & governance, consent and processing, notifications & data rights, privacy design, data breach notifications, data localization, children's online privacy considerations, and contracting & procurement (Podnar 2019). People also need to have confidence/trust in data analytics. A recent survey of 2,200 global information technology and business decision makers by KPMG (2018) reveals that only 35% of survey respondents have high level of trust in their organization's use of data analytics. On top of the technological and technical perspectives (e.g., quality, effectiveness and efficiency), transparency, communication, leadership and training could be other important factors for fostering people's trust in data analytics.

Meanwhile a process of implementing data analytics could be adopted by organizations (Charlin et al. 2018):

- Initiation: identifying key initiatives and evaluating them.
- Scope determination: answering questions such as what? where? Data available? build or buy? partners? project team?
- Prototype development: testing and evaluating the test results and improving.
- Validation in the market place.
- Scale up and roll out: integrating into the organization and building capabilities (e.g., data governance, people, technology, and change management).

However while the huge potential and benefits of Big Data are recognized, its role and influence should not be overstated. It should be remembered that "human beings are decision-makers not the machine and the big data, they are there to support us to make better decision". Big Data could make our decision making process more scientific (Lohr 2012), but the role of our experience and intuition, which is impossible (or extremely hard) for the machine to emulate and acquire, should never be diminished. Big Data & Data Analytics need to focus on solving business problems (typically focus on 1 or 2 areas), achieving outcomes and having impact, not working in silos, not simply working on data without purposes; and recognizing Good Big Data Analytics=Good business acumen+ IT+Mathematics +Data+… (Buluswar et al. 2016; Court 2015; McAfee & Brynjolfsson 2012).

What about the future of Big Data? Do you agree (partially agree) with the following Big Data Future Predictions proposed by Marr (2016)?:

- Data volumes will continue to grow.
- Ways to analyse data will improve.
- More tools for analysis (without the analyst) will emerge.
- Prescriptive analytics will be built in to business analytics software.
- Real-time streaming insights into data will be the hallmarks of data winners.
- Machine learning will be top strategic trend.

- Big data will face huge challenges around privacy.
- More companies will appoint a chief data officer.
- "Autonomous agents and things" will continue to be a huge trend.
- Big data staffing shortages will expand from analysts and scientists to include architects and experts in data management.
- The big data talent crunch may ease as companies employ new tactics.
- The data-as-a-service business model is on the horizon.
- Algorithm markets will also emerge.
- Cognitive technology will be the new buzzword.
- "All companies are data businesses now,"
- Businesses using data will see $430 billion in productivity benefits over their competition not using data by 2020.
- "Fast data" and "actionable data" will replace big data.

5.4 Blockchain Technology

Blockchain is the technology behind the Bitcoin and was developed as the main authentication and verification technology for the first decentralized crypto- digital currency even though Bitcoin is just one application of blcokchain technology (Carson et al. 2018). Some key attributes of Blockchain technology include: Decentralization (e.g., peer to peer transaction with trust and confidence without the help from third party mediators), Trust and Provenance (e.g., its indisputable mechanism to verify the data of a transaction at a specific time), and Resilience and Irreversibility (e.g., once a transaction is verified by the participating computers of the distributed network, it is highly impossible to change or alter the transaction's data) (InterSystems 2017; Morabito 2017, pp.22-23). Blockchain could have impacts on every part of the business (e.g., supply chain, finance effectiveness & contract management (e.g., smart contracts), loyal programs, identity management, digital currencies & payments, records management, and audit & compliance) (PwC 2018). Some benefits of Blockchain include enhanced transparency & traceability, faster transactions, removal of intermediaries, reducing cost, better bookkeeping & record management, improved productivity & efficiency, more efficient regulatory compliance, and greater access to services (e.g., financial services) in emerging economies (O'Donnell & Richards 2018; PwC 2018; Plansky).

What is the current status of Blockchain technology adoption and implementation? according to IDC (2019), global spending on blockchain solutions is predicted to reach $2.9 billion in 2019 (i.e., an increase of 88.7% from the $1.5 billion in 2018) and would reach $12.4 billion in 2022. Global blockchain spending will be led by the financial sector (with $1.1 billion spending) in 2019, followed by manufacturing and resources sector with spending of $653 million and $642 million respectively in 2019. The manufacturing and resources sector will see the fastest growth in blockchain spending over the 2018-2022 forecast (i.e., with compound annual growth rate over 70%). The top three countries leading in blockchain spending in 2019 are: United States ($1.1 billion), Western Europe ($674 million), and China ($319 million). Cross border payments & settlements and trade finance & post-trade/transaction settlements are the two blockchain use cases that will receive the most investment ($453 million and $285 million, respectively) in 2019, and the banking industry will be the largest investor in both use cases. Meanwhile lineage/provenance use cases and asset/good management use cases will be the favored by the manufacturing sector while identity management use cases will be the emphasis for such industries as banking, government, and healthcare provider.

Meanwhile according to PwC 2018 Global Blockchain Survey, 84% of the survey respondents suggested that their organizations had some involvement with Blockchain technology (e.g., 32% development, 20% research, 15% live, 10% pilot, and 7% paused). So far financial services (e.g., banking services provided by USAA, CBW Bank, Barclays, Santander, Citi, investment services provided by UBS, Goldman Sachs, BNY Mellon, Nasdaq, and transaction an payment services provided by American Express, First Data, PayPal) are leading in adopting Blcokchain, and some other industries include industrial products & manufacturing, energy & utilities, healthcare, government, retail & consumer, and entertainment & media are catching up (IDC 2019; O'Donnell & Richards 2018; PwC 2018; Plansky).

Countries have been working on various blockchain applications & services, including adopting blockchain for voting, improving fishing productivity, ensuring transparency & sustainability in fishing & other agricultural produces, increasing transparency in education, improving efficiency in remittances, enhancing clearance & settlement of payments & securities, managing health databases, managing global trade connectivity network, P2P energy trading, central bank digital currency, among many others (EY 2018).

Some barriers of blockchain implementation include: regulatory uncertainty, lack of trust among users, ability to brining network together, integration issues of different blockchains, inability to scale, lack of common standards, lack of clear regulations, the relative immaturity of blockchain technology, intellectual property concerns, and audit/compliance concerns (Carson et al. 2018; PwC 2018). Meanwhile recommendations for blockchain implementation include (Carson et al. 2018; EY 2018; Lacity 2018; Morabito 2017, p.35; PwC 2018; Plansky, O'Donnell & Richards 2018; Schmahl et al. 2018):

• Asking questions before embarking on blockchain: Is blockchain the right solution? How are blockchain standards being established? How can blockchain solutions deal with regulatory uncertainty? How should blockchain technology be governed? How can an ecosystem be established for the proposed blockchain solutions?

• Having a process in place: identifying the specific blockchain opportunities & focusing on specific & promising ones, optimizing strategy for identified opportunities with market positions and aligning with business strategic objectives, exploring feasibility & readiness, testing the prototype & proofs of concept thoroughly, scaling appropriately (including establishing or participating in the ecosystem of blockchain, building required capabilities, and implementing blockchain solutions) .

• Employing tactics for dealing with Trust issues: making the business case, developing an industry ecosystem, determining rules of engagement, and staying agile and responding to regulatory requirements as they evolve.

• Understanding the required time and efforts and being patient.

• Paying close attention to the blockchain standards & standard development.

• Exploring open blockchain standards.

• Scrutinizing privacy issues and other legal challenges associated with blockchain.

5.5 Knowledge Management and Knowledge Management Systems

Knowledge management is "an approach to adding or creating value by more actively leveraging the know-how, experience, and judgment [that] reside within and, in many cases, outside of an organization" (Ruggles 1998, p.80). The above definition highlights important elements of knowledge management. The know-how aspect of knowledge management emphasizes explicit knowledge, which can be easily captured and codified (Bonner 2000). On the other hand, the experience and judgment aspects of knowledge management reflect tacit or implicit knowledge, which is difficult to capture and formalize (Bonner, 2000). The definition also emphasizes that the primary purpose of knowledge management is to add or create value. Knowledge management systems such as intranets, best practice databases, corporate knowledge directories, corporate information portals, knowledge networks and maps and other applications (e.g., online communities, social networks, internal wikis, internal prediction markets, internal Google-type search engines, blogs, discussion boards, feedback forums, online live communication systems, virtual organizations & teams), can also be used to support and enhance knowledge management activities and facilitate the sharing of both tacit and explicit knowledge (Alavi & Leidner 2001; The Author's Own Knowledge).

There are four modes of tacit and explicit knowledge creation processes (Nonaka & Takeuchi 1995). The four processes are: socialisation, externalisation, combination, and internalisation (see Figure 5.1).

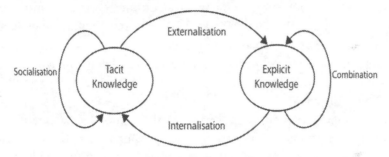

Figure 5.1 Four knowledge creation processes
(Soruce: adapted from Bolloju et al. 2002)

Socialisation refers to the conversion of tacit knowledge to tacit knowledge that is hidden knowledge and hard to communicate, such as knowledge sharing among individuals through face-to-face contacts, such as interviews, focus group, conversations in the lunch time and coffee/tea break, on-the-job training, master-fellow-relationships, formal and informal networks, and brainstorming. In this knowledge creation process, information systems can be useful in connecting people and creating and sustaining knowledge communities through teleconferencing technologies, including desk-top videoconferencing tools; online live communication systems and virtual organizations and teams; and internal knowledge marketplaces, predication markets, talent marketplaces (Junnakar & Brown 1997; Bryan & Joyce 2005; The Author's Own Knowledge).

Externalisation is the process of converting tacit knowledge to explicit knowledge in the form of metaphors, analogies, hypothesis, and models, such as articulating tacit knowledge, experience, insight, judgment, problem solving skills, obtained through observation, imitation, and practice into the format that can be used for future purpose and by who need it. The creation of explicit knowledge can be dramatically enhanced by information systems including groupware tools and electronic mail as well as wikis, blogs, discussion boards, feedback forums, and virtual organizations and teams (Junnakar & Brown 1997; The Author's Own Knowledge).

Combination is the creation of new explicit knowledge for individuals through activities of sharing, combining, organising, and processing discrete pieces of and different bodies of explicit knowledge (e.g., information through meetings & telephone conversations, information in the documents, information in the common databases, and information from electronic communication systems). Information systems such as intranets as well as internal wikis, blogs, discussion boards, feedback forums, internal Google-type search engines, internal predication markets, internal eBay type knowledge auction sites, have enabled the paperless forms of explicit to explicit knowledge transfer (Junnakar & Brown 1997; The Author's Own Knowledge).

Internalisation is a process in which explicit knowledge is absorbed and becomes part of tacit knowledge. This process regards the activities of applying knowledge in practice and reflects the concept of learning by doing (e.g., internalising the new or shared explicit knowledge through hands-on practice). Also documented knowledge can be helpful in this process, such as learning from best practice databases. Applications such as data mining tools, OLAP, internal Google-type search engines, internal predication markets, internal eBay type knowledge auction sites, for enhancing decision-makers' ability to make sense out of explicit information, especially in the presence of complex sets of data, can be very effective in this regard (Junnakar & Brown 1997; The Author's Own Knowledge).

As demonstrated in the above discussion, information systems and information technology provides essential roles and is an important enabler of knowledge management and knowledge sharing process. One related point is the discussion brought by Davenport (2010). He argues that even though there are a lot of tools available for managing knowledge, the actual information needs of knowledge workers vary and organizations should then provide them with appropriate systems in line with their tasks. He suggests there are four type of knowledge workers (by looking at the two dimensions of level of interdependence and complexity of work) requiring different kinds of support technologies/applications:

• Transaction model (low level of interdependence and low complexity of work); knowledge workers of this category mainly deal with individual and routine tasks, and need more structured-provision tools (e.g., work flow management systems, document management systems, content management systems, case management systems, business-rules or algorism to automate decisions, and business process management or monitoring systems), which have certain control of how knowledge workers get information and do job tasks (on the contrary, free access means knowledge workers can use any tools organizations can provide. The concern here is knowledge workers may know how to use the tools but may not have the skills for using (e.g., how to use different data sources for decision making and how to use different analytics tools), or for sharing the knowledge.

• Integration model (high level of interdependence and low level of complexity of work): knowledge workers under this category normally involve in collaborative groups but systematic and repeatable work, and need some free-access tools (i.e., e-mail and collaborative tools for communications) and/or semi-structured-provision tools (e.g., applications for joint-design, joint-development).

• Expert model (low level of interdependence and high complexity of work): knowledge workers of this kind mainly deal with judgment-oriented work and need to apply their expert knowledge to tasks or problems, and they typically need free access tools (e.g., telephone/video/online conferencing, virtual teams, wikis, social media, online chatting, e-mail systems) to deliver their knowledge sitting in the brain. Organizations also need to apply some structured-provision tools (e.g., expert systems) to record and automate their expertise.

• Collaboration model (high level of interdependence and high complexity of work): Knowledge workers of this type usually deal with iterative and unstructured work and depend on deep expertise across multiple function, and they typically need free access tools (i.e., group decision support systems, collaborative tools, telephone/video/online conferencing, virtual teams, online chatting, wikis, social media, email systems) to work on major plans and big ideas). But structured-provision tools (e.g., best practices & lessons learned databases, internal wikis) for knowledge reuse.

Knowledge sharing is possible in all four knowledge creation processes. The difference is in their focus (tacit, explicit, or both) and the required facilitation and support by information systems. However, resistance to knowledge sharing is probably part of human nature, especially when we believe that knowledge is power and that hidden knowledge can lead to prestige and job security (since only I know, and no one else knows; so they need me). When people are asked to share their knowledge, one question they always ask is: 'What's in it for me?. In addition, people may be reluctant to share their research and data for the following two primary reasons: (1) the fear of being criticized for possible errors and weaknesses and (2) the fear of losing the advantages arising from sharing what they know (Hubbard & Little 1997).

To foster knowledge creation and encourage collaboration and knowledge sharing, we need to take a holistic approach and take into consideration of various related factors. A good example of effectively managing knowledge is Southern Cross University's Doctor of Business Administration (DBA) program. Knowledge is important to everyone in today's knowledge-based economy, and academics will be among those who view knowledge as a very important resource since they are knowledge professionals who engage heavily in creating and delivering knowledge products (publications) and services (lectures, presentations, seminars, supervision, theses examinations), and whose performance appraisals are very much related to these knowledge products and services. For research students, similar issues will come up as they spend two to four years or even longer on their knowledge products – their research theses. Again, academics and research students may be reluctant to share their research and data for the following two primary reasons: (1) the fear of being criticized for possible errors and weaknesses; (2) the fear of losing the advantages arising from full utilization of the findings and data of their research projects (Hubbard & Little 1997). Southern Cross University's Doctor of Business Administration (DBA) program has implemented some effective pro-knowledge sharing practices to promote knowledge sharing among academics and research students. These include: (1) promoting a knowledge sharing culture and creating an environment for comfortable knowledge sharing; (2) having a pod structure for doctoral supervision with a group of candidates and supervisors working together for collaboratively; (3) putting in knowledge management systems, including the online doctoral candidates centre, doctoral supervisors centre, and Elluminate Live (an online communication and learning software); (4) providing optional colloquia for works-in-progress presentations (5) having mandatory doctoral weekend workshops/ symposia twice a year; (6) organizing social gatherings for doctoral students and supervisors; (7) providing a professional development program for supervisors; and (8) establishing a publications program to help researchers publish their work in peer-reviewed conferences and journals (Sankaran, Xu & Sankaran 2007).

An important element for successful knowledge sharing practices is the establishment of a knowledge sharing culture. Changing the existing culture and people's work habits is the main hurdle for most knowledge management programs (McDermott 1999). Previous studies (e.g., Chase 1997; The Conference Board 1999) indicate that the lack of a knowledge sharing culture is the biggest obstacle to knowledge management. The Graduate College of Management (now part of Southern Cross Business School), which runs Southern Cross University's DBA program, has been actively working on creating a pro-knowledge sharing environment (by promoting knowledge sharing in all the public places, including meetings, presentations, workshops, conferences and websites, and establishing and implementing reward programs for good knowledge sharing practices), in which supervisors and candidates feel comfortable and are happy to share their knowledge and discuss their experiences (Sankaran, Xu & Sankaran 2007).

5.6 Summary

Understanding data, information and knowledge is critical to the success of managing knowledge resources in the organization. Database technologies, data warehouses, and data centers ae available for organizations to manage their data. In the meantime, technologies such as Big Data and Blockchain provide organizations with more power to collect, manage, and analyze the collected or available massive amount of data. However dealing with large amount of data is not without costs, organizations need to do it effectively and efficiently. Finally through systematic knowledge management practices facilitated by knowledge management systems, organizations can better manage their tacit and explicit knowledge. In the next chapter, management of information systems infrastructure including hardware, software, telecommunication, and networks, will be discussed.

References

Alavi, M. & Leidner, D.E. 2001, 'Knowledge management and knowledge management systems: Conceptual foundations and research issues', *MIS Quarterly*, Vol. 25, No.1, pp. 107-146.

Barnett, R. 2018, 'Hyperscale Data Centers; What Are They and Why Should You Care', *The Raritan Blog*, February 1, 2018, Online, Available at: https://www.raritan.com/blog/detail/hyperscale-data-centers-what-are-they-and-why-should-you-care (accessed on 2 July 2019).

Biggs, P., Johnson, T., Lozanova, Y. & Sundberg, N. 2012, 'Emerging issues for our hyper-connected world', in *The Global Information Technology Report 2012: Living in a Hyper-connected World*, Dutta, S. & Bilbao-Osorio, B. eds, INSEAD & World Economic Forum, pp. 47-56. Bolloju, N., Khalifa, M. & Turban, E. 2002, 'Integrating knowledge management into enterprise environments for the next generation decision support', *Decision Support Systems*, Vol. 33, No. 2, pp. 163-176.

Bonner, D. 2000, *Leading Knowledge Management and Learning*, American Society of Training & Development, Virginia, U.S.A.

Brocchi, C., Grande, D., Rowashankish, K., Saleh, T. & Weinberg, A. 2018, 'Designing a data transformation that delivers value right from the start', *McKinsey Payments*, August 2018, pp. 52-59.

Brown, E. 2019, 'Getting started with AI in 2019: Prioritize data management', *The Enterprise Project*, January 09, 2019, Online, Available at: https://enterprisersproject.com/article/2019/1/getting-started-ai-2019-resolve-make-data-management-top-priority (accessed on 2 May 2019).

Brown, B., Chui, M. & Manika, J. 2011, 'Are you ready for the ear of big data', *McKinsey Quarterly*, October 2011, pp. 1-12.

Bryan, L. L. & Joyce, C. 2005, 'The 21st century organization', *McKinsey Quarterly*, Number 3, 2005, pp. 25-33.

Bughin, J., Livingston, J. & Marwaha, S. 2011, 'Seizing the potential of 'big data'', *McKinsey on Business Technology*, Number 24, Autumn 2011, pp. 8-13.

Buluswar, M., Campisi, V., Gupta, A., Karu, Z., Nilson, V. & Sigala, R. 2016, *How company are using big data and analytics,* McKinsey & Company, Interview April 2016, Online, Available at: https://www.mckinsey.com/business-functions/mckinsey-analytics/our-insights/how-companies-are-using-big-data-and-analytics (accessed on 20 January 2017).

Carson, B., Romanelli, G., Walsh P. & Zhumaev, A. 2018, 'Blockchain beyond the hype: What is the strategic business value', *Digital Marketing*, June 2018, pp. 1-13.

Caylar, P. L. & Menard, A. 2016, 'How telecom companies can win in the digital revolution', *Digital McKinsey*, September 2016, pp. 1-7.

Charlin, G., Gell, J., Bellefonds, N. D., Smith, T., Lui, V., Bellemare, J., Royston, J. & Sehili, C. 2018, 'Unlocking Growth in CPG with AI and Advanced Analytics', The Boston Consulting Group, 15 October 2018, Online, Available at: https://www.bcg.com/en-au/publications/2018/unlocking-growth-cpg-ai-advanced-analytics.aspx (accessed on 1 May 2019).

China Daily 2018, 'China Telecom Cloud Computing Inner Mongolia Information Park', *China Daily*, Nov 2, 2018, Online, Available at: http://subsites.chinadaily.com.cn/regional/hohhot/2018-11/02/c_288222.htm (accessed on 2 May 2019).

Chase, R.L. 1997, 'The knowledge-based organization: an international survey', *The Journal of Knowledge Management*, Vol.1, No.1, pp. 38-49.

Chui, M. & Fleming, T. 2011, 'Inside P & G's digital revolution', *McKinsey Quarterly*, November 2011, pp. 1-11.

Conway, R. 2012, 'Where angels will tread', The World in 2012, *The Economist*, January 2012, p. 123.

Court, D. 2015, "Getting big impact from big data", *McKinsey Quarterly*, January 2015, Online, Available at: https://www.mckinsey.com/business-functions/digital-mckinsey/our-insights/ getting-big-impact-from-big-data (accessed on 30 February 2017).

Datacenters.com 2019a, Micrsoft, Online, Available at: https://www.datacenters.com/ providers/microsoft (accessed on 16 July 2019).

Datacenters.com 2019b, Facebook, Online, Available at: https://www.datacenters.com/ providers/facebook (accessed on 16 July 2019).

Davenport, T. H. 2010, 'Rethinking knowledge work: A strategic approach', *McKinsey on Business Technology*, Number 21, Winter 2010, pp. 26-33.

Day, T. & Pham, N. D. 2017, 'Data Centers: Jobs and opportunities in communities nationwide', Technology Engagement Center, U.S. Chamber of Commerce, pp. 1-19.

Diaz, A., Rowshankish, K. & Saleh, T. 2018, 'Why data culture matters', *McKinsey Quarterly*, September 2018, pp.1-17.

Digital Realty 2019, *What is a data center*, Online, Available at: https://www.nature.com/ articles/d41586-018-06610-y (accessed on 16 July 2019).

Dijcks, J.P. 2012, 'Big data for the enterprise', *An Oracle White Paper*, January 2012, Oracle Corporation, USA.

Dutta, S., Bilbao-Osorio, B. & Geiger, T. 2012, 'The networked readiness index 2012: Benchmarking ICT progress and impacts for the next decade', in *The Global Information Technology Report 2012: Living in a Hyper-connected World*, Dutta, S. & Bilbao-Osorio, B. eds, INSEAD & World Economic Forum, pp. 3-34.

Energystar 2019, *12 Ways to save energy in data centers and server rooms*, Online, Available at: https://www.energystar.gov/products/low_carbon_it_campaign/12_ways_save_energy_data_ center (accessed on 15 July 2019).

EY 2018, *Industrializing Blockchain in Asean: Unblocking the potential Blockchain across Organizations*, Ernst & Young 2018, pp. 1-17.

Fleming, O., Fountaine, T., Henke, N. & Saleh, T. 2018, 'Ten red flags signaling your analytics program will fail', *McKinsey Analytics*, May 2018, pp. 1-8.

Forbes Insights 2018, *Is your data center holding you back*, pp. 1-5.

Fulton, S. 2019, 'How hyperscale data centers are reshaping all of IT', *Zdnet*, April 5, 2019, Online, Available at: https://www.zdnet.com/article/how-hyperscale-data-centers-are-reshaping-all- of-it/ (accessed on 1 July 2019).

Google 2019, Data Center Locations, Online, Available at: https://www.google.com/ about/datacenters/inside/locations/ (accessed on 16 July 2019).

Grone, F., Peladeau, P. & Samad, R. A. 2019, 'Tomorrow's data heroes', *Strategy+Business*, February 2019, pp. 1-13.

Haag, S., Baltzan, P. & Phillips, A. 2008, *Business Driven Technology*, 2nd edn, McGraw-Hill Irwin, Boston, USA.

Hagström, M. & Gill, N. 2012, 'The wisdom of the cloud: Hyper-connectivity, big data, and real-time analytics', in *The Global Information Technology Report 2012: Living in a Hyper-connected World*, Dutta, S. & Bilbao-Osorio, B. eds, INSEAD & World Economic Forum, pp. 97-103.

Hapler, F. 2017, 'Advanced analytics: Moving toward AI, Machine Learning, and Natural Language Processing', *Best Practices Report*, TDWI, Q3 2017, pp. 1-35.

Henke, N., Bughin, J., Chui, M., Manyika, J., Saleh, T., Wiseman, B. & Sethupathy, G. 2016, *The Age of Analytics: Competing in a Data-driven World*, McKinsey Global Institute, December 2016.

Hubbard, R. & Little, E.L. 1997, 'Share and share alike? A review of empirical Evidence concerning information sharing among researchers', *Management Research News*, Vol. 20, No.1, pp. 41-49.

IBM 2013, *The State of Graph Databases*, Online, Available at: https://www-01.ibm.com/ common/ssi/cgi-bin/ssialias?htmlfid=IMM14205USEN& (accessed on 30 June 2017).

IDC 2019, *Worldwide Blockchain Spending Forecast to Reach $2.9 Billion in 2019,* 4 March 2019, IDC, Online, Available at: https://www.idc.com/getdoc.jsp?containerId=prUS44898819 (accessed on 12 July 2019).

InterSystems 2017, *Blockchain and Preparing for Future Market Demand*, InterSystems.com, 2017, pp. 1-6.

Jones, N. 2018, 'How to stop data centres from gobbling up the world's electricity', *Springer Nature*, 13 September 2018, Online, Available at: https://www.nature.com/articles/d41586-018-06610-y (accessed on 10 June 2019).

Junnarkar, B. & Brown, C.V. 199), 'Re-Assessing the Enabling Role of Information Technology in KM', *Journal of Knowledge Management*, Vol. 1, No. 2, pp. 142-148.

Kannan, H. & Thomas, C. 2018, 'How high-tech suppliers are responding to the hyperscaler opportunity', *High Tech Practice*, October 2018, McKinsey & Company, pp. 1-10.

Kidd, C. 2018, 'What is a Hyperscale Data Center', *BMC Blog*, July 11, 2018, Online, Available at: https://www.bmc.com/blogs/hyperscale-data-center/ (accessed on 1 July 2019).

KPMG 2018, *Guardians of Trust: Who is responsible for trusted analytics in the digital age*, pp. 1-41.

Kumar, P., Sedra, R., Casanova, J. B. 2019, 'Winning with a data-driven strategy', *Strategy+Business*, June 5, 2019, pp. 1-10.

Lacity, M. C. 2018, 'Addressing key challenges to making enterprise blockchain applications a reality', *MIS Quarterly Executive*, Vol. 17, No. 3, pp. 201-222.

Laudon, K.C. & Laudon, J.P. 2005, *Essentials of Management Information Systems: Managing the Digital Firm*, 6th edn, Prentice Hall.

Laudon, K.C. & Laudon, J.P. 2012, *Essentials of Management Information Systems: Managing the Digital Firm*, 12th edn, Prentice Hall.

Leonard, D. & Sensiper, S. 1998, 'The role of tacit knowledge in group innovation', *California Management Review*, Vol. 40, No. 3, pp.112-132.

Lohr, S. 2012, The Age of Big Data, *The New Your Times*, February 11, 2012, Online Available at: http://www.nytimes.com/2012/02/12/sunday-review/big-datas-impact-in-the-world.html?pagewanted=all (accessed August 11, 2012).

MacDuffie, J. P. & Fujimoto, T. 2010, 'Why Dinosaurs Will Keep Ruling the Auto Industry', *Harvard Business Review*, June 2010, Online, Available at: https://hbr.org/2010/06/why-dinosaurs-will-keep-ruling-the-auto-industry (accessed on 4 September 2017).

Macias-Lizaso, G. 2018, 'Building an effective analytics organization', *McKinsey Payments*, August 2018, pp. 60-67.

Manyika, J. 2009, 'Hal Varian on how the Web challenges managers", *McKinsey Quarterly*, January 2009, Online available at: https://www.mckinseyquarterly.com/Strategy/Innovation/ Hal_Varian_on_how_the_Web_challenges_managers_2286 (accessed July 23, 2012).

Manyika, J., Chui, M., Brown, D., Bughin, J., Dobbs, R., Roxburgh, C. & Byers, A. H. 2011, *Big Data: The Next Frontier for Innovation, Competition, and Productivity*, McKinsey Global Institute, McKinsey & Company. Marr, B. 2017, '17 Predictions about the future of Big Data everyone should read', *Forbes*, March 15, 2016, Online, Available at: https://www.forbes.com/sites/bernardmarr/2016/03/15/17-predictions-about-the-future-of-big-data-everyone-should-read/#41fef91f1a32 (accessed on 30 September 2017).

Marr, B. 2016, '17 Predictions about the Future of Big Data Everyone Should Know', *Forbes.com*, March 15, 2016, Online, Available at: https://www.forbes.com/sites/bernardmarr/2016/03/15/17-predictions-about-the-future-of-big-data-everyone-should-read/#4fd888591a32 (accessed on 12 December 2019).

McAfee, A. & Brynjolfsson, E. 2017, 'Big Data: The Management Revolution', *Harvard Business Review*, October 2012, Online, Available at: https://hbr.org/2012/10/big-data-the-management-revolution (accessed on 20 September 2017).

McDermott, R. 1999, 'Why information technology inspired but cannot deliver knowledge management', *California Management Review*, Vol. 4, No. 4, pp. 103-117.

Moody, D. L. & Shanks, G.G. 199), 'Using knowledge management and the internet to support evidence based practice: a medical case study', *Proceedings of the 10th Australasian Conference on Information Systems,* Wellington, New Zealand, December 1-3, 1999, pp. 660-676.

Morabito, V. 2017, *Business Innovation Through Blockchain: The B³ Perspective*, Springer International Publishing, pp.21-39.

Nonaka, I. & Takeuchi, H. 1995, *The Knowledge-Creating Company-How Japanese Companies Create the Dynamic of Innovation*, Oxford University Press, New York.

O'Brien, J. A. & Marakas, G. M. 2011, *Management Information Systems*, 10th Edition, McGraw-Hill, New York, USA.

Oracle 2012, 'Driving innovation through analytics', *Executive Strategy Series*, Oracle Corporation, USA.

Plansky, J., O'Donnell, T., Richards, K. 2018, 'A Strategist's Guide to Blockchain', *Strategy+Business*, Issue 82, Spring 2016, pp. 1-10.

Podnar, K. 2019, 'How to survive the coming data privacy tsunami', *TDWI.org*, June 17, 2019, Online, Available at: https://tdwi.org/articles/2019/06/17/dwt-all-how-to-survive-data-privacy-tsunami.aspx (accessed on 2 July 2019). Polanyi, M. 1962, *Personal Knowledge: Toward a Post-Critical Philosophy*, Routledge and Kegan Paul, London, UK.

Polanyi, M. 1967, *The Tacit Dimension*, Archor Books, Doubleday, Garden City, New York, USA.

Pollard, S., Rajwanshi, V., Murphy, M. R., Auty, S., Huang, T. T., Anmuth, D., Yao, A., Hariharan, G., Willi, A. & Coster, P. 2017, *An Investor's Guide to Artificial Intelligence*, Global Equity Research, J.P. Morgan, 27 December 2017, pp. 1-112.

PwC 2018, Blockchain is here: What is your next move, Global Blockchain Survey 2018, August 2018, pp. 1-14.

Rayome, A. D. 2017, 'Here are the 10 skills you need to become a data scientist, the no.1 job in America', *Techrepublic.com*, September 22, 2017, Online, Available at: https://www.techrepublic.com/article/here-are-the-10-skills-you-need-to-become-a-data-scientist-the-no-1-job-in-america/ (accessed on 30 October 2017).

Ruggles, R. 1998, 'The state of the notion: knowledge management in practice', *California Management Review*, Vol. 40, No. 3, pp. 80-89.

SAP AG 2012, 'Harnessing the power of Big Data in real time through in-Memory technology and analytics', in *The Global Information Technology Report 2012: Living in a Hyper-connected World*, Dutta, S. & Bilbao-Osorio, B. eds, INSEAD & World Economic Forum, pp. 89-96.

Schmahl, A., Mohattala, S., Burchardi, K., Egloff, C., Govers, J., Chan, T. & Giakoumelos, M. 2019, *Resolving the Blockchain Paradox in Transportation and Logistics*, Boston Consulting Group, January 2019, pp. 1-14.

Shankar, S., Xu, J. & Sankaran, G. 2007, 'Knowledge sharing in doctoral research', *International Technology Management Review*, Vol. 1, No. 1, pp. 34-42.

Siegele L. 2012, 'Welcome to the yotta world', The World in 2012, *The Economist*, January 2012, p. 122.

Spender, J. C. 1996, 'Organizational knowledge, learning, and memory: three concepts in search of a theory', *Journal of Organizational Change Management*, Vol. 9, pp. 63-78.

Stafford, P. 2012, 'How big data can turn the smallest business into Moneyball?', *Smart Company*, Online Available at: http://www.smartcompany.com.au/information-technology/051244-best-of-the-web-how-big-data-can-turn-the-smallest-business-into-moneyball.html?utm_source=SmartCompany&utm_campaign=8ca827ec42-TechCompany_16_August_201216_08_2012&utm_medium=email (accessed August 16, 2012).

Sveiby, K.E. 1997, *The New Organizational Wealth: Managing and Measuring Knowledge-Based Assets*, Berrett-Koehler Publishers, San Francisco, USA.

Synergy Research Group 2017, *Hyperscale Data Center Count Approaches the 400 Mark; US Still Dominates*, December 20, 2017, Online, Available at: https://www.srgresearch.com/articles/hyperscale-data-center-count-approaches-400-mark-us-still-dominates (accessed on 1 July 2019).

Technavio Blog 2018, 'Top 10 Data Center Companies in the World', *Technovio Blog*, 10 Oct 2018, Online, Available at: https://blog.technavio.com/blog/top-10-data-center-companies (accessed on 1 June 2019).

The Conference Board 1999, *Beyond Knowledge Management: New Ways to Work and Learn*, The Conference Board Inc, New York, USA.

Upsite Technologies 2019, 'Top 20 Data Center Trends and Predictions to Watch for in 2019', *Upsite Technologies Blog*, Jan 16, 2019, Online, Available at: https://www.upsite.com/blog/top-20-data-center-trends-and-predictions-to-watch-for-in-2019/ (accessed on 2 April 2019).

Wikipedia 2019, Graph Database, 21 June 2019, Online, Available at: https://en.wikipedia.org/wiki/Graph_database (accessed on 2 July 2019).

Chapter 6

Managing Infrastructure for Information Systems

This chapter will review current practices and future trends of computer hardware, software, and telecommunication networks; discuss Internet of Things, 5G, Self-driving vehicles, Cloud computing, Edge computing, Mobile computing, and Quantum computing; and look at management challenges associated with managing information systems infrastructure.

6.1 Hardware and Software Management

Computer hardware and software can either improve or impede organizational performance. They are major organizational assets. Therefore it is necessary to properly manage their acquisition and use. Hardware is the equipment, the machinery, the tangible components of information systems. Software is the instructions that tell the hardware what to do. Although managers and business professionals do not need to be experts of hardware and software, a basic understanding of the role of hardware and software will assist them in making good technology decisions thus enhancing business performance and organizational productivity (Laudon & Laudon 2005, p. 192). Some questions on hardware and software in the organization are addressed in the following Table 6.1.

Table 6.1. Some questions on hardware and software

Component	What	Who	Where	How
Hardware	What hardware do we have?	Who manages it?	Where is it located?	How is it used?
	What computer processing and storage	Who uses it?	Where is it used?	How should we acquire and

	capability does our organization need to handle its information and business transactions			manage the firm's hardware assets?
	What arrangement of computers and computer processing would best benefit our organization?	Who owns it?		How would the new technologies benefit our organization?
	What criteria should we use to select our hardware?			
	What new hardware technologies are available?			
Software	What software do we have?	Who manages it?	Where is it located?	How is it used?
	What new software technologies are available?	Who uses it?	Where is it used?	How should we acquire and manage our firm's software assets?
	What kinds of software and software tools do we need to run our business?	Who owns it?		How would the new software technologies benefit our organization?
	What criteria should we use to select our software technology?			
	What new software technologies are available?			

(Sources: Developed from; Laudon & Laudon 2005, pp. 225–226; Pearlson & Saunders 2004, p.134; Pearlson & Saunders 2010, p.169; Pearlson & Saunders 2013, p.229)

Trends of hardware and software

The trend of hardware is towards user-friendly, mobile, interoperable, and connected devices. The trend of software is towards easy-to-use, Internet based, and device-independent systems and applications. One particular trend is demands such as "the Internet in the pocket", "the Internet on the move", "personal computer in the pocket", and "personal computer on the move". Device manufacturers and software developers need to address such demands by working on devices (especially tablets, smart phones) and applications for mobility. Bisson, Stephenson and Patrick Viguerie (2010) suggest that the percentages of mobile phone users have jumped from 3% of the world population to 50% in 15 years' time and nearly 50% of all new mobile phones purchased in developed markets are smartphones; and within just three years of iPhone's launch developers have done more than 200,000 applications. IDG Connect (2012) finds out that a majority (71%) of business and information systems executives around the world own tablets. Meeker (2017) argues that the trend of enterprise software is Perpetual, On-premise Software>>>Cloud-based SaaS (software-as-a-service) Apps>>> Mobile Smart Apps.

Evaluation of hardware and software

How do companies evaluate and select hardware and software? When making decisions on hardware, there is much more to look at than deciding the fastest and cheapest computer devices. Many factors for software evaluation would be the same as those used for hardware evaluation since software and hardware are intertwined (e.g., without software hardware can do nothing while without hardware software is useless). Many vendors of hardware and software and other firms offer a variety of information systems services to end users and organisations. When organizations are evaluating hardware, software, and service options, some specific questions have to be asked and evaluated (refer to Table 6.2).

Table 6.2. Evaluation of hardware, software and services

Evaluation Subject	Evaluation Criteria
Hardware	• Performance: speed, capacity, throughput? • Cost: lease or purchase price, cost of operations and maintenance?

	• Reliability: risk of malfunction, maintenance requirements, error control and diagnostic features? • Compatibility: with existing hardware and software? with hardware & software provided by competing suppliers? • Connectivity: easily connected to networks that use different types of network technologies and bandwidth alternatives? • Scalability: can it handle the processing demands of end users, transactions, queries, & other processing requirements? • Software: is system and application software available that can best use this hardware? • Support: is support available? • Ergonomics: user-friendly? safe, comfortable, easy to use? "human factors engineered"? • What is the total hardware cost (e.g. desktops, servers, mobile platforms, printers, archival storage, technical support, administration, training, informal support, and retirement cost)? • Technology: year of product life cycle? Does it use a new, untested technology? Does it run the risk of obsolescence?
Software	• Quality: bug free? • Efficiency: well-developed system of program code that does not use much CPU time, memory capacity, or disk space? • Flexibility: Can it handle our processes easily without major modification? • Security: Does it provide control procedures for errors, malfunctions, and improper use? • Connectivity: Web-enabled? • Language: Is the programming language familiar to internal software developers? • Documentation: well-documented? Help screens and helpful software agents? • Interoperability: can work with open source software? mobile apps? cloud-based solutions? • Hardware: Does existing hardware have the features required to best use this software? • What is the total software cost (e.g. operating systems,

	office suite, database, proprietary, technical support, administration, training, and informal support)?
	• Other factors: Setup decision, software delivery practices, software management practices, software development practices, required architecture, talent, performance, cost, reliability, availability, compatibility, modularity, technology, human-centric design, ergonomics, scalability, and support characteristics?
Information Systems Services	• Performance: record of past performance?
	• Systems Development: Are website and other e-business developers available? What are their quality and cost?
	• Maintenance: Is equipment maintenance provided? What are its quality and cost?
	• Conversion: What systems development and installation services will they provide during the conversion period?
	• Training: Is the necessary training of personnel provided? What are its quality and cost?
	• Total cost of ownership: What is the total cost of using the service?
	• Backup: Are similar computer facilities available nearby for emergency backup purposes?
	• Accessibility: Dose the vendor provide local or regional sites that offer sales, systems development, and hardware maintenance services? Is a customer support centre at the vendor's website available? Is a customer hot line provided?
	• Business Position: Is the vendor financially strong, with good industry market prospects?
	• Hardware: Do they provide a wide selection of compatible hardware devices and accessories?
	• Software: Do they offer a variety of useful e-business software and application packages?
	• Security, Privacy and Risk Management: What are the vendor's security, privacy and risk management policies and processes?
	• Data management and Governance: Has the vendor put in place of effective data management policies and governance mechanism?

(Sources: Gnanasambandam et al. 2017; Morrison 2018; O'Brien & Marakas 2006, pp.420-422; Pearlson & Saunders 2013, p.229; Toesland 2019):

On a related note, by surveying 3,124 global IT and business professionals, IDG Connect (2012) identifies five factors important for owners and potential owners of tablets, including functionality, applications availability, branding, appearance and price.

6.2 Networks and Telecommunications Management

Telecommunications and network technologies are connecting and revolutionising business and society. We are now live in a world of "The Global Grid": everyone and everything is connected (Bisson, Stephenson & Patrick Viguerie 2010). Many organisations today could not survive without a variety of interconnected computer networks to service their information processing and communications needs. Businesses have become networked enterprises, where the Internet, intranets and extranets are networking to business processes and employees and linking them to their customers, suppliers and other business stakeholders (O'Brien & Marakas 2011, p. 218).

Trends of telecommunications

As Eric Schmidt, Former Google Senior Executive argues (reported in Manyika 2008), in the digital world and the networked economy, the cost of transmission and distribution of information has becoming lower and lower even though it is still very costly to build underlying infrastructure (in fact it is a long term investment. The Internet we have today is largely a result of the investments made about 30 years ago during the first wave of Internet booming). To survive and grow in the rapidly evolving digital world, telecommunication firms should (1) reinvent their core business by digitizing all the touch points and channels interacting with their customers and becoming a multiple service provider; (2) move into adjacent businesses (e.g., financial services, IT services, media, healthcare, utilities, automotive, retail/e-commerce); (3) developing required talent and capabilities (e.g., skills in Big Data and Data Analytics, Big Data IT Architecture, and Lean Digital Processes); (4) revamping IT (e.g., focusing on agility, speed, flexibility, scalability, simplicity, automation), and (5) taking the customer-centric approach-whatever we do is to understand and meet the needs of our customers) (Caylar & Menard 2016).

Currently a consortium of more than 300 universities, government agencies and private businesses are collaborating to find ways to make the Internet more efficient and are working on the project of the next generation of Internet – Internet2 (http://www.internet2.edu). The primary goals of the Internet2 project are: creating a leading edge very-high speed network for the research community, enabling revolutionary Internet applications, and ensuring the rapid transfer of new network services and applications to the broader Internet community. Internet2 is a high-performance network that uses an entirely different infrastructure than the public Internet we know today. But Internet2 was never intended to replace the current Internet, rather its purpose is to build a roadmap that can be followed when the next stage of innovation to the current Internet takes place. Most institutions and commercial partners are connected via Abilene, a network backbone that will soon support throughput of 10 gigabits per second. Internet2 is all about high-speed telecommunications and infinite bandwidth. What do you think the Internet will 'look' like in the future? On a related note, while IPV4 has around 4 billion (2X 32 IP addresses), IPV6 (2X 128 IP addresses) could allocate each human being on the earth a few IP addresses (Biggs et al. 2012, p.52).

6.3 The Internet of Things

The Internet of Things refers to objects embedded with sensors and actuators and linked with wired and wireless network (Chui, Löffle & Roberts 2010). They have the ability to sense the environment and deliver large volume of data through networks. According to Bisson, Stephenson and Patrick Viguerie (2010), there are more than 35 billion of Internet Things (including sensors, routers, cameras, and the like), and the number is growing very quickly.

The Internet of Things could assist organizations' efforts of Information & Analysis and Automation & Control (Chui, Löffler & Roberts 2010):

• Tracking behaviour: monitoring the behaviour of persons, things, or data through space and time (e.g., targeted advertising based on the location of the users of smart phones; real-time information of movement of packages from warehouse to end user).

• Enhanced situational awareness: realizing real-time and accurate information of physical environment (e.g., utilizing sensor networks that combine video, audio and vibration detectors to identify unauthorized individuals and crime suspects).

• Supporting decision making via sensor-driven business analytics: supporting long-range and more complex planning and decision making (e.g., remote monitoring and controlling oil & gas operations; remote monitoring and controlling medical procedures).

• Optimizing resource consumption and management: monitoring and controlling resource consumption across the network (e.g., managing consumption (and pricing) of water, electricity and energy via networked sensors and automatic feedback mechanism).

• Improving processes: automating processes by having much better information granularity (e.g., automation of chemical plants by utilizing sensors and actuators along the production lines).

• Enhanced ability (especially in open environments with great uncertainty): rapid and real-time sensing and responding systems (e.g., sensors in the two cars could detect and avoid potential collision between them).

It is estimated that the potential economic impact of IoT applications could be up to $11.1 trillion per year in 2025 from nine settings (Manyika et al. 2015):

• Human (e.g., devices to monitor and maintain human health and wellbeing).

• Home (e.g., smart home applications).

• Retail environment (e.g., automated checkout, location-based mobile user assistance applications, in-store personalized promotion, real-time inventory monitoring and replacement systems).

• Offices (e.g., security management & access control in the office, augmented training, employee monitoring, office asset management).

• Factories (e.g., production and warehouse management systems).

• Worksites (e.g., workplace health and safety management, predicative maintenance, operation optimization)

• Cities (e.g., smart city applications).

• Outside (e.g., self-driving vehicles, GPS applications).

On a related note, it is estimated that business-to-business (B2B) IoT applications create more value than pure consumer applications (i.e., 70% vs. 30%). The IoT technology spending can be divided into areas such as integration services (20-40% of total spending), software/app development (20-35%), software infrastructure (5-20%), connectivity (0-10%), and hardware (20-30%). Meanwhile some enablers and barriers of IoT include (Manyika et al. 2015):

• Better and affordable technology is essential (e.g., cheaper sensors and better analytical software).

• Interoperability between different types of devices and sensors and between data from different sources, is required. Interoperability is critical to maximizing the value of the Internet things and accounts for up to 40% of the total value.

- Privacy and confidentiality issues (e.g., can consistent privacy policies and practices be applied to all the connected devices and parties?).
- Security concerns (e.g., arising from very wide connections).
- Intellectual property issues (e.g., arising from devices and data from different vendors and sources).
- Organization and talent perspectives (e.g., are organizations ready or suitable for IoT implementation? do organizations have required expertise?).
- Public policy (e.g., have appropriate regulations been complied with or regulatory approvals been sought for IoT connections?).

6.4 5G

5G is the next evolution of the mobile (wireless) network. It offers much faster speed (e.g., gigabits a second) and highly reliable connections & data communications, and it cuts down latency (so we can have (near) real-time communication) and enable Internet of Things applications and networks with much lower power and cost (Brake 2016; Grijpnil, Nattermann & London 2019). 5G is a critical element of the new data economy with more than 50 billion connected things coming from various areas (e.g., smart cities, connected health, smart home, smart agriculture, smart media, industry 4.0 and automation) (Intel 2019). It is estimated that 5G will enable $12 trillion of global economic activity, generate $3.5 trillion global gross value chain output, and support 22 million jobs in 2035(Campbell et al. 2017). Some critical services will be supported by 5G include: autonomous vehicles, drones, industrial automation, remote patient monitoring/telehealth, and smart grid (Campbell et al. 2017). Some performance criteria for 5G include: latency in the air link (<1ms), latency end-to-end (device to core) (<10ms), connection density (100 times faster compared with 4G LTE), area capacity density (1 Tbit/s/km^2), system spectral efficiency (10b its/s/Hz/cell), peak throughput (downlink) per connection (10 Gbit/s), and energy efficiency (>90% improvement over LTE) (GSA 2015). Countries and regions such as the U.S., Europe, South Korea, Japan and China and businesses such as Nokia, Huawei, Ericsson, Samsung, Qualcomm, Intel, ZTE, and LG have been actively working on 5G initiatives (Nokia 2016).

According to a McKinsey worldwide 5G Survey in 2018 (reported in Grijpnil Nattermann & London 2019), many 5G deployments will be coming in the near future (e.g., 92% respondents are planning 5G deployment by 2022). Another forecast (reported in GSA 2015), by 2025, there will be over 270 networks (local or regional areas) worldwide with full 5G capacity. However it can be argued that the global implementation of 5G is still in the early stage (Fisher 2019). One of the biggest challenges of rolling out 5G networks is the cost of establishing 5G networks. For example, 5G typically operates at the high frequency ranges, and consequently the density of the network is significantly higher (e.g., typically up to 30-45 base stations per square kilometre in the urban areas) (Grijpnil Nattermann & London 2019). Another significant challenge is the standardization of 5G technology (GSA 2015). Without agreed 5G technology standards, the future 5G networks will not be efficient and interoperable. Some other challenges include: lack of suitable spectrum, delay in providing terminals/handsets, difficulties in establishing business cases, technical complexity, and lack of compelling use cases (GSA 2015). On the other hand, 5G technologies and networks could increase the exposure to radio frequency electromagnetic fields (RF-EMF) and could have potential hazards for human health and the environment (Wagner 2019).

6.5 Self-driving Vehicles

It can be said that the development, deployment and acceptance of self-driving vehicles is still in the early stage, but it is predicted by 2030, up to 80% of Chinese, European and US miles will be at or approaching self-driving (Heineke et al. 2019); by 2030, 42% of vehicle transport in China, 21% in Europe and 5% in the U.S., will be autonomous (Kuhnert 2019). One of the interesting issues associated with self-driving vehicles is insurance, and it is expected that the first autonomous/self-driving vehicle insurance policies will be written by 2019 even though the insurance firms are still catching up with the advances in technology and the changes in the operating environment (e.g., changing nature of mobility, losing control over the data, cyberattacks on transportation systems or accidents resulting from system failures, and lack of regulations on self-driving car accidents, other unknowns) and working on the pricing and risk management models(Heineke et al. 2019; Martin, Schwartz & Garfinkel 2017).

To fully roll-out self-driving vehicles, self-driving vehicle ecosystem has to be established (Heineke et al. 2017; Heineke et al. 2019; The Author's Own Knowledge):

• Vehicles and Manufacturers: the vehicle has to equipped with latest technologies & systems (e.g., IoT applications, 5G connections, AI systems), and the price of the vehicle is affordable. Some key sensor systems include: global position systems (GPS), light detection and ranging, cameras, radio detection and ranging radar, infrared sensors, ultrasound sensors, dedicated sensors, dedicated short-range communication, inertial navigation system, prebuilt maps, and odometery sensors.

• Road: power/battery charging stations and wireless connections as well as networked sensors (e.g., sensors for vehicle to vehicle, vehicle to pedestrian, vehicle to network) on the road need to be in place for self-driving vehicles.

• Customers/Consumers: are they ready for being the passenger in the self-driving vehicles? do they have the knowledge to deal with system failures and traffic accidents? are they willing to share the self-driving vehicles with other people whom they may not know?

• Insurance firms: are they ready for writing insurance for self-driving vehicles?

• Police forces: are they ready for assessing and investigating road accidents involving self-driving vehicles?

• Utility industry: can the electricity produced by self-driving vehicles integrate with exists grids? and get paid for?

• Societal issues: is mobility a common thing in the community? how and where people live and consume?

• Public policies: have legislations for regulating self-driving vehicles and services for self-driving vehicles been established? how about legislations for using and sharing the data generated from self-driving vehicle networks established? how about legislations for dealing with accidents between pedestrians and self-driving vehicles?

6.6 Cloud Computing

Cloud computing basically is another type of outsourcing (Phelan 2018) and refers to lease computing resources (including software, networks, servers, storage, processing, operation systems, applications, services) on the networks (especially the Internet) as per usage, and it can deploy in the models of private cloud (solely for one firm and could be managed by the organization or a third party on its premise or off its premise), public cloud (is made to the general public or a large industry group and is owned by an organization selling cloud services), and hybrid cloud (the combination of private and public) (Compuware 2010; Trend Micro 2010).

By adopting cloud-computing, organizations could (1) better utilize their IS/IT investments; (2) have better flexibility, quicker responses to changes, enhanced ability for information systems to scale up, better ability of disaster recovery and business continuity; and (3) focus on their core business (especially for small and medium firms). One good example (reported in Roberts, Sarrazin & Sikes 2010) is by using Amazon's cloud computing facilities, The New York Times digitalized and catalogued more than 100 years of archived articles in a 24-hour period, avoiding the need to configure and run a set of servers for a onetime effort. In line with the rapid progress and huge potential of cloud computing, major ICT firms have committed significant resources to cloud computing developments.

Some typical technologies associated with cloud computing include virtualization and service-oriented architecture. It could be argued that the approach of clouding computing is not really new (e.g., thinking about the example of mainframe computer to individual users of it). The difference is between sharing computing resources on the networks (there are more than 50 million servers and most of them operates only at 15% of capacity (Intel Corporation 2011; Harvard Business Review 2010)) and sharing the main-frame computer. Some characteristics of cloud computing consist of: (1) on-demand self-service (for example, required computing resources could be run automatically without human interaction once the parameters and instructions are set); (2) broad network access (can access via various devices such as mobile devices, personal computers, laptops); (3) resource pooling (the provider's computing resources are pooled to serve multiple clients simultaneously by using a multi-tenant model); (4) rapid elasticity (the ability of quickly scaling out and scaling in according to the changes in demand); and (5) measured service (adopting metering capability for transparency in monitoring, controlling and reporting) (Compuware Corporation 2010).

Cloud service models include (Compuware Corporation 2010; Intel Corporation 2011; Rouse 2017, 2018, 2019; Toesland; Trend Micro 2010):

• Cloud Software as a Service (SaaS): it provides customer with the capability to use the provider's applications sitting on a cloud infrastructure. Examples of SaaS include Google's Gmail system and Microsoft's Office 365.

• Cloud Platform as a Service (PaaS): it provides customer with the capability to deploy applications on the cloud platform using programming languages and tools supported by the cloud provider, who has full control of the cloud infrastructure. Examples include Microsoft's Windows Azure and Google App engine.

• Infrastructure as a Service (IaaS): the customer has the ability to access processing, storage, networks and other fundamental computing resources and run arbitrary software such as operating systems and applications. But such computing resources controlled by the customer are typically for securing their own virtual machines and applications & data residing on them, the cloud provider still controls the underlying cloud infrastructure. Examples include Amazon EC2 and vCloud.

• Anything as a service (XaaS): the customer can access many services provided by cloud service providers and manage its IT infrastructure management via click-and-play environment via the web on the network. Examples include: M5 Networks and Microsoft. One related concept is serverless computing model which refers to a cloud service provider runs the servers for the customer and is in charge of managing the allocation of the customer's computing resources (Violino 2019).

Meanwhile some top concerns of cloud computing are: security, privacy, and availability & performance as well as cost uncertainty, vendor lock-in and compliance/governance issues (Casey 2017; Compuware 2010, Intel Corporation 2011; Meeker 2017; Phelan 2019; Schwenderman, Horner & Shah 2019; Trend Micro 2010). Security and privacy issues are critical and typical for cloud computing since you have put your critical information/data in other people's properties and you have no good idea and have no effective control regarding what is going to happen to your data/information. According to Symantec 2019 cloud security survey among 1,250 security decision makers worldwide, 73% of the respondents suggested immature cloud security practices are responsible cloud security incidents and 93% of the respondents believed that their organizations need to work on enhancing cloud security skills.

Furthermore issues such as multi-tenancy (you are completely unaware of your neighbour's identity, security profile or intention), data access control and protection (the cloud provider could easily move around your data for their purposes), and data romance (there is no clear standard on how the cloud provider should recycle memory and disk space). So it is likely the next user of your ex-rented cloud computing resources could have your critical and confidential data), and data privacy issues (for example, data losses/leakage and breaches are top security concerns of cloud computing, especially for public cloud) further highlight the need for effective security management of information/data in the cloud.

Organizations need to put in place effective security management process and tools (e.g., encryption, good security/encryption key management access control, auditing) to protect the information in the cloud. Availability & performance issues are logic concerns when you are relying on other people's services. At the moment, even you host applications/systems in your organization, the availability is around 99% since the networks are controlled by the telecoms, and while you put your applications/systems with the cloud service provider, the availability may become 99% X 99% X 99%..... since problems may come from each part of the cloud chain. One effective way to deal with such issues are to sign a service level agreement (SLA) with cloud service provider.

Another concern is the hidden costs in the cloud, and organizations need to pay close attention to data transfer charges, which could increase dramatically once required cloud service and computing power grow to a certain level (Harvard Business Review 2010). Some other concerns (or required actions) include evaluating the current IT portfolio, understanding the need for adapting business processes & operating models to cloud applications, addressing issues with integration and interoperability with the firm's computing infrastructure, adjusting technology governance processes (e.g., policies for control, monitoring) for cloud applications, having a cloud migration plan and/or a cloud strategy, identifying the right vendors, adopting new KPIs for IT (e.g., standardization and automation vs. availability), working on change management & organizational changes, and developing the required skills for managing cloud applications (Boommadevara, Del Miglio & Jansen 2018; Boommadevara, Kaplan & Starikova 2016; Dutta, Grewal & Hrishikesh 2019; Gnanasambandam et al. 2017; Roberts & Sikes 2011). Cloud platform choice is another issue (e.g., Amazon Web Services vs. Microsoft Azure), organizations could examine factors such as: commercial terms (e.g., up-front cost of onboarding, recurring expenses and contract flexibility), ease of use (e.g., the ability to onboard quickly, ongoing support), platform features (e.g., data complexity, compliance flexibility, platform architecture), and data sovereignty considerations (Gnanasambandam et al. 2017).

Hybrid cloud and multi-cloud are two popular cloud systems. Hybrid cloud is a combination of in-house systems (for some core functions) supplemented by cloud-based applications, and it is becoming quite popular for reasons such as: organizations need improved abilities (e.g., optimized productivity, improved functionality and real-time decision making analytics) but don't want to add to or change the in-house legacy system as well as the argument that cloud-based solutions (another type of outsourcing) work for some scenarios only despite the push from the cloud vendors (CompuData 2015; Phelan 2018; Rimini Street 2018; Rimini Street 2019). Multi-cloud is about using cloud services from different providers to meet specific workload needs or application requirements (Casey 2017). When organizations are embarking on multi-cloud, they need to choose the right vendors and have thorough understanding of pricing, security, compliance, integration and other perspectives of potential cloud platforms.

On a related note, grid-computing and virtualization are closely related to the cloud computing. The former looks at utilizing the shared computing resources of computer networks while the latter refers to distribute your available computing resources among many users or environment (e.g., divide your servers into sub-servers for different dedicated purposes/applications or run multiple systems on a single hardware system) (Red Hat 2019; Strickland 2019). Computing approaches such as grid computing, cloud computing, and virtualisation, can enable businesses to (1) have better inter-operability and integration of their various applications from different vendors in different languages, formats, platforms, (2) better utilise and streamline their information systems resources, (3) look at delivering computing as a service rather than a product; and (4) thus improve the efficiency and effectiveness of their information systems investments.

6.7 Edge Computing

The massive amount of data received from Internet of Things (IoT) networks (or arguably Internet of Everything networks) have really tested the limit of the existing computing facilities (e.g., data centres/the clouds), especially for those use cases needing reliable and swift (if not real-time responses) computing and are quite far away from central computing capabilities located in the data centres/the clouds. Edge computing is about bringing computational capabilities (e.g., data collection & processing, data storage, backup, and data analytics) closer to the end users or the locations by utilizing micro-type data centres or other smaller version of central computing facilities, without sending all the data to the data centres/the clouds and relying on the computing capabilities of the data centres/the clouds (the data or the critical data can be sent to the central computing facilities later (e.g., on the daily basis)) (Brown 2018; Butler 2017; Chabas et al. 2018; Fabel 2019; Harris 2019; MSV 2017; Oveby 2019a; Overby 2019b; Wikipedia 2019).

A good analogy is a popular hot food service provider will have smaller branches in suburbs to deal with orders from suburbs instead of delivering every order from its central city shop since the hot food may become cold when it arrives at the address in the suburb and it would be expensive to do so from its central city shop as well (Overby 2019a). Some drivers of edge computing include: unstable connectivity & data mobility issues, the need for real-time or swift decision making, requirement for localized computing power on light weighted devices, storage and security needs arising from data collected from remote and mobile devices, and the issues of power and infrastructure variations in different areas and regions (Chabas et al. 2019). Some top use cases include: Travel, transportation, and logistics (e.g., location-based advertising & retailing, drones, self-driving cars); Global energy and materials (e.g., health & safety in mining, offer shore drilling, predictive maintenance); and Public sector and utilities (e.g., public transportation monitoring, water quality monitoring) (Brown 2018; Butler 2017; Chabas et al. 2019; Harris 2019).

Some key concerns/issues of edge computing include: security (e.g. edge devices could be vulnerable), cost (e.g., difficulties in deciding on the total cost. For example, network cost could be underestimated), and ongoing support and maintenance requirements (e.g., to ensure, continuous, frictionless and dynamic connection, delivery and computing of massive amount data, the ongoing deployment and maintenance of edge computing assets is critical) (Bulter 2017; Oveby 2019b; The Author's Own Knowledge).

Even though the development, adoption and diffusion of these technologies (e.g., cloud computing, edge computing, quantum computing) methodologies, and approaches have grown rapidly in recent years, however a lot more has to be done or to happen (e.g., standards & standardization, governance, integration, open interface, training & development, skills update, talent management, network reliability, organization's readiness).

6.8 Mobile Computing

El-Darwiche, Singh & Genediwalla (2012) suggest that more people today have access to a mobile phone than to electricity. Bold and Davidson (2012, p.71) suggest that the installed base of smartphones exceeded that of PCs in 2011 and is growing more than three times faster than personal computers, for example, the expected shipment of the former and the latter in 2019 are 1,745.4 million and 257 million respectively (Garner 2019b). Today's smartphones deliver increasing rich experiences to consumers, including full web-browsing and computing capabilities, high-definition video, 3D gaming, access to social networks, and many other compelling services. Garner reported in May 2011 (cited in Bold & Davidson 2012, p. 72) that total download of mobile applications reached 8 billion in 2010 and should surpass 100 billion by 2015. Ericsson estimates (cited in Dutta, Bilbao-Osorio & Geiger (2012, p.3)) there will be more than 50 billion connected devices in the world by 2020. It is reported (cited in Berman & Bell 2011) by the end of 2011, smart phones and tablet-computers will overtake personal computer shipments; and downloads of mobile applications (Apps) are expected to surge from 11 billion in 2010 to 77 billion in 2014. Meanwhile it is estimated that by 2025 up to $2.5 trillion potential economic impact could be generated from mobile services (Henke et al. 2016, p.9).

Mobility is becoming an important agenda for organizations as a result of the wide adoption of mobile devices (especially smart phones and tablets), the availability of fast cabled and wireless networks (e.g., 3G, 4G, 5G), and the explosion of innovative mobile applications. According to a recent McKinsey survey of 250 CIOs on their organizations' mobile strategies (cited in Akella et al. 2012), 56% of respondents reported demand from employees to support a wide range of mobile devices, 77% were going to allow staff to use personal mobile devices to access company data and applications, and nearly 100% expected to deploy more than 25 mobile applications in the next two years. The survey also identified top three challenges for mobile computing: (1) security concerns (wireless communication is more vulnerable than wired one, and the mobile devices have higher chance of getting lost or stolen because of their smaller size);(2) costs (including costs for devices, connectivity, applications, maintenance & support); and (3) associated organizational challenges (e.g., fit with existing structure, process, information systems development & management, infrastructure, and governance required for mobile computing). In line with the results of the survey, Akella et al. (2012) suggest four steps for implementing a holistic mobility strategy: (1) defining your mobile policy, (2) developing the support/required infrastructure for mobile computing, (3) identifying priority user segments and meeting their needs (e.g., field people and sales/marketing people will be the major users for whom extensive access to firms' data and applications should be provided while for others access to email, calendar and other simple applications or long-tail applications could be provided), and (4) integrating mobility into computing capabilities of the organization (and making mobile computing a part of information systems governance).

Another trend of mobile computing is bring-your-own-device (BYOD) phenomenon. BYOD could involve both hardware (e.g., mobile phones, tablets, laptops, desktops, wearables) and software (e.g., cloud storages, chat systems, online collaboration tools, social networking sites, online app stores, modified and original applications) (Steelman, Lacity & Sabherwal 2016). When embarking on the journal of BYOD, organizations should encourage and support the initiatives of BYOD; explore opportunities of BYOD; use BYOD for innovative activities & projects; conduct thorough testing; pay close attention to information & system security and data privacy &governance issues; establish and execute processes and policies for BYOD; have required organizational adjustments (e.g., cultural and structural adjustments); balance freedom, control, compatibilities and security perspectives (e.g., more control and security could result in reduced functionality and compatibility); and promote the benefits of BYOD (e.g., cost saving, gains in productivity, and innovation) & provide incentives for the benefits arising from BYOD (Steelman, Lacity & Sabherwal 2016; The Author's Own Knowledge).

6.9 Quantum Computing

Quantum Computing has attracted a lot attention in recent years, and it is estimated that the quantum computing market will exceed $5 billion by 2020(Srivastava, Choi & Cook 2016). Quantum computers adopt quantum mechanism for their basic operations and are difficult to build (Shor 1998; Srivastava, Choi & Cook 2016). The commercialization of quantum computers is still not certain, but a number of firms (e.g., D-Wave Systems, Regetti Consulting, IBM, Microsoft, Google, Intel, NTT, Alibaba, Zapata Computing, Cambridge Quantum Computing, IonQ, Qutech, Tellus Matrix Group, Quantika) and countries (e.g., China, USA, Germany, UK, Japan, Canada, Australia) have been actively investing into developing quantum computers over the years. IBM recently announced that it will deliver its first commercialized quantum computers in next 3-5 years (Loeffier 2019).

Some critical properties of quantum computer include (Fursman & Gerbert & Ruess 2018, p.5; IBM 2017; Srivastava, Choi & Cook 2016; Zaribafiyan 2017):

• Quantum bits (Qubits): Qubits take on arbitrary values between the state "0" and state "1" while the bits of the classical computers choose either state "0" or state "1" (i.e., on and off position of transistors).

• Superposition: An overlay of the states of "0" and "1".

• Entanglement: Qubits occupy intertwined states while the bits class computers are kept separated (i.e., either 0 or 1).

• Quantum gates: Representing logical operations based on entangled quantum states.

• Interference: Quantum states can interfere with each other.

• Measurement: The rich information of a computational state cannot be directly read, but collapses to a discrete state with some probability (i.e., quantum answers are probabilistic with multiple possible answers being considered in a given computation).

One key attributes for quantum computers' fast computing power is the quantum parallel computing enabled by its critical properties (i.e., quantum computers can operate in multiple states at the same time while classic computer can only involve one defined path) (Fursman & Zaribafiyan 2017; Poo & Wang 2018). Some assessment criteria for quantum computer performance consist of: number of physical qubits on a chip (current range: 2-20), number of logical qubits used for fault-tolerant quantum computing (current range: 0), qubit lifetime (current range: $50\mu s$-50s), gate fidelity for two-qubit operation (current range: 90-99.9%), gate operation time for two-qubit operation (current range: 1ns- 50 μs), connectivity between qubits (current range 1:1- n:n), scalability (current range: low to high), and maturity of technology readiness level (current range: TRL 1-5) (Gerbert & Ruess 2018, p.14).

However it can be said that quantum computers are not intended to replace classical computers, but to complement each other; and quantum computers are more for complex problems that beyond the capabilities of classical/traditional computers (IBM 2017; Marr 2017; Poo & Wang 2018). Some potential use cases of quantum computing include: High tech (e.g., machine learning, search, bidding strategies for advertisements, cybersecurity, software verification and validation), Industrial goods (e.g., material design, fault analysis, production optimization, traffic simulation, logistics & production scheduling, utility system distribution optimization), Healthcare, Chemistry & Pharma (e.g., drug development, bioinformatics, patient diagnosis, cancer & drug discovery, individually tailored treatments, protein folding), Business & Finance (e.g., trading strategies, advertising scheduling & advertising revenue maximization, portfolio optimization, risk analysis, market simulation, fraud detection, scenario analysis), and Energy (e.g., network design, energy distribution, oil well optimization) (Fursman & Zaribafiyan 2017; Gerbert & Ruess 2018, p.9; IBM 2017; Poo & Wang 2018; Srivastava, Choi & Cook 2016).

Some recommended action plans regarding implementing quantum computing in the organization include (Fursman & Zaribafiyan 2017):

• Short-term plan: (1) exploring available tools and their capabilities, (2) identifying areas suitable for quantum computing, (3) testing initial use cases, and developing a timeline for how these tested use cases can scale up with quantum computing advancements.

• Long-term plan: (1) developing a roadmap, (2) having someone to monitor and report the trends regularly, and (3) building and testing quantum-ready applications and preparing for putting into the use when the suitable conditions evolve.

6.10 Management Challenges

Understanding Global ICT Industry

The worldwide IT spending will reach $3.9 trillion in 2020, with $270 billion on data centre systems, $462 billion on enterprise software, $677 billion on devices, $1,065 billion on IT services, and $1,513 billion on communication services (Gartner 2019a). According to a study by the consulting firm Booz & Company on Global ICT (information and communication technology) companies reported in Acker, Gröne and Schröder (2012), top ten ICT leaders are (in the order): Microsoft, Oracle, IBM, HP, Cisco Systems, Apple, SAP, Xerox, Accenture and CSC. The ranking is completed by looking at each firm's performance in the perspectives of: financial performance (i.e., how is the ability of sustaining the profitability needed to make future investments), portfolio strength (i.e., how good is the mix of different products/services), go-to-market footprint (i.e., how is the sales and delivery capabilities in the top markets for ICT), and growth potential (i.e., how is innovation capacity? presence in the emerging markets? the ability to attract new customers?).

In addition, in the above-mentioned study by Booz & Company reported in Acker, Gröne and Schröder (2012), they have grouped top 50 ICT firms into four categories:

• Hardware and infrastructure firms: including HP, Apple, Samsung, Dell, Fujitsu, Cisco Systems, NEC, Ericsson, Xerox, and Alcatel Lucent

• Software and Internet firms: including Microsoft, Oracle, Google, SAP, Yahoo, SAP, Yahoo, Symantec, Intuit, Adobe, Amdocs, and Convergys

• Information systems service providers (Global firms, regional providers, and offshore firms in emerging markets): including IBM, Accenture, CSC, Capgemini, First Data, Tata Consulting Services, Hitachi, Wipro, Atos, Infosys, Logica, Cognozant, Capita, Unisys, IT Holdings, HCL, Indra, Steria, and Tieto

• Telecom operating firms (mobile, landline, Internet and television): including NTT, AT & T, Verizon, Deutsche Telecom, Telefonica, Vodafone, France Telecom, KDDI, British Telecom, and KPN.

Meanwhile the emerging trends in the ICT industry are:

• Hardware and infrastructure firms such as Apple, HP, Dell, Cisco Systems and Xerox while they are still focusing on their core business (e.g., building more powerful and affordable devices and equipment), they are also working hard on differentiation strategy and branching out into Software and Service areas.

• Software and Internet firms are expanding into other areas selectively. Large firms are either entering certain new territories (e.g., Alibaba and Amazon offering cloud services, Microsoft and Google embarking on hardware business) or focusing on enhancing their lead in the industry (e.g., via acquisition and consolidation)-an example is Oracle's move to the complete integration skills through acquisition of Sun Microsystems to seek for markets traditionally owned by system integrators and information systems service providers). Other smaller players are trying to be specialized & sufficiently distinctive and create relatively protected platforms for growth.

• Global information systems service providers (such as IBM and CSC) are starting offering some telecom services (e.g., telephony services by IBM and conferencing solutions by CSC) while they are keeping their large scale and industry leading position. Regional service providers (e.g., Atos in France, Logica in the UK, and Unisys in the US) are working on expanding their market share and increasing their scale (e.g., through mergers and acquisitions) while offshore firms (especially firms in India such as HCL, Infosys and Wipro) are actively entering ICT developed markets (including the U.S., the U. K., Japan, Germany, France-these five markets contributed 60% of Global ICT sales in 2011) by leveraging advantages of large pool of talent with lower salaries. In addition, the "follow-the-sun" delivery (e.g., a project could be worked on from different locations in different zones 24 hours a day) become a reality as a result of global connectedness.

• Although Telecom firms have not been active in investing in innovating as a result of the on-going investments required for network structure and dividend commitments, they are starting cross boundaries and entering into information systems service areas (e.g., Verizon and NTT's offerings for cloud computing services).

• Integration is an important information systems service area for ICT firms for reasons such as the wide adoption of cloud-based applications and the ever increasing demand for enterprise mobility. ICT firms working in or intending to embark on service areas should upgrade or complete their integration skills.

• For most ICT firms their main revenue are still coming from classic ICT products and services, and the financial performance of new (or so called next generation) products and services (e.g., highly specialized services, RFID solutions, near-field communications, cloud computing, mobile computing, and social computing) will be realized in the future.

• As ICT firms compete across boundaries, the winners are those firms that are more innovative, more responsive to customers, and better able to deliver more with lower costs. In order to stay ahead of the competition, they have to be fast-moving, flexible and with something distinctive that no other firms can duplicate/copy.

• ICT firms also need to be aware non-ICT firms could be major competitors and venture into areas of ICT firms, for example Amazon is providing many products and services traditionally covered by ICT firms.

The trends of global ICT industry (including hardware & infrastructure firms, software & Internet firms, IT service providers, and Telecom operators as per the classification by Acker, GrÖne & SchrÖder 2012) can be summarised as the increasing of attention and efforts on building the business ecosystems (also called digital ecosystems) to survive the tough competition, stay ahead of the game, and generate sustainable growth and provide flexible and modular (or service-based) architecture, infrastructure and software delivery (Dias et al. 2017). On top of building business ecosystems, ICT firms need to focus on creating value for their customers (e.g., via building a dominant position in a relatively narrow product or service category, mergers & acquisitions, developing and introducing new products and services, offering personalized and customized solutions, and lowering the costs of competitive services) (Acker, Groene & Schroeder 2016).

Meanwhile new technologies typically work together to provide maximized benefits to the organization. For example, the sensors of Internet of Things (IoT) networks could provide comprehensive and real-time data for automated business processes, and the collected data are then stored in the cloud and analysed via artificial intelligence (AI) technologies and applications, and the outcomes of data analytics by AI can in turn inform (and predict) and better manage performance of the automated business processes (George, de Boer & London 2019). Another interesting thing is the interplay between software and hardware (e.g., between virtual stuff of social networks and hard physical sensors and devices/machines of Internet of Things networks) (Grijpnil Nattermann & London 2019).

Another emerging trend in the ICT industry is the fight for standards (including standards in operation systems) and patents even though it could be common to other industries. The fight between Apple's iOS and Google's Android operation systems and the fight between Apple and Samsung on patents of mobile phone design and features are just two interesting cases among many others (to come!). In addition, cloud-based options, open source solutions and custom app development have become more and more popular and reliable (Morrison 2018).

Some questions needed to be asked about information systems infrastructure

Information systems infrastructure is fundamental to the effective deliveries of required information systems capabilities for the business and critical to the organizational performance (especially in today's networked/digital economy). To successfully manage information systems infrastructure, organizations need to look at their management practices and ask themselves a few question in this regard (Kaplan 2011; Markus 2012; The Author's Own Knowledge):

• How to effectively manage the increasing demand and the cost for better infrastructure?: While business leaders are demanding better technology capacity to support business/revenue growth, organizations need to make informed decision by effectively managing demand (e.g., via prioritizing the demand as per strategic objectives and goals of the business) and taking advantages of emerging/new technologies (e.g., technologies for social, mobile and location computing as well as cloud-computing and global connectedness).

• What is the contingency plan for the current economic situation or even worse one?: Organizations need to look at how they work on their information systems investments in the unstable economic situations and should be ready for scenarios such as how can we get required IS/IT capabilities and stay with the competition with reduced budget (10%? 20%? 30%?....)?

• Which and how much infrastructure capability will be needed in the near term?, medium term?, and long term?: Organizations need to have short, medium, and long term plans to survive, grow and prosper.

• What is required infrastructure for our globalization efforts?: A global infrastructure strategy needs to be properly planned and executed by taking into consideration of political, technological, economic and social (including cultural elements) factors of different markets (especially those large emerging markets).

• What are our approach in dealing with the capabilities of new technologies and associated risks?: New and emerging technologies such as cloud computing applications could bring benefits (including lower costs and increased agility) to organizations (especially to small and medium enterprises while concerns and risks such as availability, privacy, security could be brought serious damage/ham to the business). However, organizations should not stay away from new technologies just because they are not 100% risk free. In fact, organizations should actively look at leveraging the advantages and opportunities arising from new technologies with a well-thought plan and process (i.e., looking at perspectives of adopting new technologies such as demand, value, architecture, organization & governance, and vendor selection), while having an effective risk management strategy in place (and allocating sufficient resources for it).

• What is your approach and process to manage IS/IT investments?: Organizations need to have an effective process for selecting and measuring IS/IT investments and should have an IS/IT investment committee or steering committee, which involves relevant stakeholders from business and IT areas.

• Have we managed good relations with regulators and relevant agencies?: To some extent (less for some industries and more (even much more) for other industries), organizations' IS/IT infrastructure investments are a result of regulatory requirements. Having good relations with regulators and relevant agencies will definitely make the job of complying with regulations easier, reduce the cost of doing it, and put organizations in better position for anticipating and preparing for the expected/informed changes!.

Centralisation or decentralisation

Centralised computing can give organisations benefits such as: more control since all processing is accomplished by centralized computing facilities (e.g., main frame computer), consistent standards & common data, economies of scale & shared services, access to large capacity, better recruitment and training of information systems professionals, and better bargaining power when negotiating with suppliers; on the other hand, it may lead to such issues as not meeting local needs, slow support for strategic initiatives, tension between business and information systems function, and lack of business unit control over overhead costs (Laudon & Laudon 2005, p.192; O'Brien & Marakas 2006, p.481; Pearlson & Saunders 2010, p.233;).

On the other hand, distributed computing, such as client/server, peer to peer (P2P), and grid computing, distributes computing powers among computers in different locations/functions. The benefits of this approach include: giving more power for local operations, departments, divisions and end users; looking after local needs, closer partnership between business and information system, better flexibility; and better cost control. Meanwhile it can also lead to issues such as lack of consistency of standards, loss of control, duplication of staff & data, difficulty in getting preferred contracts/agreements, and higher costs (Laudon & Laudon 2005, p.192; O'Brien & Marakas 2006, p.481; Pearlson & Saunders 2010, p.233). So what is the best? How much to centralise or distribute? Answers vary for different needs of various organisations. Organisations should choose the computing model compatible with organisational goals, and they also should assess the costs and benefits. For example, networked computers and centralised computing could increase management's control, but what happens if there is a failure in network? (Laudon & Laudon 2005, p.192).

Selecting appropriate technologies for enterprise networking

Internet technologies (e.g., different networks and network services, XML and Java) have dramatically enhanced organisations' capacity for connectivity and integration of various applications. However, there is still a lot to do. Many companies are facing the challenge of integrating and coordinating various applications and systems (Laudon & Laudon 2005, p.266).

There are different standards for linkage with different networks. Networks operated on one standard may not be able to link to those networks based on other standards. Addressing this problem leads to investment on additional equipment and management overheads. Furthermore, integration of business applications from different vendors may require integration software (e.g., middleware) that can support the firm's business processes and data structures. Open standard for interoperability of applications from different vendors is a way to go. For example, Open Mobile Alliance (OMA), which includes more than 300 companies representing mobile operators, device and network suppliers, information technology companies, and content providers, has actively pursued the Open Standard for interoperability of various mobile data services from different vendors across devices, geographies, service providers, operators, and networks.

Networks and telecommunications technologies that meet today's requirements may lack the connectivity for domestic or global expansion in the future (Laudon & Laudon 2005, p.266). Strategic telecommunications planning, which can be a part of a firm's strategic information systems planning, can ensure the firm's telecommunications and networks address the business needs, respond to the market changes, and plan for the connectivity and application integration needed (Laudon & Laudon 2005, p.287). For example, wireless (mobile) technologies promise to be the next major development in e-commerce for both business and consumer markets (B2B and B2C). Businesses should closely examine how wireless technologies can support their operations, enhance their business performance, and generate new opportunities through mobile business/mobile commerce. Organisations also should take a broader perspective on infrastructure development and can no longer develop and implement telecommunications networks confined to organisational boundaries. The new information systems infrastructure for a networked enterprise should connect the whole enterprise and link it with other organisations and the public. Balancing network reliability and availability against mushrooming network costs also needs to be considered (Laudon & Laudon 2005, p.266). On the one hand, networking is the foundation of digital economy/society. Although telecommunication transition costs are decreasing, total network capacity (bandwidth) requirements are growing very fast, which will lead to massive increases in costs to business (Laudon & Laudon 2005, p.266).

Another very important role of telecommunications & networks planning is to help managers with decisions about selecting telecommunications technologies and services to enhance the performance of the firm. Laudon and Laudon (2005, p. 288; 2012, pp.224-225) suggest some factors to consider when a business is embarking on new telecommunications technologies. These factors include:

• Distance: Are future telecommunication needs primarily local or long distance?

• Services: range of functions and services needed? (e.g., email? electronic data interchange? wireless? voice mail? videoconferencing? graphics & multimedia transition? need of integration of different services?).

• Point of access: number of locations needed for services and capabilities?

• Utilisation: anticipated frequency and volume of communications?

• Security and reliability of the proposed new telecommunications systems

• Scalability of the proposed new telecommunications systems: not only for current demand but also for future demand.

• Connectivity: How easy or difficult (e.g., required time, money and effort) is it to connect disparate components of network or networks?

• Flexibility/adaptability: Can the proposed telecommunications applications be adapted to the changes in the market place?

• Purchasing & maintaining its own Or renting from external suppliers?: What are benefits? risks? benefits versus risks?

• Cost: What is the cost of proposed telecommunication technology?, What are some variable costs?, How about fixed cost?, Any hidden cost?, direct and indirect costs?, and what is total cost of ownership (hardware, software account for only about 20% of total cost of ownership! Other costs include: installation, training, support, maintenance, infrastructure, downtime, space and energy. Total cost of ownership can be reduced through the adoption of cloud services, greater centralization, and standardization of hardware and software resources).

On a related note, some typical components of total cost of ownership include (Laudon & Laudon 2012, p. 226):

- Hardware acquisition: purchase price or lease costs of computer hardware equipment including computers, terminals, storage, and printers.
- Software acquisition: purchase price or license fees of software for each user.
- Installation: cost to install computers and software (large organizations normally do this themselves via their information systems operation/function).
- Training: cost to provide training for information systems specialists and end users
- Support: cost to provide on-going technical support, help desks and so forth.
- Infrastructure: cost to acquire, maintain, and support related infrastructure, such as networks and specialized equipment (including storage backup units).
- Downtime: cost of lost productivity if hardware and software failures cause the system to be unavailable for processing and user tasks.
- Space and Energy: real estate and utility costs for housing and providing power for the technology (e.g., data centres for large organizations).

Integration

When organizations are embarking on exciting opportunities and capabilities offered by various technologies and leveraging advantages from multiple channels (e.g., call centres, stores/branches, online operations, mobile applications, videos, fax machines, agents and third parties), one critical factor is integration. They need to appropriately integrate various applications/systems with their information systems infrastructure or/and existing applications/systems and unify different channels to share information across the organization. Technologies (e.g., service-oriented architecture) can create a unified business-service layer for channels and front-end processes to share (customer) information. For example, if a customer calls before walking into a store, if such information is not managed and shared across the organization and multiple channels, then the opportunity of wining the customer could be gone (Wang 2010). One particular relevant point is to integrate mobile devices (such as smart phones, tablets) into the IS/IT infrastructure so the owners of those mobile devices could securely and smoothly access the required information and use corporate applications from them (mobile devices) (Kleiner 2012).

The next generation of the Internet standards such as HTLM5 will provide the access to all programs and applications via a web browser from any device anytime, anywhere. HTML5 arguably is the most significant evolution yet in web standards, and it could locally store 1,000 times more data in browsers than they currently do (Korkmaz, Lee & Park 2011). It allows programs/applications to run through web browsers and communicate different multimedia content without requiring plug-in software and other workarounds.

6.11 Summary

An information system is composed of hardware, software, people, data, and telecommunications networks. Hardware is a vital part of computer systems and provides the underlying physical foundation for firms' information systems infrastructure. Other infrastructure components of software, data and networks require hardware for their storage and operation. To be useful, hardware needs software, which gives instructions that control the operation of a computer system. Networks enable large and small businesses to communicate internally between staff and externally with suppliers, customers, government and the marketplace. Networks are fundamental to online businesses and digital enterprises. Making the right decision in relation to information systems infrastructure is vital to the success of the business. In the next chapter, the need for cross-functional information systems will be looked at and how organizations can use enterprise resource planning systems for improving internal operational efficiency will be discussed as well.

References

Acker, O., Gröne, F. & Schröder, G. 2012, 'The Global ICT 50: the supply side of digitization', *Strategy + Business*, July 2012, pp. 1-9.

Acker, O., Groene, F. & Schroeder, G. 2016, 'The new game of global tech', *Strategy+Business*, Issue 85, Winter 2016, pp.1-7.

Akella, J., Brown, B., Gilbert, G., & Wong, L. 2012, 'Mobility disruption: A CIO perspective', *Business Technology Office, McKinsey & Company*, September 2012, Online Available at: https://www.mckinseyquarterly.com/Business_Technology/BT_Strategy/Mobility_disruptio n_A_CIO_perspective_3019 (accessed Sep 20, 2012).

Biggs, P., Johnson, T., Lozanova, Y. & Sundberg, N. 2012, 'Emerging issues for our hyper-connected world', in *The Global Information Technology Report 2012: Living in a Hyper-connected World*, Dutta, S. & Bilbao-Osorio, B. eds, INSEAD & World Economic Forum, pp. 47-56.

Bisson, P., Stephenson, E. & Patrick Viguerie, S. 2010, 'The global grid', *McKinsey Quarterly*, June 2010, pp. 1-7.

Blake, D. 2016, 5G and Next Generation Wireless: Implications for Policy and Competition, Information Technology & Innovation Foundation, June 2016, pp.1-22.

Bold, W. & Davidson, W. 2012, 'Mobile Broadband: Redefining Internet access and empowering individuals', in *The Global Information Technology Report 2012: Living in a Hyper-connected World*, Dutta, S. & Bilbao-Osorio, B. eds, INSEAD & World Economic Forum, pp. 67-77.

Boommadevara, N., Del Miglio, A. & Jansen, S. 2018, 'Cloud adoption to accelerate IT modernization', *Digital McKinsey*, December 2018, pp.12-19.

Boommadevara, N., Kaplan, J. & Starikova, I. 2016, 'Leaders and laggards in enterprise cloud infrastructure adoption', *Business Technology Office*, McKinsey & Company, pp.1-8.

Brown, M. 2018, '4 impacts of the growth of edge computing', *Bowery Capital* , 04/07/2018, Online, Available at: https://bowerycap.com/blog/insights/4-impacts-edge-computing/(accessed on 10 January 2019).

Butler, B. 2017, 'What is edge computing and how it's changing the network', *Insights, Network World*, pp. 1-5.

Campbell, K., Diffley, J., Flanagan, B., Morelli, B., O'Neil, B. & Sideco, F. 2017, 'The 5G economy: How 5G technology will contribute to the global economy', *Economic Impact Analysis*, IHS Econonics/HIS Technology, January 2017, pp. 1-34.

Caylar, P. L. & Menard, A. 2016, 'How telecom companies can win in the digital revolution', *Digital McKinsey*, September 2016, pp. 1-7.

Casey, K. 2017, 'Multi-cloud vs. hybrid cloud: What is the difference', *The Enterprise Project*, July 07, 2017, Online, Available at: https://enterprisersproject.com/article/2017/7/multi-cloud-vs-hybrid-cloud-whats-difference (accessed on 8 July 2019).

Chabas, J.M., Gnaaasambandam, C., Gupte, S. & Mahdavian, M. 2018, 'New demand, new markets: What edge computing means for hardware companies', *High Tech Practice*, October 2018, pp. 1-8.

Chui, M. Löffler, M. & Roberts, R. 2010, 'The Internet of Things', *McKinsey Quarterly*, Number 2 2010, pp. 1-9.

Compuware Corporation 2010, 'Performance in the Cloud', *White Paper: Cloud Computing 2010*, Corpuware Corporation USA, pp. 1-6.

CompuData 2015, *Outgrowing ERP: Why Hybrid Cloud ERP May Be Your Next Step*, Online, Available at: http://www.compudata.com/outgrowing-erp/ (accessed on August 10, 2017).

Schwenderman, M., Horner, W. & Shah, S. 2019, *Crunch time 8, The CFO guide to cloud*, Deloitte Consulting, pp.1-28.

Dias, J., Hamiton, D., Paquette, C. & Sood, R. 2017, 'How to start building your next generation operating model', *Digital McKinsey*, March 2017, Online, Available at: https://www.mckinsey.com/business-functions/digital-mckinsey/our-insights/how-to-start-building-your-next-generation-operating-model (accessed on 2 July 2019).

Dutta, S., Grewal, G. & Hrishikesh, H. 2019, Six simple steps pave the way to the cloud, The Boston Consulting Group, 27 February 2019, Online, Available at: https://www.bcg.com/en-au/publications/2019/six-simple-steps-pave-way-to-cloud.aspx (accessed on 1 July 2019).

Fabel, S. 2019, 'The cloud in 2020: Enterprise compatibility with edge computing, containers and serverless', *Cloud Tech News*, 21 February 2019, Online, Available at: https://www.cloudcomputing-news.net/news/2019/feb/21/cloud-2020-enterprise-compatibility-edge-computing-containers-and-serverless/ (accessed on 2 June 2019).

Gartner 2019a, 'Gartner says global IT spending to grow 1.1% in 2019', Press Release, News Room, April 17, 2019, Online, Available at: https://www.gartner.com/en/newsroom/press-releases/2019-04-17-gartner-says-global-it-spending-to-grow-1-1-percent-i (accessed on 1 July 2019).

Gartner 2019b, 'Gartner says global device shipment will decline 3% in 2019, Press Release, News Room, July 17, 2019, Online, Available at: https://www.gartner.com/en/newsroom/press-releases/2019-07-17-gartner-says-global-device-shipments-will-decline-3-- (accessed on 1 August 2019).

Gerbert, P. & Ruess, F. 2018, *The Next Decade in Quantum Computing*-and *How to Play*, Boston Consulting Group.

George, K., de Boer, E. & London, S. 'The future of manufacturing', *Operations Practice*, McKinsey & Company, pp. 1-9.

GSA 2015, *The Road to 5G: Drivers, Applications, Requirements and Technical Development*, Global Mobile Suppliers Association, November 2015, pp. 1-29.

Gnanasambandam, C., Harryson, M., Mangla, R. & Srivastava, S. 2017, "An executive guide to software development", *High Tech*, Feb 2017, McKinsey & Company, pp.1-6.

Grijpnil, F., Nattermann, P. & London, S. 2019, *Who wins in a 5G world?*, The Podcast Transcript, February 2019, McKinsey & Company, February 2019, pp. 1-13, Online, Available at: https://www.mckinsey.com/industries/telecommunications/our-insights/who-wins-in-a-5g-world (accessed on 2 June 2019).

Fisher, T. 2019, '5G Spectrum and Frequencies: Everything You Need to Know', *Lifewire*, July 01, 2019, Online, Available at: https://www.lifewire.com/5g-spectrum-frequencies-4579825 (accessed on 9 July 2019).

Fursman A. & Zaribafiyan, A. 2017, 'Innovating with Quantum Computing', *Accenture Labs*, pp.1-15.

Haag, S., Baltzan, P. & Phillips, A. 2006, *Business Driven Technology*, 1st edition, McGraw-Hill Irwin, Boston, U.S.A.

Harris, R. 2019, 'Understanding Edge Computing', *App Development Magazine*, 24 July 2019, Online, Available at: https://appdevelopermagazine.com/understanding-edge-computing/ (accessed on 25 July 2019).

Harvard Business Review 2010, 'Idea Watch: Cloud Computing', Harvard Business Review, June 2010, pp. 24-30.

Henke, N., Bughin, J., Chui, M., Manyika, J., Saleh, T., Wiseman, B. & Sethupathy, G. 2016, *The Age of Analytics: Competing in a Data-driven World*, McKinsey Global Institute, December 2016.

Heineke, K., Kampshoff, P., Mkrtchyan, A. & Shao, E. 2017, 'Self-driving car technology: When will the robots hit the road', *Automotive & Assembly*, May 2017, McKinsey & Company, pp.1-11.

Heineke, K., Padhi, A., Pinner, D. & Tschiesner, A. 2019, 'Reimagining mobility: A CEO's guide', *McKinsey Quarterly*, February 2019, pp.1-11.

IBM 2017, Quantum Computation, ATPESC 2017, pp. 1-58.

IDG Connect 2012, *The Global Shift to Android: Businesses & IT Professionals*, IDG Connect, June 2012, Online Available at:

Intel Corporation 2011, *The New CIO Agenda: Inter Cloud Computing Insights 2011*, Intel Corporation USA, pp. 1-14.

Intel Corporation 2019, *The 5G Effect: Your 5G Business Opportunity*, Online, Available at: https://www.intel.com.au/content/www/au/en/wireless-network/5g-business-opportunity-infographic.html (accessed on 10 July 2019).

Kaplan, J. M. 2011, 'Nine questions technology leaders should be asking themselves about infrastructure', *McKinsey on Business Technology*, Number 22, Spring 2011, pp. 2-5.

Kleiner, A. 2012, 'The thought leader interview: Bob Carrigan(CEO IDG Communications)', *Strategy + Business*, Issue 66, Spring 2012, pp. 1-8.

Korkmaz, B., Lee, R. & Park, L. 2011, 'How new Internet standards will finally deliver a mobile revolution', *McKinsey Quarterly*, April 2011, pp. 1-9.

Kuhnert, F. 2019, 'Competing for consumers in driverless cars', *Strategy+Business*, Consumer & Retail, June 4, 2019, Online, Available at: https://www.strategy-business.com/blog/Competing-for-consumers-in-driverless-cars?gko=06226 (14 June 2019).

Laudon, K.C. & Laudon, J.P. 2005, *Essentials of Management Information Systems: Managing the Digital Firm*, 6th edn, Prentice Hall.

Laudon, K.C. & Laudon, J.P. 2012, *Essentials of Management Information Systems: Managing the Digital Firm*, 12th edn, Prentice Hall.

Loeffler, J., 'IBM Expects Commercialization of Quantum Computers in 3 to 5 years', *Interesting Engineering*, May 25, 2019, Online, Available at: https://interestingengineering.com/ibm-expects-commercialization-of-quantum-computers-in-3-to-5-years (accessed on 1 July 2019).

Manyika, J. 2008, 'Google's views on the future of business: An Interview with CEO Eric Schmidt', *McKinsey Quarterly*, September 2008, Online available at: https://www.mckinseyquarterly.com/Googles_view_on_the_future_of_business_An_interview_with_CEO_Eric_Schmidt_2229 (accessed Aug 2, 2012).

Manyika, J., Chui, M., Bission, P., Woetzel, J., Dobbs, R., Bughin, J. & Aharon, D. 2015, *The Internet of Things: Napping the value beyond the hype*, June 2015, McKinsey Global Institute.

Markus, D. 2012, 'IT systems: Right size or wrong size, elastic or fixed cost: what does this all mean for IT and productivity", *Smart Company*, July 12, 2012, Online Available at: http://www.smartcompany.com.au/tech-strategy/right-size-or-wrong-size-elastic-or-fixed-cost-what-does-this-all-mean-for-it-and-productivity.html (accessed Aug 20, 2012).

Marr, B. 2017, 'What is Quantum Computing? A Super-easy explanation for anyone', *Forbes*, July 4, 2017, Online, Available at: https://www.forbes.com/sites/bernardmarr/2017/07/04/what-is-quantum-computing-a-super-easy-explanation-for-anyone/#7bed0d201d3b (accessed on 2 February 2019).

Martin, C., Schwartz, A. & Garfinkel, H. 2017, 'Who will insure self-driving cars', *Strategy+Business*, Issue 86, Spring 2017, pp. 1-3.

Meeker, M.2017, *Internet Trends 2017-Code Conference*, Kleiner & Perkins, May 31, 2017, Online, Available at: http://www.kpcb.com/internet-trends (accessed on 30 July 2017).

Morrison, A. 2018, 'Are you spending way too much on software', *Strategy+Business*, Thought Leaders, August 6, 2018, Issue 92, Autumn 2018, Online Available at: https://www.strategy-business.com/article/Are-You-Spending-Way-Too-Much-on-Software?gko=88503 (accessed on 1 June 2019).

MSV, J. 2017, 'Edge computing: Redefining the enterprise infrastructure', Frobes.com. February 7, 2107, Online, Available at: https://www.forbes.com/sites/janakirammsv/2017/02/07/edge-computing-redefining-the-enterprise-infrastructure/#b1f3af575499 (accessed on 20 June 2018).

Nokia 2016, *5G Technology Aspects*, pp. 1-30.

O'Brien, J.A. & Marakas, G.M. 2006, *Management Information Systems*, 7th edn, Irwin/McGraw-Hill, Boston.

O'Brien, J. A. & Marakas, G. M. 2011, *Management Information Systems*, 10th Edition, McGraw-Hill, New York, USA.

Overby, S. 2019a, 'How to explain edge computing in plain English', *The Enterprise Project*, July 22, 2019, Online, Available at: https://enterprisersproject.com/article/2019/7/edge-computing-explained-plain-english (accessed on 25 July 2019).

Overby, S. 2019b, 'Edge Computing: 6 things to know', *The Enterprise Project*, July 24, 2019, Online, Available at: https://enterprisersproject.com/article/2019/7/edge-computing-6-key-facts (accessed on 25 July 2019).

Pearlson, K.E. & Saunders, C.S. 2004, *Managing and Using Information Systems: A Strategic Approach*, 2nd edn, Wiley, Danvers.

Pearlson, K. E. & Saunders, C. S. 2010, *Managing and Using Information Systems: A Strategic Approach*, Fourth Edition, John Wiley & Sons, USA.

Pearlson, K.E. & Saunders, C.S. 2013, *Managing and using information systems: A strategic approach*, 5th edn, John Wiley & Sons Inc. USA.

Phelan, P. 2018, 'The World of Enterprise Applications is Changing: Is it time to reroute your ERP Roadmap', *Research Report, Rimini Street*, pp. 1-16.

Poo, M.M. & Wang, L. 2018, 'Andrew Chi-Chih Yao: The future of quantum computing', *National Science Review*, Issue 5, 2018, pp. 1-5.

Rimini Street, 2018, 'Examining SAA's Cloud Strategy', *White Paper, Rimini Street*, pp. 1-23.

Rimini Street, 2019, 'How SAP Customers rea responding to the planned 2025 End of ECC6 Mainstream Maintenance Deadline', *Survey Report, Rimini Street*, pp. 1-14.

Roberts, R. & Sikes, J. 2011, 'How IT is managing new demands: McKinsey Global Survey results', *McKinsey on Business Technology*, Number 22, Spring 2011, pp. 24-33.

Roberts, R. Sarrazin, H. & Sikes, J. 2010, 'Reshaping IT management for turbulent times', *McKinsey on Business Technology*, Number 21, pp. 2-9.

Red Hat 2019, *What is virtualization*, Red Hat 2019, Online, Available at: https://www.redhat.com/en/topics/virtualization/what-is-virtualization (accessed on 1 July 2019).

Rouse, M. 2017, *Platform as a Service (PaaS)*, Techtarget.com, September 2017, Online, Available at:https://searchcloudcomputing.techtarget.com/definition/Platform-as-a-Service-PaaS (accessed on 8 July 2019).

Rouse, M. 2018, *Infrastructure as a Service(IaaS)*, Techtarget.com, September 2018, Online, Available at: https://searchcloudcomputing.techtarget.com/definition/Infrastructure-as-a-Service-IaaS (accessed on 8 July 2019).

Rouse, M. 2018, *Software as a Service (SaaS)*, Techtarget.com, February 2019, Online, Available at: https://searchcloudcomputing.techtarget.com/definition/Software-as-a-Service (accessed on 8 July 2019). Shor, P. W. 1998, 'Quantum Computing', *Documenta Mathematica,* Extra Volume ICM 1998 I, pp. 467-486.

Srivastava, R., Choi, I. & Cook, T. 2016, *The Commercial Prospects for Quantum Computing*, Issue 1, December 2016, pp. 1-47.

Steelman, Z. R., Lacity, M. & Sabherwal, R. 2016, 'Charting your organization's bring-your-own-device voyage', *MIS Quarterly Executive*, Vol. 15, Issue 2, pp. 85-104.

Strickland, J. 2019, *How Grid Computing Works*, Howstuffworks.com, Online, Available at: https://computer.howstuffworks.com/grid-computing3.htm (accessed on 1 July 2019)

Symantec 2019, 'Adapting to the New Reality Evolving: Cloud Threats', *Executive Summary, Cloud Security Threat Report*, Volume 1, June 2019, pp. 1-9.

Toesland, F. 2019, 'Xaas models are reshaping the future of outsourcing', *ComputerWeekly.com*, 08 May 2019, Online, Available at: https://www.computerweekly.com/feature/XaaS-models-are-reshaping-the-future-of-outsourcing (accessed on 11 June 2019).

Trend Micro 2010, 'The Need for cloud computing security', *Trend Micro White Paper July 2010*, Trend Micro Inc. USA, pp. 1-7.

Violino, B. 2019, 'How and where to use serverless computing', *Networkworld*, April 22, 2019, Online, Available at: https://www.networkworld.com/article/3390116/how-and-where-to-use-serverless-computing.html (accessed on 24 June 2019).

Wagner, P. 2019, '5G Health Risks: The War between Technology and Human Beings', Gaia.com, May 14, 2019, Online, Available at: https://www.gaia.com/article/5g-health-risks-the-war-between-technology-and-human-beings (accessed on 1 July 2019).

Wang, K. W. 2010, 'Creating Competitive Advantage with IT Architecture', *McKinsey on Business Technology*, Number 18, Winter 2010, pp. 18-21.

Wikipedia 2019, *Edge Computing*, 23 July 2019, Online, Available at: https://en.wikipedia.org/wiki/Edge_computing (accessed on 25 July 2019).

Chapter 7

Using Information Systems for Enhancing Internal Operation

This chapter will review functional information systems, explain why there is a trend towards cross-functional information systems, identify the major cross-functional information systems in business and their main roles, explain the need for enterprise resource planning (ERP) systems in business, discuss implementation issues of ERP systems, and look at merging trends of ERP systems.

7.1 Functional and Cross-functional Information Systems

Traditionally businesses are operated by dividing the organisation into various functions in a silo structure with each having its own information system and tending to work in isolation. Functional information systems support the business functions of: Accounting, Finance, Marketing, Productions/operations management, and Human resource management. In the real world information systems are typically integrated combinations of functional information systems (O'Brien & Marakas 2011, p.287).

The functional (silo) approach to information systems allows organisations to optimise expertise and avoid redundancy in expertise. It also makes it easier to benchmark with other organisations, develops core competencies, and provides functional efficiency (Pearlson & Saunders 2004, p.106; Pearlson & Saunders 2010, p.140). On a related note, people could feel more trust in silos (e.g., they will trust people they know well) (DeGrandis 2019). However there are some problems with this approach, such as information recreation, information errors, communication gaps among departments, loss of information arising from inaccurate information, and not-timely shared information, and lack of consistent services to customers. In order to deal with these problems of silo approach, managers need to think beyond the walls of the organisation. Thus there is a need for a cross-functional approach, which focuses on business processes and customer services and is supported by cross-functional information systems that cross the boundaries of several business functions (O'Brien & Marakas 2011, p. 275). It is noted that the term of cross-functional also includes cross-channel integration (e.g., integrating online shops, physical stores, call centers and other channels).

Cross-functional information systems are a strategic way to use information systems to share information resources and focus on accomplishing fundamental business processes in concert with the company's customer, supplier, partner, and employee stakeholders. Some typical examples of cross-functional information systems include: enterprise resource planning systems, customer relationship management systems, supply chain management systems, and knowledge management systems. These four systems have different focuses: enterprise resource planning systems emphasize on internal efficiency; customer relationship management systems concentrate on customer relations; supply chain management systems focus on managing relations with suppliers and business partners; and knowledge management systems facilitate managing tacit and explicit knowledge of the organization. Meanwhile these four systems are inter-related (e.g., accurate customer information is critical to the success of supply chain management systems and enterprise planning systems; knowledge sharing facilitated by knowledge management systems is important to all the aspect of business including the success of supply chain management systems, enterprise planning systems, customer relationship management systems).

Another two commonly used cross-functional information systems are transaction processing systems and enterprise collaboration systems. Transactions are events such as sales, purchases, deposits, withdrawals, refunds, and payments. Transaction processing systems are cross-functional information systems that capture and process data describing business transactions (O'Brien & Marakas 2011, p. 278). Enterprise collaboration systems are information systems that use a variety of information technologies to help people work together, including electronic communications tools (e.g., e-Mail, instant messaging, voice mail, faxing, web publishing, paging), electronic conferencing tools (e.g., data conferencing, voice conferencing, video conferencing, discussion forums, chat systems, electronic meeting systems), and collaborative work management tools (e.g., calendaring & scheduling, task & project management, workflow systems, document sharing, and knowledge management) (O'Brien & Marakas 2011, p. 281). Enterprise collaboration systems enhance communication (e.g., sharing information with each other), coordination (e.g., coordinating individual work efforts and use of resources with each other), and collaboration (e.g., working together cooperatively on joint projects and assignments) across the organisation (O'Brien & Marakas 2011, p.280).

7.2 Enterprise Resource Planning Systems

Evolution of enterprise resource planning systems

Enterprise resource planning (ERP) has its origin in the material requirements planning (MRP) (to manage inventory in production) then MRPII, which are mainly for manufactures to plan all the resources for its production. Enterprise resource planning systems can be seen as an extension of MRPII systems with integrated functions/modules (such as accounting and finance, human resource management, manufacturing, logistics, and distribution). Nowadays ERP systems can be found in all kinds of organisations (e.g., universities, governments, service providers) including those that are not primarily involved in manufacturing. The latest version of ERP systems has included web-based ERP applications (including cloud-based) and integrated other applications/components/modules, such as supply chain management, customer relationship management, and business intelligence. Major ERP software vendors are SAP, PeopleSoft, Oracle, JD Edwards, Infor, and Microsoft.

Like any other information systems, EPR systems can be looked at from dimensions of usefulness (also called functionality) and ease of use/user friendliness (also called usability) (Lippincott 2018):

• High Usefulness and High Ease of Use/User Friendliness: Acumatica, Syspro, Orcale NetSuite, Microsoft Dynamics 365 Finance and Operations, Deltek, Orcale ERP Cloud, SAP S/4HANA.

• High Usefulness and Low Ease of Use/User Friendliness: Epicor, IFS, Roots tock, QAD, and Aptean.

• High Ease of Use/User Friendliness and Low Usefulness: Qualic, FiancialForce, Microsoft Dynamics 365 Business Central, Unit 4, and SAP Business by Design.

• Low Ease of Use/User Friendliness and Low Usefulness: Plex, VAI, IQMS, and Sage.

On top of the above mentioned considerations of usefulness and ease of use/user friendliness, when organizations are looking at ERP systems, they also ask some key questions such as: (1) does the EPR system address business needs?;

(2) what benefits will the system generate?; (3) what is the total cost and timeframe of the implementation?; (4) how disruptive to the organization will the ERP implementation be?; (5) how quickly people will adopt and use the system; and (6) more importantly do the organization really know the organizational needs before jumping on ERP system? (Boyce 2019; Shacklett 2019).

ERP systems have been implemented in many large corporations, and more and more SMEs are embarking on ERP systems. The EPR market is large and significant, for example in 2011, the ERP systems market was worth more than US$ 36 billion (Krigsman et al. 2010). Haag, Baltzan and Phillips (2008, p. 136) suggest the three primary forces driving the explosive growth of enterprise resource planning systems are:

• ERP system is a logical solution to the mess of incompatible applications that had sprung up in most businesses.

• ERP system addresses the need for global information sharing and reporting.

• ERP system is used to avoid the pain and expense of fixing legacy systems.

Business values of ERP system

Enterprise resource planning (ERP) system is a cross-functional enterprise system that integrates and automates many of the internal business processes of a company, particularly those within the manufacturing, logistics, distribution, accounting, finance, and human resource functions of the business (O'Brien & Marakas 2011, p 320). ERP systems track business resources and the status of commitments made by the business and give real-time cross-functional view of its core business processes. (O'Brien & Marakas 2011, p.333). It features a set of integrated software modules and normally a central database that allow data to be shared by many different business processes and functional areas throughout the enterprise (Laudon & Laudon 2005, p.333). The primary purpose of an ERP system is to collect, update, and maintain enterprise-wide information, so the same information can be shared across different departments and functions of the organization. And the shared information enables different departments and function work together (so they don't work in silos).

Successful implementation of ERP systems can provide organisations with many benefits. Examples include: (O'Brien & Marakas 2011, p. 324; Haag, Baltzan & Phillips 2008, p.398):

• Quality and efficiency enhancement by helping improve the quality and efficiency of customer service, production, and distribution by creating a framework for integrating and improving internal business processes.

• Decreased costs by replacing old legacy systems, reductions in transaction processing costs, hardware, software, and information systems support staff, and reduction in inventory.

• Decision support assistance through providing cross-functional information on business performance to assist managers in making better decisions.

• Enhanced enterprise agility through breaking down many walls and creating a more flexible organisational structure, managerial responsibilities, work roles and integrated financial information.

The costs of ERP system implementation

Costs involved in implementing ERP systems are considerable. Hardware and software costs are a small part of the total costs. O'Brien and Marakas (2011, p. 325) point out the costs of developing new business processes (reengineering) and preparing employees for the new ERP system (training and change management) could be very high (more than 50% of the total implementation costs). Data conversion (i.e. converting from previous legacy systems to the new cross-functional ERP system) could also be very expensive. Consulting fees, process reworking, customisation, testing, and integration could also be costly. The breakdown (in percentage) of typical costs of implementing a new ERP system includes: engineering (43%), software (15%), data conversion (15%), training and change management (15%), and hardware (12%) (O'Brien & Marakas 2011, p.325). ERP system implementation costs also could be viewed from another perspective and includes up-front costs (e.g., hardware, software, consulting fees), recurring annual costs (e.g., for license and support), upgrade costs (e.g., for newer version and added functionalities), implicit costs (e.g., internal information systems resources costs), and additional costs (e.g., cloud applications, increasing security expenditure, additional support) (Krigsman et al. 2010). A survey of 63 SMEs and large firms indicates that the average total cost of ownership of an ERP system is $15 million. Total cost of ownership ranges from 400,000 to 30 million (Haag, Baltzan & Phillips 2006, p.282; Pearlson & Saunders 2004, p.118). Another recent study by Aberdeen group, which surveyed 1,680 manufacturing companies of all sizes, cited in Koch and Wailgum (2008), found that companies with less than US$ 50 million in revenue should expect to an average of US$ 384, 295 in total ERP system costs, just over US$ 1 million for companies with US$ 50 million to 100 million in revenue, just over US$ 3 million for companies with US$ 500 million to 1 billion in revenue, and nearly US$ 6 million for companies with more than US$ 1 billion in revenue. On a related note, on average it will take one to three years to have real transformation resulting from ERP system implementation (but the emphasis is not focusing on how long it will take but on understanding why you need it and how you will use to improve the business of the organization) (Koch & Wailgum 2008). In addition, according to 2011 ERP report produced by Panorama Consulting Solutions cited in Kimberling (2011) the average ERP system implementation time reduced to 14 months in 2010 (from 18 months in 2009) and the average total costs of ERP system implementation fell to 4.1% of implementing firms' annual revenue (from 6.1% in 2009). Meanwhile according to CIO Magazine (cited in NetSuite 2015), the average cost of an Oracle or SAP deployment can be between $12 million to $17 million. Panorama Consulting Solutions (2013) indicate (cited in ZiffDavis 2014), over the last 4 years (until 2013) the average cost of an ERP implementation could be $7.3 million with the average duration of 16.6 months.

Challenges and issues of ERP system implementation

ERP systems affect an entire organisation simultaneously rather than a single department (Reimers 2003). However, developing and implementing a new ERP system is definitely not as simple as installing the software package and required hardware. The implementation of ERP systems is a difficult and costly process that has caused serious business losses for some companies, who typically underestimated the importance of planning, development, training, and required organizational adjustments. Some reported causes of ERP system implementation failures are (Krigsman 2010; NetsSuite 2015; O'Brien & Marakas 2011, pp.326-327; Rimini Street 2019a; Rimini Street 2019b; The Author's Own Knowledge):

• Unrealistic implementation expectations and underestimating the complexity of planning, development, training, and required organizational adjustments & change management.

• Failure to involve affected employees from the beginning of the implementation process.

• Trying to do too much, too fast in the conversion phase.

• Insufficient training for the new work tasks required by the ERP system.

• Failure to do enough data conversion and testing.

• Lack of ERP system implementation expertise or over-reliance on external expertise (e.g., consultants, vendors).

- Lack of fit between ERP system and business needs: too many ERP implementation failures resulting from failures in fulfilling the real needs of the organization.
- Lack of business leaders' buy-in and support.
- Have the tendency to over-customization, which either costs you very much or indicates you have chosen the wrong software. A rule of thumb for customization is less than 30% (ideally 20%).
- Inflexibility of ERP packages which sometime lock companies into rigid processes that make it hard, if not impossible, to adapt quickly to changes in the marketplace or in the structure. The embedded best practices in ERP packages may not be able to apply to all the businesses.
- Forced upgrades and migrations by ERP vendors.
- High cost but poor support by ERP vendors.
- The risk/threat of end of support from ERP vendors.
- Also be aware of the maintenance costs (e.g., between 50% -90% of a typical IT budget is spent on maintenance, not innovation).

While ERP system implementation failures could have been due to technical issues, most of the time they are due to change management and business process implementation issues (Turner 2004). ERP systems require a fundamental transformation of a company's business processes. People, processes, policies, and the company's culture are all factors that should be taken into consideration when implementing a major enterprise system (such as EPR systems). ERP systems often changes the way an organisation operates because ERP developers typically include industry best practices in the system and create the system without knowing the exact requirements of their future customers (Reimers 2003). Davenport (1998, p. 123) expresses the view that "Enterprise systems are basically generic solutions even though they integrate industry best practices in many cases. Of course some degree of customisation is possible, but major modifications are very expensive and impractical. As a result, most companies installing enterprise systems will have to adapt or rework their processes to reach a fit with the system". On the other hand, inflexibility of ERP packages may sometime lock companies into rigid processes which make it hard, if not impossible, to adapt quickly to changes in the marketplace or in the structure of the organisation. The embedded best practices in ERP packages may also not be able to apply to all businesses (Pearlson & Saunders 2004, p. 118). Many companies are still adjusting themselves to the concept of 'cross-functional integration', using a centralised database. Furthermore, while the costs and risks of failure in implementing a new

ERP system could be substantial, it also takes time to realize benefits (Haag, Baltzan & Phillips 2008, p. 398).

In order to avoid ERP system implementation failures, organisations should (Blick & Quaddus 2003, Cook 2015; Krigsman 2010; O'Brien & Marakas 2011, pp 326-327; Pearlson & Saunders 2004, p.121; Tippit 2008; Turner 2004; ZiffDavis 2014; The Author's Own Knowledge):

• Know what they want the ERP system to do and understand specific business problems the organization needs to solve with ERP implementation.

• Involve staff in the ERP project from the beginning.

• Understand and commit to change management.

• Have a balanced project management team (business acumen & technical skills and inside & outside expertise) with an unswerving project champion

• Develop an effective project plan to look after scope, timeframe and resources aspects of the ERP system implementation.

• Hire consultants with proven track records.

• Conduct extensive data conversion and test thoroughly.

• Understand the very complex nature of the enterprise resource planning system implementation.

• Define realistic scope and goals.

• Gain support from top management

• Provide people with sufficient training and allocate sufficient resources

• Put in place effective ERP system performance measurement metrics and benefits realization strategy, and have designated people responsible for them.

• Realistic delivery date based on the project not external pressures.

• Effective communication both up and down the organization regarding the ERP implementation.

• Establish benefit realization strategy and closely evaluate the realized benefits of the implementation.

• Have a contingency plan (e.g., many projects have exceeded their planned budgets, planned durations, and have not received expected benefits).

Pearlson and Saunders (2004, pp.119–120) point out that sometimes organisations have to make a decision between (1) letting the ERP system drive business process redesign or (2) re-designing the business process first then implementing ERP system. The former approach is suitable for new businesses, or for businesses whose processes are not sources of competitive advantage, or for businesses whose current systems are in crisis and there is not enough time, resources or knowledge within the firms to fix them. The latter approach can be applied when business processes, which have to be designed in-house not from the package, give a firm competitive advantage, or when features of available packages and the needs of businesses do not fit. On a related note, organisations also can use data warehouses (poor man's ERP) if they don't want to pay for the costs and risks involved in the ERP system implementation (Pearlson & Saunders 2004, p.120).

Meanwhile for organizations of different sizes the emphasis of the ERP implementation could be varied, such as on-going operational support for small firms, selecting right software for mid-size firms, and integration & implementation for large firms (Krigsman et al. 2010). Furthermore as mentioned earlier, selecting a right vendor is critical to the success of ERP implementation. When organizations are embarking on looking for candidates of potential ERP system suppliers, organizations could look at the following perspectives (Krigsman et al. 2010):

• Kinds of customers they typically serve: small or large?, industry?, and region?

• Appropriate references from various reliable sources.

• Process and methodology for implementation.

• Facilitating process for improvement or reengineering during the implementation.

• Approach and expertise in handling change management.

• Process for controlling project scope and budget.

• Ways of responding to identified mismatch between business requirements and software package's functionalities.

• Definition and measures of the success of implementation.

• Benefit realization strategy and execution.

• Experience and background of the proposed team members for the ERP system implementation project.

Integration issues

Most organisations have various systems and applications from multiple vendors. Often organisations take the approach of best-of-breed for the reason that no one vendor can respond to all an organisation's needs (Haag, Baltzan & Phillips 2008, p.138). Organisations, which are looking for optimal solutions for individual areas, are more likely to go for the best-of-breed approach for richer functionalities.

One of the most popular integration tools is enterprise application integration (EAI) (Haag, Baltzan & Phillips 2008, p.138). EAI is a software (a kind of middleware), which enables two business applications to communicate and to exchange data (Laudon & Laudon 2005, p.217; O'Brien & Marakas 2011, p.277). EAI can integrate front-office and back-office applications to allow for quicker, more effective responses to business events and customer demands, thereby improve customer and suppler experience with the business (O'Brien & Marakas 2011, p.277). Laudon and Laudon (2005, p.217) point out that, compared to the traditional approach of integrating where you need to have different and customised software to connect one application to another, EAI connects disparate applications and multiple systems through a single software hub using a special middleware.

Emerging trends of ERP Systems

In the future we will see more open and flexible software packages, such as more customisable interfaces to suit individual needs (Haag, Baltzan & Phillips 2008, p. 401). In line with the wide accessibility of the Internet and rapid development of the Internet and digital technologies, more and more organizations will be looked at web-based (cloud-based) ERP systems (Haag, Baltzan & Phillips 2008, p.401; O'Brien & Marakas 2011, p.327; Krigsman et al. 2010). A mixed or hybrid model, which combines in-house deployment of ERP system components and web-based (cloud) ERP system modules, will be adopted by more and more organizations. Another future trend for ERP systems is the development of inter-enterprise ERP systems that provide web-enabled links between key business systems of a company and its customers, suppliers, distributors, and others (O'Brien & Marakas 2011, p.327). Meanwhile, allowing users to access an organization's ERP system via mobile devices (also called enterprise mobility) will be another emerging trend (Haag, Baltzan & Phillips 2008; Krisgman et al. 2010). Social web computing capabilities to meet with the demand of exponentially growing social networks is another area organizations' ERP systems should cover. Haag, Baltzan and Phillips (2008) suggest that in the future lines between SCM, CRM, and ERP systems will continue to blur, and their view is supported by the fact that ERP vendors are adding more and more modules/components into their ERP packages (one recent emphasis is Business Intelligence as a result of the increasing importance of better understanding customers and the availability of Big Data & Data Analytics). ERP software companies have developed modular, web-enabled software suites (e.g., oracle's E-business suite) that integrate ERP, CRM, SCM, procurement, decision support, enterprise portals, and other business applications and functions.

Although originally designed for manufacturing businesses, ERP systems have been widely adopted in the service industry and other industries (including public sector). Another emerging/future trend is the web-based On Demand ERP Services (e.g., renting the required ERP services rather than owning and maintaining in house). An example of On Demand ERP Services is SAP Business ByDesign, which charges fees according to usage of per user, per month for the software, infrastructure, services and support.

Second wave of ERP systems

Graham Shanks of University of Melbourne, Australia believes that the first wave of ERP was a more IS/IT view of projects: let's get the software in and working; second wave implementation will see the process more as a business project where you have the opportunity to realign your business processes, change the way you do things with IS/IT as an enabler (Turner 2004, p.5).

While it is true that most of the Fortune 500 companies have already adopted ERP systems, the next target for growth are the small and medium enterprises (SMEs) and industry-specific solution markets. EPR software vendors have been working hard to target SMEs to install ERP systems and have released less-expensive, modular and hosted versions of their software. Vendors' strategy is to make the systems more user-friendly to SMEs so that they can avoid customisation, which can really drive up costs. SAP Business One is an example of ERP Solutions for Small and Midsize Enterprises. Another cut-down version for small business is Open ERP (open source ERP system).

The latest trend is to have a cloud-based ERP system (to reduce cost and have more flexibility, scalability and mobility) or a hybrid ERP system (to have the best of both in-house and cloud-based applications). A hybrid ERP system is a combination of in-house ERP (for some core functions) supplemented by cloud-based ERP applications, and it is becoming quite popular for reasons such as: organizations need improved ERP abilities (e.g., optimized productivity, improved functionality and real-time decision making analytics) but don't want to add to or change the in-house legacy system as well as the argument cloud-based solutions (another type of outsourcing) work for some scenarios only despite the push from the ERP vendors (CompuData 2015; Phelan 2018; Rimini Street 2018; Rimini Street 2019a). Some challenges of hybrid ERP approach include: (1) smooth integration of in-house ERP applications with cloud-based applications and (2) the decision-making about what will be in the cloud and what stays in-house (Nadeau 2017). Another interesting future consideration is Intelligent ERP systems, which facilitate agility, continuous learning, innovation, better efficiency, and enhanced integration of the external & internal and frontend & backend operations through working with technological advances (e.g., machine learning, artificial intelligence, cloud computing, Internet of things, Big data and business analytics) (Boggs & Rizza 2018; Rizza 2018).

On a related note, some people argue that ERP (and other enterprise systems) are obsolete since they are too old and there are many new things available or emerging (e.g., Cloud Computing, Mobile Computing, Big Data and Data Analytics, The Internet Of Things, Artificial Intelligence), some aspects to consider are: (1) whether ERP software or the terms of ERP or Enterprise Systems are obsolete, organizations also need a single and accurate and complete and real-time view of their customers so they can better understand them and meet their demands; (2) the traditional (in-house) ERP applications should be able to work with new applications (e.g., some core functions (such as manufacturing and accounting & finance) could be served by in-house ERP applications) while other applications needing more flexibility and mobility (e.g., human resources, distribution, e-commerce) could be looked after by cloud-based ERP applications); Or (3) new applications modules could integrate with in-house ERP applications (e.g., recent ERP applications-they typically have the built-in capabilities to scale and integrate with other applications (i.e., plug-in when needed and plug-out when not needed) and have been evolving to respond to rapidly changing business environments). It could be argued an evolving ERP systems is the way forward in the foreseeable future, and such ERP system could provide continuous support to organizational endeavors in digital transformation, productivity improvement, enhanced agility, strengthened competitive advantages and cost efficiencies (Phelan 2018). More integration between ERP systems and other advanced technologies will be seen in the future, for example ERP vendors are looking at integrating blockchain with ERP systems (e.g., using smart contract function of blockchain for managing supply chain management function in ERP systems) (Stackpole 2019a; Stockpole 2019b). Meanwhile in the digital era, ERP enabled digital transformation could help organizations develop new business models while the traditional EPR implementation primarily looks at technology upgrades and efficiency improvement (Kimberling 2019).

7.3 Summary

In this chapter, functional information systems and the need for cross-functional information systems were discussed. Enterprise resource planning systems and different perspectives of ERP systems, including benefits, costs, features, implementation, trends and future directions, were looked at. In the next chapter, two popular cross-functional information systems for improving external relations: customer relationship management (CRM) systems and supply chain management (SCM) systems, will be examined.

References

Blick, G. & Quaddus, M. 2003, *Benefit Realization with SAP: A Case Study*, Graduate School of Business, Curtin University of Technology, Australia, pp. 1-16.

Boggs, R. & Rizza, M. N. 2018, 'Small and Midsize Businesses Put ERP at the Center of Digital Transformation Strategies', *IDC Analyst Connection*, January 2018, pp.1-5. Boyce, A. 2019, 'Choosing cloud ERP vendors: Know what you need before going in', *ERP Comparison Guide: SAP vs. Infor vs. Microsoft vs. Orcale*, TechTarget, pp. 14-22.

CompuData 2015, *Outgrowing ERP: Why Hybrid Cloud ERP May Be Your Next Step*, Online, Available at: http://www.compudata.com/outgrowing-erp/ (accessed on August 10, 2017).

Cook, R. 2015, 'Secrets of Highly Effective ERP Implementations', *Toolbox.com Blogs*, Inside ERP, May 1, 2015, Online Available at: http://it.toolbox.com/blogs/inside-erp/secrets-of-highly-effective-erp-implementations-66540 (Accessed June 1, 2015).

DeGrandis, D. 2019, 'Why silos are not the enemy', *The Enterprises Project*, January 24, 2019, Online Available at: https://enterprisersproject.com/article/2019/6/devops-why-silos-are-not-enemy (accessed on 27 June 2019).

Davenport, T. 1998, 'Putting the enterprise into the enterprise system', *Harvard Business Review*, July/August 1998, pp. 121–131.

Haag, S., Baltzan, P. & Phillips, A. 2006, *Business Driven Technology*, 1st edition, McGraw-Hill Irwin, Boston, U.S.A.

Haag, S., Baltzan, P. & Phillips, A. 2008, *Business Driven Technology*, 2nd edn, McGraw-Hill Irwin, Boston, USA.

Kimberling, E. 2011, 'Who are top ERP vendors in 2011', *Panorama Consulting*, Online Available at: http://panorama-consulting.com/who-are-the-top-erp-vendors-in-2011/ (accessed August 20, 2012).

Kimberling, E. 2019, '7 Critical ERP digital transformation questions CIOs must answer', *SearchERP.com*, 21 March 2019, Online, Available at: https://searcherp.techtarget.com/feature/7-critical-ERP-digital-transformation-questions-CIOs-must-answer (19 June 2019).

Koch, C. & Wailgum, T. 2008, 'ERP definition and Solutions', *CIO*, Online Available at: http://www.cio.com/article/print/40323 (accessed August 20, 2012).

Krigsman, M. 2010, 'Lessons from ERP Implementation Failures', *Focus Research*, Online Available at: http://www.ithound.com/abstract/lessons-erp-implementation-failures-6935 (accessed July 15, 2012).

Krigsman, M., Fauscette, M., Kimberling, E., Simon, P, & Sommer, B. 2010, 'The 2011 Focus Experts' Guide to Enterprise Resource Planning', *Focus Research*, Online Available at: http://www.sbaconsulting.com/research/ERP-Expert-Guide-final-4.pdf (accessed July 15, 2012).

Laudon, K.C. & Laudon, J.P. 2005, *Essentials of Management Information Systems: Managing the Digital Firm*, 6th edn, Prentice Hall.

Lippincott, S. 2018, *ERP Technology Value Matrix 2018*, Nucleus Research, pp. 1-17.

Nadeau, M. 2017, 'Hybrid ERP matures as companies develop better strategies', *CIO*, February 22, 2017, Online, Available at: https://www.cio.com/article/3173028/hybrid-cloud/hybrid-erp-matures-as-companies-develop-better-strategies.html (accessed on August 20, 2017).

NetSuite 2015, *8 Ways Legacy ERP Harms Businesses*, pp. 1-26.

O'Brien, J. A. & Marakas , G. M. 2011, *Management Information Systems*, 10th Edition, McGraw-Hill, New York, USA.

Pearlson, K.E. & Saunders, C.S. 2004, *Managing and Using Information Systems: A Strategic Approach*, 2nd edn, Wiley, Danvers.

Pearlson, K. E. & Saunders, C. S. 2010, *Managing and Using Information Systems: A Strategic Approach*, Fourth Edition, John Wiley & Sons, USA.

Phelan, P. 2018, 'The World of Enterprise Applications is Changing: Is it time to reroute your ERP Roadmap', *Research Report, Rimini Street*, pp. 1-16.

Reimers, K. 2003, 'Implementing ERP Systems in China', *Communications of the Association for Information Systems*, Vol. 11, pp. 335–356.

Rimini Street, 2018, 'Examining SAA's Cloud Strategy', *White Paper, Rimini Street*, pp. 1-23.

Rimini Street, 2019a, 'How SAP Customers rea responding to the planned 2025 End of ECC6 Mainstream Maintenance Deadline', *Survey Report, Rimini Street*, pp. 1-14.

Rimini Street, 2019b, 'Is your Organization Delivering on a Business-Driven Roadmap', *White Paper, Rimini Street*, pp. 1-11.

Rizza, M. N. 2018, 'Why Intelligent ERP is Key to Mastering the Complexity of the Digital Age', *IDC Analyst Connection*, January 2018, pp.1-5.

Shacklett, M. 2019, 'Comparing SAP ERP ROI to Oracle, Microsoft and Infor', *ERP Comparison Guide: SAP vs. Infor vs. Microsoft vs. Orcale*, TechTarget, pp. 2-13.

Stockpole, B. 2019a, 'Vendors step up efforts to marry blockchain and ERP', *SearchERP.com*, 08 May 2019, Online, Available at: https://searcherp.techtarget.com/feature/Vendors-step-up-efforts-to-marry-blockchain-and-ERP (accessed on 2 July 2019).

Stockpole, B. 2019b, 'Challenges slow the union between blockchain and ERP', *SearchERP.com*, 15 May 2019, Online, Available at: https://searcherp.techtarget.com/feature/Challenges-slow-the-union-between-blockchain-and-ERP (accessed on 2 July 2019).

Tippit Inc. (2008) *Inside ERP: Midmarket ERP Solutions Buyer's Guide*, Online Available at: http://www.inside-erp.com/ (accessed July 15, 2012).

Turner, A. (2004). 'ERP Rides the Second Wave', *The Sydney Morning Herald*, 10 February, Online Available: http://www.smh.com.au/articles/2004/02/09/1076175092011.html (accessed 20 March 2006).

ZiffDavis, 2014, *ERP: The Buyer's Guide*, White Paper, pp. 1-7.

Chapter 8

Using Information Systems for Improving External Relations

This chapter will explain benefits from effective customer relationship management (CRM) and CRM systems, review different types of CRM applications/systems, discuss challenges & issues involved in implementing CRM systems as well as the future trends in the development of CRM systems, explain benefits from effective supply chain management (SCM) and SCM systems, review different types of SCM applications/systems, and discuss challenges & issues involved in implementing SCM systems as well as the future trends in the development of SCM systems.

8.1 Customer Relationship Management Systems

The customer-focused business strategy

A customer-focused business strategy is not a matter of choice – rather it is a matter of necessity, and technology makes this possible. Technologies, especially internet technologies, have been increasingly used to reach customers and interact with them. Two great examples of winning the competition by applying customer–focused strategy are Apple and Google, both of them are focusing on user experience even though the former puts more emphasis on Steve Job's intuiting the experience of customers while the latter has more focus on using data-driven and iterative approach to provide better products and services customers want and like (Shapiro 2012). Today's customers can quickly change from one company's product offering to that of other companies with a click of a mouse or a touch of screen. Businesses have come to realise that the relationships that they build with customers are their most valuable assets (O'Brien & Marakas 2011, p.309). The

169

focus of competition has shifted from who sells the most products and services to who owns the customers and who can attract the customer's (limited) attention (especially online). The digital channel has huge impact on the consumer's purchase decision (e.g., digital could influence up to 60% of luxury sales (Abton et al. 2016, p.4).

Good understanding of customers

A critical aspect of successfully implementing customer-focused strategy is to have good understanding of customers. Organizations could develop good understanding of customers' needs through applying good research (via both qualitative and quantitative methods) on customers, gaining market insights, and using intuition based on experiences (Edelman 2010b; Shaprio 2012).

In addition, a good understanding of the customer/consumer decision journey/process and how technologies can assist in different parts/stages of the journey/process is essential as well. The customer decision journey can be grouped into three categories (Edelman 2010a, 2010b; Divol, Edelman & Sarrazin 2012; Laudon & Traver 2012, pp. 397-398; Turban et al. 2012, p.433; The Author's Own Knowledge):

• Pre-purchase activities: including awareness/need recognition (i.e., considering something because of external influences (such as advertisements, peer-influence, word of mouth) and/or actual needs), and searching for suitable products & services, and evaluation of alternative options. On top of the traditional media of TV, radio, print media, print advertisements, catalogues mass media, networks and other things (such as store visits and sales people's push), technologies & applications (especially Internet based) such as banners advertisements, interstitials, video ads, permission emails, e-newsletters, social networks, search engines, blogs & micro-blogs, online forums, online chatting, online communities, virtual/online catalogues, information intermediaries and site visits, could provide assistance in this stage.

• Purchase/Buy activities: including buying online (via firms' own sites or third-party platforms), buying in the store, paying online, and picking-up in the store, buying online via kiosks or other computing devices in the store, online payment systems, and online delivery (arrangements). Technologies/applications such as digital payment systems, online shopping sites & systems for taking and processing online orders and online payments, third-party trading platforms, online logistic management systems, content management systems, and online coupon and discount systems, could assist in this stage.

- Post-purchase activities: including enjoying/experiencing the product/ service, advocating the product/service, having the bond with the product/service, and repurchasing the product/service. On top of traditional measures of warranties, service calls, repairs, returns, refunds, and customer groups & networks, technologies & applications such as social networks, blogs & micro-blogs, online forums, online user groups, online chatting, online communities, e-mails, newsletters, follow-ups & updates, radio frequency identification tags, online behaviour tracking and monitoring systems, business intelligence/business analytics, could be useful in this stage.

It could be argued that the Internet has been particularly useful to customers in the areas of (pre-purchase) search & evaluation and (post-purchase) reviews & advocacy. It also could be said search engines (especially Google) have been effective in helping us find information even though the results are not perfect-most of the search results (normally after first page) don't really match with what we are looking for. There is just too much information there on the web, and our (eyeball) attention is limited. Businesses that can effectively grasp our attention for information and advertisements at the right time at the right place will be doing fine. In fact, according to Hal Varian, Google's Chief Economist (reported in Manyika 2009), Google has developed its entire business model around the notion.

In addition, for the majority of businesses (at least now and in the near future) applying a mix of online and offline communications is the most effective way, and the combination of digital and non-digital channels is still the way to go (and it will be true for many years to come) since the technology is not their core business and is only used for supporting their business processes and operations. Organizations need to adopt a "omni-channel" approach (Rigby 2011), which takes advantages of both digital and non-digital channels (e.g., 24/7 availability, convenience, wider selection, easy comparison, customer reviews, social engagement for digital channel; and shopping experience, tangible feeling, personal human help, convenient return, instant access to products/services for non-digital(traditional) channel).

Some other useful customer strategies include: Embracing data analytics & other new technologies, Having comprehensive understanding of your customers, locking your customers with distinctive identity and reputation (e.g., via value proposition, capabilities, offerings, services); Focusing on the market segments you can reasonably win the competition, Building long-term relationship with customers, Leveraging your ecosystems and work with your partners to provide better products and services on the continuous basis with efficiency and effectiveness, Providing excellent delivery services, Reorganizing the organization around your customers, and Ensuring your culture is aligned with your customer-centric strategy (Ripsam & Bouguet 2016).

Using social technologies

Social technologies (including social networking sites, video sharing, photo-sharing, blogs & microblogs, forums, social gaming, social commerce, ratings and reviews, crowdsourcing, shared work spaces, RSS, Podcasts, and wiki applications) have been becoming popular in recent years. Social networks such as Youtube, Flickr, Linkedin, Facebook, Instagram, Twitter, and Wechat connect people with specified interests and provide them with a suite of tools to allow them to more easily interact and sharing online with other individuals with similar interests (e.g., exchanging information & disseminating knowledge, sharing videos & photos, connecting with the people).

In addition, according to McKinsey Global Institute's recent surveys (reported in Bughin, Hung Bayers & Chui 2011; Chui et al. 2012, pp. 1-2), organizations are using social technologies for such purposes as: scanning external environment, finding new ideas, managing projects, developing strategic plan, allocating resources, matching employees to tasks, assessing employee performance, improving intra-inter-organizational collaboration and communication, providing services to customers, gathering customer insight, supporting marketing and sales activities, conducting social commerce, and determining compensation.

Social commerce (SC) refers to the delivery of e-business/digital buisness activities and transactions through social networks/platforms (Turban et al. 2015, p.314). You may have never heard of WeChat, but it's the most important app in China right now. WeChat users can do just about anything, including sending messages, sharing news & photos/videos, establishing communities, making voice & video calls, playing games, mobile shopping & mobile commerce, order food & services, making payments, transferring money, business to-business & enterprise communications, and so on. And WeChat is a leader in social commerce. WeChat equals to WhatsApp+ Facebook+ Timeline+Group Chat + See someone nearby to look for new friends + Shopping+ Games+ Scan Code (You can send messages in Web Browser and download something (QR Code), Get the Price of any goods (Barcode))+Get the Street View of Any places)+Translate any words+ Incredible Amount of News Feed+ Get any services like getting the take out+ Transfer money between you and other guys (Multiple transferring supported)+many other integrated functions (Heath 2015; Wikipedia 2019).

Businesses therefore need to allocate more technology resources in these areas to attract and retain customers. Businesses have started increasingly using social networks for commercial purposes (e.g., marketing and advertising), and they believe the notion when a customer "likes" (e.g., Like function in Facebook) a company or interacts with it he/she is more likely to buy its products and services (Kleiner 2012). Meanwhile businesses need to ensure they have processes and action plan to deal with misleading information and inappropriate comments on their social media sites.

Excellent customer service

One good example of excellent customer service is Zappo.com, which has seven practices of exceptional customer services (Hsieh 2010):

- Organizations should make customer service a priority of the whole firm.
- Organizations should empower customer service representatives/people
- Organizations should fire bad customers who are abusive and unreasonable.
- Organizations should not measure call time, should not upsell, and should not use scripts for phone conversations with customers.
- Organizations should be keen in talking to customers: provide phone number and make it visible to customers.
- Organizations should treat cost of serving customers via phone/call centers as an investment but not an expense.
- Organizations should celebrate and share stories of exceptional customer service across the organization.

According to an IDC 2019 research surveying 1,957 midsize companies (with 100-1,000 employees) worldwide, some customer experience/service challenges companies are facing include (in the order of the importance): Ability to manage customer data amid privacy and GDPR regulation; Identifying and optimizing sales channels, Timely responding to customer; Building and managing an effective digital business presence; Examining and targeting appropriate customer segments and markets; Generating sufficient sales leads and establishing sales pipeline; Managing sales opportunities & measuring sales performance; Managing and measure the efficiency & effectiveness of marketing campaign; and Providing proper and timely field service. In the same study, some identified technologies & techniques for enhancing customer experience include (in the order): Big Data & Data Analytics, Customer journey mapping, Chatbots & Conversational AI applications, Automated self-help services, Integrating all customer-facing systems, AI/Machine Learning (for anticipating individual customer's needs), and

Providing sales teams with access to complete customer data to enable better communications with customers.

Another important dimension of customer service in today's environment is timely and effectively addressing customers' complains and problems/service mishaps, especially online complains (Collier & Beinstock 2006; Tripp &Gregoire 2011). One latest example is the video clip posted on Youtube titled "United Break Guitars", which has been viewed more than 10 million times. Organizations need to quickly identify the issues and take appropriate actions (normally with quite short timeframe). They need to provide complaining customers with the opportunity to talk to a person, fair & transparent processes, policies and procedures of dealing with complains, and compensations & apologies.

One important part of customer services is dealing with customers' complaints about unsatisfactory services. It can be argued that many (if not most) customers will try to contact the organization for unsatisfactory services, and if they don't receive reasonable responses from the organization, they will take their complaints to digital channels and platforms, which can disseminate information to much larger audience in a very short time frame. Organizations should respond within 24-hour timeframe. On a related note, people tend to discuss with friends and families regarding their unhappy experiences as they do when they are making purchase decision (Bjørnland et al. 2015; Leggett 2016). According to a recent Forrest research on consumers in the U.S. (reported in Leggett 2016, p.4), some channels customers use to make their service complaints include (in the order of the importance): Telling friends and family members about the negative experience; Writing negative reviews online at consumer review sites (e.g., Yelp), Posting on Facebook page, Posting in the online customer community, Posting on a blog sponsored by the business, Posting on a blog not sponsored by the business, Posting on Twitter page, and Posting on the business's Twitter page. The same research also indicates that consumers are increasingly using self-service channels for customer service (e.g., using a self-service mobile phone application or help).

Meanwhile, even though digital plays more important role in the customer's journey with organization, for most retailing businesses in-store experience is and will be critical for many years to come. For example, according to a recent research on retailing businesses in the U.S (reported in eMarketer 2016a), the most important customer experience channels include: In-store (45% of the respondents), Social media (19%), Web (14%), Call Center (11%), Mobile & text (6%), and E-mail (5%).

Customer relationship management

Haag, Baltzan and Phillips (2008, p.127) state that 'Customer relationship management (CRM) is a business philosophy based on the premise that those organizations that understand the needs of individual customers are best positioned to achieve sustainable competitive advantages in the future'. O'Brien and Marakas (2011, p.309) suggest that CRM is the business focus and is an enterprise-wide effort to acquire and retain customers. It focuses on building long-term and sustainable customer relationships that add value for both the customer and the firm.

Through applying technology that collects and examines customer information from a multifaceted perspective, CRM could provide customer-facing employees with a single, complete view of every customer at every touch point and across all channels while giving the customer a single, complete view of the company (Laudon & Laudon 2005, p.65). By applying a set of integrated applications and modules, CRM can address all aspects of the customer relationship, including customer services, sales, and marketing, provide consistent and personalised services to individual customers (mass customisation). CRM contributes to building long-term customer relations, and identifying the best and most profitable customers (Laudon & Laudon 2005, p.65).

Laudon and Laudon (2005, p.65) suggest that through effective customer relationship management, organisations are able to identify answers for such questions on their customers as: what is a value of a particular customer to the firm over his or her life time?, who are our most profitable customers?, what do these most profitable customers want to buy?, what is the past, present and future potential of individual customers?, at what price level am I winning and losing business?, what quotes did the customer previously accept or reject?, which competitors has the customer used?, and what is the cost of shipping?. At the same time, effective customer relationship management plays an important role in business success, for example (O'Brien & Marakas 2011, p.312):

• It costs six times more to sell to a new customer than to sell to an existing one.

• A typical dissatisfied customer will tell 8 to 10 people about his/her experience.

• A company can boost its profit 85% by increasing its annual customer retention by only 5%.

• The odds of selling to a new customer are 15%; an old customer 50%.

- 70% of complaining customers will do business with the company again if it takes care of a service mishap.

Customer management relationship systems

O'Brien and Marakas (2011, p.309) note that customer relationship management systems are cross-functional enterprise systems that integrate and automate many of the customer serving processes in sales, marketing, and customer service. They also point out a CRM system develops an information systems framework, which integrates processes of sales, marketing, and customer service with the rest of the company's business operations, tracks all of the ways in which a company interacts with its customers, and helps analyse these interactions. CRM systems could assist in organizations' activities of acquiring new customers, enhancing relations with customers, and retaining customers (O'Brien & Marakas 2011, p.315). Major CRM software application vendors include: Siebel, Oracle, PeopleSoft, Saleforce.com, SAP, IBM, Amdocs, and Nortel/Clarify.

A typical CRM system for a financial business could be described as follows (Laudon & Laudon 2005, p.406; The Author's Own Knowledge). The system capture customer information from customer touching-points and channels (e.g., branch, telephone, email, online, mobile, customer service desk, conventional mail, point-of-purchase) and other sources (e.g., third-party service providers, available public or published information). Then it merges and aggregates the collected data into a customer data repository (e.g., data warehouse, cloud) where it is cleansed and prepared for subsequent data analysis. The collected data then are processed and examined via tools and techniques (e.g., data mining, OLAP, Big Data & Data Analytics, Artificial Intelligence) to understand customers' behaviors and profiles and predict their future intentions. The outcomes of data analysis could be used by production, sales, marketing, and customer services functions to generate better products and services.

Challenges and issues of customer relationship management systems

While CRM systems can bring organisations benefits such as those stated in Haag, Baltzan and Phillips (2006, p.114), the failure rates of CRM system implementations can be as high as 55 to 75% (Laudon & Laudon 2005, p. 357). Many companies have found CRM systems difficult to implement. One common and key reason for the failure of CRM systems is the lack of understanding and preparation. Some other identified reasons include (IDC 2019; Laudon & Laudon 2005, pp.357–358; O'Brien & Marakas 2011, p.316; Zikmund et al. 2003, p.163):

• Difficulty in being able to see a 'total picture' of a customer, especially managing global customers with different languages, time zones, currencies, and regulations.

• Poor user acceptance (e.g. asking sales people to share their customer information could be hard since their income is largely based on commission. Other concerns include fears about job security and management control).

• The required shift from a product-centric view to customer centric, which could be very challenging.

• Many failures when firms try to create a cross-functional enterprise system that requires integrating data from a wide array of departments into one system.

• Required changes in their culture and business processes to facilitate cross-functional integration.

• Failures to provide proper project focus and the lack of adequate project management skills.

• The lack of ability to manage customer data amid new privacy and GDPR regulation.

Failures in providing consistent services to customers from various touch points and channels could be another reason. As per a survey conducted by Royal Bank of Canada, the largest bank in Canada, when convenience is very important to customers (e.g., convenience of online banking), what customers wanted was a bank which cares for its customers, values their businesses, and recognised them as the same individuals no matter what parts or/and which touch points of the bank they did business with (Gulati & Oldroy 2005). Organisations have to understand that CRM is more than just technology, it touches on the various aspects of the organization, and it requires enterprise-wide support. Technology itself is not able to manage customer relationships unless associated managerial and organisational issues have been properly dealt with (Laudon & Laudon 2005, p.357).

But how to ensure a successful CRM system implementation? Some suggestions provided by Haag, Baltzan and Phillips (2008, p.131) include:

• Clearly communicating the CRM strategy.
• Defining information needs and flows.
• Building an integrated view of the customer.
• Implementing in iterations.
• Having scalability for organisational growth.

Some other suggestions are (Gulati & Oldroy 2005, Laudon & Laudon 2005, pp.357–358; Zikmind et al. 2003, p.163):

- Conducting a survey to determine how the organisation responds to customers
- Carefully considering the components of CRM system and only choosing what you need.
- Concentrating on how CRM system can help but not too much on what it can do (i.e., place business before technology).
- Deciding a strategy: refining existing processes or reengineering.
- Evaluating all levels in organisations but giving more attention to the front line.
- Prioritising CRM system requirements, classifying them into must, desired, or not so important.
- Selecting appropriate CRM system from various vendors: best-of-breed approach or a single package?
- Having clear performance measures.
- Adopting staged system development and phased implementation.
- Gaining top management's support and commitment.
- Having sufficient financial commitments: total cost of ownership of the implementation can be very high.
- Making required changes in organizational culture, structure, and business processes.
- Promoting early success, carefully design the tasks involved and set up the links between units so as to minimize conflict.

When organizations are selecting new CRM systems, some issues they should look at (Mycustomer 2019):

- Do we really need a new CRM system?
- What is wrong with our existing CRM system?
- Do we need a CRM consultant to help us choose and implement a CRM system?
- How to properly solicit requirements for the new CRM system?: You need to look at such areas as business challenges needed to be addressed, main business objectives, business processes to be supported by the new CRM system, and functional requirements, implementation plan & required resources, data flow models, data migration and integration requirements, reporting requirements, and vendor selection and roles of the vendor.
- How to select a vendor?-You need to look at issues such as data migration and integration process, support, customization, contract terms, implementation timeframe, consultancy costs (e.g., on average, 3.5 times of the purchased CRM technology), and cloud costs (e.g., cloud-based implementation could be faster

than on-the-premise implementation (17 months on average for the former and 36 months on average for the latter)).

Future trends of customer relationship management systems

There is no doubt that in the future CRM will continue to be a major strategic focus for companies. CRM systems no doubt will adopt new technologies such as big data and business analytics, artificial intelligence, cloud computing, mobile computing, and social computing to help them have good understanding of customer needs and better manage customer experience & expectation through mastering the customer journey with the organization, creating an integrated view of each customer, and fully linked business processes across the organization (e.g., from CRM front-end systems to order management)(IDC 2019). On-demand CRM services are emerging and are becoming more popular for benefits such as better flexibility, enhanced agility & scalability, reduced costs, and less demand for internal expertise. However data security & privacy issues will be remained as top concerns for such on-demand services provided by third parties. Mobile CRM applications are becoming more and more popular, and in the future virtual applications (e.g., augmented and virtual reality) will attract more attention (Abton et al. 2016, p.4). Conversational commerce enabled/supported by technologies (such as Chatbots and conversational artificial intelligence applications) and voice-assisted interactions (e.g., via Amazon Echo, Google Home, and Alibaba's Genie) will gain more adoption in the future to help organizations with engage better with their customers (IDC 2019; Maxwell, Dahlhoff & Moore 2019; Reblin & Schröder 2017). The 5G and beyond could give us (near) real-time data transmission and communication in the multiple formats of voice, text and video (Vollmer & Gross 2018).

Personalization is another area attracting more and more attention. The rapid development in digital technologies has made personalization more personal (Boudet et al. 2019). Digital technologies (such as big data and business analytics, machine learning, artificial intelligence, augmented reality, virtual reality) can help organizations digitize some elements/components of processes and services, have better empathy ability to understand another person's emotions and enhance realtionships), and provide better products and services to customers via more closely collaborating with and working with stakeholders in the ecosystem (e.g., changing the liner relationships to hub-type communications). In addition to the technological perspectives, organizations also should embark on tools & techniques such as customer journey mapping, which allows organizations to have deep understanding of every possible way a customer can interact with them across his/her journey with the organization (Davey 2019), to further enhance their capabilities of understanding and meeting the needs of their customers. With the help of the available techniques/tools and digital technologies, organizations can develop a deep understanding of each customer's unique needs and then offer tailored products/services and experiences around digital and human channels/ touch points (Brodski et al. 2019).

In the future, businesses need to work harder on its delivery services since delivery services could make or break a business, for example a recent research on Australian digital consumers (reported in eMarketer 2016b) indicates that online buyers in Australia demand convenient shipping: 75% of digital buyers in Australia expect digital retailers to offer guaranteed weekend or after-hours delivery, 80% expect to be able to choose a specific time slot to receive their items, and 85% expect retailers offer same-day shipping. In addition, new technologies (such as drones, robotics, autonomous delivery vehicle, droid, Van/drone integrated system, smart doorlock, trunk delivery, autonomous vans, EV, parcel box, parcel locker) will be included in the delivery options (Joerss, Neuhaus & Schöder 2016; Schröder et al. 2018).

8.2 Supply Chain Management Systems

Supply chains

Turban et al. (2006, p. 279) define supply chain as 'the flow of materials, information, money, and services from raw material suppliers through factories and warehouses to the end customers'. Supply chains have existed for thousands years. The silk road from China to other parts of the world is a good example of a very old supply chain. Laudon and Laudon (2005, p. 347) suggest that supply chains can be viewed from a push-based or pull-based perspective. The push-based model is basically the traditional build-to-stock approach while pull-based model is the strategy of build-to-order – 'make what we sell not sell what we make' (e.g. Dell computer's model).

A complete supply chain typically consists of three parts (Turban et al. 2006, p.280, Haag, Baltzan & Phillips 2008, p.118):

• Upstream supply chain: including activities of a manufacturing company with its suppliers. The major activity is procurement.

- Internal supply chain: including in-house processes for transforming the inputs from the suppliers into the outputs. Main concerns are production management, manufacturing, and inventory control.

- Downstream supply chain: including delivering the products to the final customers. And the attention is on distribution, warehousing, transportation and after-sale services.

Some typical problems along the supply chain include (Turban et al. 2006, p.283):

- Slow and prone to errors because of the length of the chain involving many internal and external partners.
- Large inventories without the ability to meet demand.
- Insufficient logistics infrastructure.
- Quality problem or difficulties in controlling quality.

Lacking an effective information sharing mechanism is a major cause of failures of supply chains, and minor inaccurate information in demand could be amplified to become a much big one while it moves along the supply chain (called "bullwhip effect") (Laudon & Laudon 2005, p.340).

Supply chain management

Supply chain management (SCM) is a cross-functional inter-enterprise effort that uses information systems to help support and manage the links between some of a company's key business processes and those of its suppliers, customers and business partners. Some basic elements of supply chain management include: plan, source, make, deliver, and return (Haag, Baltzan & Phillips 2008, p. 119). Through using a fast, efficient, and low cost supply chain, organisations can enhance their agility and responsiveness in meeting the demands of their customers and needs of their suppliers (O'Brien & Marakas 2011, p. 330). Some SCM benefits reported in Haag, Baltzan and Phillips (2008, p.118) include: cost/control savings, productivity improvement, reductions in inventory levels, enhanced visibility of demand & supply, improved quality, and maintaining/gaining competitive advantages. O'Brien and Marakas (2011, p.330) and Laudon & Laudon (2005, p 348) add some other benefits, including faster, more accurate order processing, faster time to market, lower costs, and better relationships with suppliers, and better cash flow arising from supply chain efficiency.

Traditional SCM thinking involved 'I buy from my suppliers, and I sell to my customers'. Today, organisations are quickly realising the tremendous value they can gain from having visibility throughout their supply chain. Knowing immediately what is transacting at the customer end of the supply chain, instead of waiting days or weeks for this information to flow through, allows the organisation to react immediately (Laudon & Laudon 2005, p.340). The role of SCM is evolving and it is not uncommon for suppliers to be involved in collaborative activities (e.g., in product development) and for distributors to act as consultants in brand marketing.

Supply chain management systems

Supply chain management (SCM) systems, including systems for supply chain planning and systems for supply chain execution, automate the flow of information between members of a supply chain so that they can use it to make better decisions about when and how much to purchase, produce or ship (Laudon & Laudon 2005, p. 341). Supply chain planning (SCP) software can improve the flow and efficiency of the supply chain while reducing inventory by applying advanced mathematical applications. Supply chain execution (SCE) software is able to automate the different steps and stages of the supply chain (Haag, Baltzan & Phillips 2008, p.121).

Apart from the above mentioned supply chain planning systems and supply chain execution systems, some other technologies that can be used for managing supply chains include: extranets, intranets, corporate portals, electronic data interchange (Internet based), intra-enterprise & inter-enterprise collaboration tools, radio frequency identification tags, business to business e-business applications (e.g., buy sites, sell sites, exchanges), and many others.

Challenges and issues of supply chain management systems

Some identified challenges and issues of SCM system implementations include (Bailey et al. 2019; Cohen 2005; Laudon & Laudon 2005, p.349; Mercier et al. 2018; Mishkis, Moder & Toepert 2017; O'Brien & Marakas 2011, p.38; The Author's Own Knowledge):
• Lack of proper demand planning knowledge, tools, and guidelines, which is a major source of SCM system implementation failure.
• Inaccurate or overoptimistic demand forecasts, which will cause major production, inventory, and other business problems, no matter how efficient the rest of the supply chain management processes are.
• Inaccurate production, inventory, and other business data, which is another frequent cause of SCM system implementation failures.

- Lack of adequate collaboration among marketing, production, and inventory management departments within a company, and with suppliers, distributors, customers and other parties involved in the supply chain.
- Immature SCM systems, which are hard to implement.
- Lack of required changes in organizational adjustments (e.g., business processes, culture and structure): implementation of SCM must be accompanied by improvements in the supply chain processes and other required organizational changes.
- Lack of effective supply chain risk management in place.
- Lack of senior management support.
- Lack of advanced and modern data management and data analytics capabilities.
- Firms' reluctance to share information.
- Underestimating the amount of training: users must have in-depth knowledge of how the system works so they can properly interpret its results when they make the decisions.
- Global supply chain issues (including geographic distances and time differences; additional costs for transportation, inventory, and local taxes; foreign government regulations; cultural differences; varied performance standards; quality control issues; intellectual property concerns; and local talent recruitment and retention challenges).

So what are some solutions to various SCM system implementation challenges and problems? Some suggestions and industry best practices include (Cohen 2005; Haag, Baltzan & Phillips 2008 p. 123; Paulonis & Norton 2008; Lee 2004; Mercier et al. 2018; Mishkis, Moder & Toepert 2017; Sheffi 2005; Turban et al. 2006, pp. 284–285; Vohra, Kamath & Lyer 2018):

- Sharing information along the supply chain.
- Developing the trust among partners though it is not easy to achieve.
- Building relationships with your partners (especially long-term and important partners). Face-to-face communication is very important.
- Building an adaptable supply chain with the ability to spot trends and the capability to change supply chain (adaptability).
- Taking care to align the interest of all the firms in the supply chain with your own to create incentives for better performance and develop trust (alignment).
- Changing linear supply to hub structure (agility).
- Obtaining senior leadership's commitment.
- Preparing for a new way of working by making necessary organizational adjustments/changes (e.g., performance-oriented culture).

- Mastering data management and data analytics.
- Consolidating suppliers (e.g., not having too many suppliers and considering the option of using third party specialist aggregators).
- Bundling services and materials into a single contract.
- Using intermediaries, who normally have access to a network of suppliers and customers, to develop new partners to complement existing ones.
- Evaluating needs of ultimate consumers not just immediate customer to avoid being a victim of the 'bullwhip effect'.
- Determining where your products stand in terms of technology cycles and product life cycles to decide approximate markets and supply chains for every product and service.
- Having clear and continuous communications with suppliers and clearly specifying the roles, tasks, and responsibilities of all parties.
- Sharing risks, costs and rewards (e.g., compensate for the loss to retailers as a result of new product development, and buy back the excess books by publishers).
- Creating supply chains that respond to sudden and unexpected changes in markets
- Establishing supply chain collaboration (e.g., Collaborative Planning, Forecasting and Replenishment (CPFR) program; integrated product-development systems) and with your suppliers and customers.
- Using inventories to solve problem: optimize and control inventories (e.g., only maintaining a stockpile of inexpensive but key components).
- Drawing up contingency plans and developing crisis management teams.
- Effectively engaging with IT and Integrating IS/IT systems between suppliers and business partners.
- Thoughtfully selecting and implementing digital tools & required IT architecture and infrastructure (e.g., for high-speed data analytics for large amount of data from various sources) and adopting Internet-based applications for sourcing, transportation, communications, and international finance for global SCM.
- Establishing effective management (both recruitment and retention) of local talent and a talent pipeline.
- Monitoring economies all over the world to spot new supply bases and markets.

Laudon and Laudon (2005, p.343) and Haag, Baltzan and Phillips (2008, p.123) also stress the importance of the need to measure the performance of the supply chain. The measurement can be done by examining factors of fill rate (ability to fill the orders by due day), on-time deliveries, average time from order to delivery, total supply chain costs, number of delays of supply in inventory, supply chain response time, forecast accuracy and source/make cycle time, cash-to-cycle time, among many others (Laudon & Laudon 2005, p.343).

Furthermore, Chopra and Meindi (2004, pp.524–525) point out when organisations are making decisions on SCM systems, they should only select information systems that address a firm's key success factors(e.g., inventory in PC business (demand is unstable and short product life cycle)) versus inventory in oil company (demand is fairly stable and long product life cycle)), take incremental steps (e.g., demand planning functions then supply planning applications instead of installing a complete SCM system), align the level of sophistication with the need for sophistication (trading off between ease of implementation and the system's complexity), use information systems to support decision making but not to make decisions, and have information systems for both current needs and future needs.

Organizations also need to pay close attention to supply chain risk management. Some examples of supply chain risks include: changes in macroeconomic environment, lack of data transparency, production process being not robust, cost & time exceeding forecast, supply short fall, supply stoppage, factory shutdown or slow down, process disruption (e.g., lower-than expected yield), illegal interference from third party (e.g., pilferage), and failure to meet regulations (e.g., on environment, quality, health & safety) (Bailey et al. 2019). Some steps in managing known supply chain risks consist of: identifying and documenting risks, establishing a risk management framework to evaluate the likelihood and consequences of identified risks as well as the organization's preparedness to deal with identified risks), monitoring risk, and instituting governance and regular review; meanwhile building strong defenses via effective risk management process, standards, competence, organization as well as risk-aware culture is the key to deal with unknown supply chain risks (Bailey et al. 2019).

Future trends of supply chain management systems

Similar to previous discussion of future trends of CRM systems, new technologies such as cloud-computing, mobile computing, social computing, Big Data & Data Analytics, Internet of Things, Artificial Intelligence, will be more adopted into supply chain management systems. In addition, integration of various internal systems and external issues would be a major focus for future supply management systems (as well as previously discussed customer relationship management systems).

O'Brien and Marakas (2011, p.341) believe that the trends in the use of supply chain management systems today are the adoption of three possible stages in a company's implementation of SCM systems. They are:

• First stage: improving internal supply chain processes and external processes and relationships with suppliers and customers.

• Second stage: working on links among suppliers, distributors, customers, and other trading partners.

• Third stage: developing and implementing collaborative supply chain management applications/systems.

Laudon and Laudon (2014) argue that the future Internet-drive supply chain operates like a digital logistics nervous system. Such system provides multidirectional communication among firms, networks of firms, and e-marketplaces so that entire networks of supply chain partners can immediately make adjustments on inventories, orders, and capacities.

8.3 Summary

In this chapter, two other major cross-functional information systems of CRM systems and SCM systems were looked at closely. Their benefits, roles, challenges, and future trends were discussed. In the next chapter, information systems for decision making will be discussed.

References

Abtan, O., Bartan, C., Bonelli, F., Gurzki, H., Mei-Pochtler, A., Pianon, N. & Tsusaka, M. 2016, *Digital or Die: The Choice for Luxury Brands*, The Boston Consulting Group, September 2016, pp.1-12.

Bailey, T., Barriball, E, Dey, A. & Sankur, A. 2019, 'A practical approach to supply-chain risk management', *Operations Practice*, McKinsey & Company, pp.1-6.

Berman, S.J. & Bell, R. 2011, 'Digital Transformation: Creating New Business Models Where Digital Meets Physical', *IBM Global Business Service Executive Report*, IBM Institute for Business Value, pp. 1-17.

Bjørnland, D. F., Ditzel, C., Esquivias, P., Visser, J., Knox, S. & Sánchez-Rodríguez, V. 2015, *What Really Shapes the Customer Experience*, bcg.perspective, The Boston Consulting Group, September 2015, Online Available at: https://www.bcgperspectives.com/content/articles/ marketing-brand-strategy-what-really-shapes-customer-experience/ (accessed on May 1, 2016).

Boudet, J., Gregg, B., Rathje, K., Stein, E. & Vollhardt, K. 2019, 'The future of personalization-and how to get ready for it', *Marketing & Sales,* June 2019, McKinsey & Company, Online, Available at: https://www.mckinsey.com/business-functions/marketing-and-sales/our-insights/the-future-of-personalization-and-how-to-get-ready-for-it (accessed on 1 July 2019).

Brodski, S., Desmangles, L., Fanfarillo, S., Khodabandeh, S., Palumbo, S. & Santinelli, M. 2019, *What does personalization in banking really mean?,* The Boston Group, 12 March 2019, Online, Available at: https://www.bcg.com/en-au/publications/2019/what-does-personalization-banking-really-mean.aspx (accessed on 1 June 2019).

Bughin, J, Hung Byers, A & Chui, M 2011, 'How Social Technologies Are Extending the Organization', *McKinsey Quarterly*, November 2011, pp. 1-10.

Chopra, S. & Meindl, P. 2004, *Supply Chain Management: Strategy, Planning, and Operations*, 2nd edn, Prentice Hall, New Jersey.

Cohen. S. 2005, 'Moving to China', *Supply Chain Strategy (a news letter of Harvard Business Review)*, Vol. 1, No. 2, pp. 4–6.

Chui, M. & Fleming, T. 2011, 'Insight P & G's Digital Revolution', *McKinsey Quarterly*, November 2011, pp. 1-11.

Chui, M., Manyika, J., Bughin, J., Dobbs, R., Roxburgh, C., Sarrazin, H., Sands G. & Westergren, M. 2012, *The Social Economy: Unlocking Value and Productivity through Social Technologies*, McKinsey Global Institute, July 2012, pp. 1-170.

Collier, JE & Beinstock, CC 2006, 'How do Customers Judge Quality in an E-tailer?' *MIT Sloan Management Review*, Vol. 48, No. 1, pp. 35–40.

Mycustomer 2019, *CRM Buyer's Guide 2019: Key points to consider when selecting CRM solution for your business*, Mycustomer.com, pp. 1-20.

Davey, N. 2019, 'What is customer journey mapping and why it is so important', *Customer Journey Mapping: A 2019 Guide*, Mycustomer.com, Online, Available at: https://www.mycustomer.com/resources/customer-journey-mapping-a-2019-guide (accessed on 1 July 2019).

Divol, R., Edelman, D. & Sarrazin, H., 2012, 'Demystifying social media', *McKinsey Quarterly*, April 2012, pp. 1-11.

Edelman, DC 2010a, 'Branding in Digital Age', *Harvard Business Review*, December 2010, pp. 62-69.

Edelman, DC 2010b, 'Four Ways to Get More Value from Digital Marketing', *McKinsey Quarterly*, March 2010, pp. 1-8.

eMarketer 2016a, 'The In-Store Channel Still the Top Priority for Retailers', *Retail & E-Commerce*, June 10, 2016, Online Available at: http://www.emarketer.com/Article/In-Store-Channel-Still-Top-Priority-Retailers/1014072 (accessed June 15, 2016).

eMarketer 2016b, 'Digital Buyers in Australia Demand Convenient Shipping', *Retail & E-Commerce*, March 10, 2016, Online Available at: http://www.emarketer.com/Article/Digital-Buyers-Australia-Demand-Convenient-Shipping/1013684 (accessed March 11, 2016).

Gulati, R. & Oldroyd, J.B. 2005, 'The Quest for Customer Focus', *Harvard Business Review*, April 2005, pp. 92–101.

Haag, S., Baltzan, P. & Phillips, A. 2008, *Business Driven Technology*, 2nd edn, McGraw-Hill Irwin, Boston, USA.

Heath, A. 2015, 'An app you've probably never heard of is the most important social network in China', *Business Insider*, November 1, 2015, Online, Available at: https://www.businessinsider.com/what-is-wechat-2015-10?r=AU&IR=T (accessed on 1 July 2018).

Heish, T. 2010, 'Zappo's CEO on Going to Extremes for Customers', *Harvard Business Review*, July-August 2010, pp. 41-45.

IDC 2019, *The Customer Experience Role in Best-Runm Midsize Companies: Embedding Intelligence to Drive CX*, An IDC InfoBrief, February 2019, pp.1-12.

Joerss, M., Neuhaus, F. & Schöder, J. 2016, *How customer demand are reshaping last-mile delivery*, McKinsey & Company, October 2016, Online Available at: http://www.mckinsey.com/industries/travel-transport-and-logistics/our-insights/how-customer-demands-are-reshaping-last-mile-delivery (Accessed on November 5, 2016).

Kleiner, A. 2012, 'Brand transformation on the Internet', *Strategy + Business*, June 25, 2012, Online Available at: http://www.strategy-business.com/article/00117?pg=all (accessed July 20, 2012).

Kleiner, A. 2012, 'The thought leader interview: Bob Carrigan (CEO IDG Communications)', *Strategy + Business*, Issue 66, Spring 2012, pp. 1-8.

Laudon, K.C. & Laudon, J.P. 2005, *Essentials of Management Information Systems: Managing the Digital Firm*, 6th edn, Prentice Hall.

Laudon, K.C. & Traver, C.G. 2012, *E-commerce in 2012: Business, Technology, Society*, 7th edn, Addison Wesley, Boston, USA.

Laudon, K.C. & Laudon, J.P. 2014, *Management Information Systems: Managing the Digital Firm*, 13th edn, Global Edition, Pearson, U. K.

Lee, H. L. 2004, 'The Triple-A Supply Chain', *Harvard Business Review*, October 2004, pp. 102–112.

Leggett, K. 2016, *Trends 2016: The Future of Customer Service-Vision: The Contact Centers for Customer Service Playbook*, Forrester, pp. 1-14.

Manyika, J. 2009, 'Hal Varian on how the Web challenges managers', *McKinsey Quarterly*, January 2009, Online available at: https://www.mckinseyquarterly.com/Strategy/Innovation/Hal_Varian_on_how_the_Web_challenges_managers_2286 (accessed July 23, 2012).

Maxwell, J., Dahlhoff, D. & Moore, Claire-Louise 2019, 'Competing for Shoppers' Habits', *Strategy+Business*, Issue 91, Summer 2019, Online, Available at: https://www.strategy-business.com/feature/Competing-for-Shoppers-Habits?gko=ccc17 (accessed on 14 June 2019).

Mercier, P. 2018, Knizek, C., Sieke, M. & Dunn, S. 2018, *Is your supply chain planning already for digital*, The Boston Group, 22 October 2018, Online, Available at: https://www.bcg.com/en-au/publications/2018/supply-chain-planning-ready-for-digital.aspx (accessed on 1 June 2019).

Mishkis, L., Moder, M. & Toepert, M. 2017, 'Use precurement's data to power your performance', *Operations Extranet*, McKinsey & Company, September 2017, pp.1-5.

Mycustomer 2019, Customer journey mapping: A 2019 Guide, Online, Available at: https://www.mycustomer.com/resources/customer-journey-mapping-a-2019-guide (accessed on 20 July 2019).

O'Brien, J. A. & Marakas, G. M. 2011, *Management Information Systems*, 10th Edition, McGraw-Hill, New York, USA.

Paulonis, D. & Norton, S. 2008, 'McKinsey global survey results: Managing global supply chains', *McKinsey Quarterly*, July 2008, pp. 1–9.

Rigby, D. 2011, 'The Future of Shopping', *Harvard Business Review*, December 2011, pp. 65-76.

Reblin, J. & Schröder, S. M. 2017, 'Chatbots: engaging with your customers like a friend', *Performance*, Vol. 9, Issue 3, pp.1-11.

Ripsam, T. & Bouquet, L. 2016, '10 Principles of Customer Strategy', *Strategy +Business*, Marketing, Media & Sales, September 26, 2016, Online, Available at: http://www.strategy-business.com/article/10-Principles-of-Customer-Strategy?gko=083a5 (Accessed on November 1, 2016).

Schröder, J., Heid, B., Neuhaus, F., Kässer, M., Klink, C. & Tatomir, S. 2018, 'Fast forwarding last-mile delivery-implications for the ecosystem', *Travel, Transport, and Logistics and Advanced Industries*, July 2018, McKinsey & Company, pp.1-17.

Shapiro, A. 2012, 'Are you making the most of your company's software layer', *McKinsey Quarterly*, April 2012, pp. 1-6.

Sheffi, Y. 2005, 'Creating Demand-Responsive Supply Chains', *Supply Chain Strategy (a news letter of Harvard Business Review)*, Vol. 1, No. 2, pp.1–4.

The Economist (2012), 'The world in figures: industries', The World in 2012, *The Economist*, January 2012, pp. 117-118.

Trip, T.M. & Gregoire, Y. 2011, 'When Unhappy Customers Strike Back on the Internet', *MIT Sloan Management Review*, Vol. 52, No. 3, pp. 37-44.

Turban, E., King, D., Viehland, D. & Lee, J. 2006, *Electronic Commerce 2006: A Managerial Perspective,* International edn, Prentice Hall, Upper Saddle River, NJ.

Turban, E., King, D., Lee, JK, Liang, T.P. & Turban, D. 2012, *Electronic Commerce 2012: A Managerial and Social Networks Perspective*, International edn, Prentice Hall, Upper Saddle River, NJ.

Turban, E., King, D., Lee, J.K., Liang, T. P., Turban, D.C. 2015, *Electronic Commerce: A Managerial and Social Networks Perspective*, Eighth Edition, 2015, Springer, Germany.

Zikmund, W.G., McLeod, R. Jr. & Gilbert, F.W. 2003, *Customer Relationship Management: Integrating Marketing Strategy and Information Technology*, John Wiley, Danvers, MA.

Vohra, R., Kamath, P. & Lyer, K. 2018, *Don't give up on strategic supplier management*, The Boston Group, 06 December 2018, Online, Available at: https://www.bcg.com/en-au/publications/2018/do-not-give-up-on-strategic-supplier-management.aspx (accessed on 1 June 2019).

Vollmer, C. & Gross, D. 2018, 'Oath CEO Tim Armstrong in the Promises of the Mobile' Consumer, *Strategy+Business*, Thought Leaders, June 13, 2018, Online, Available at: https://www.strategy-business.com/article/Oath-CEO-Tim-Armstrong-Believes-in-the-Promise-of-the-Mobile-Consumer?gko=b177a (accessed on 14 June 2019).

Wikipedia 2019, WeChat, Online, Available at: https://en.wikipedia.org/wiki/WeChat (accessed on 5 July 2019).

Chapter 9

Using Information Systems for Supporting Decision Making

This chapter will explain the importance of information quality for decision making, review various information systems for decision support, and discuss business intelligence/business analytics, artificial intelligence for supporting & enhancing decision making.

9.1 Enabling the Organization-Decision Making

Organisations today can no longer use a 'cook book' approach to decision making. In order to succeed in business today, companies need information systems that support the diverse information and decision-making needs of their operations. The rapid development of the Internet and other information technologies has further strengthened the role of information systems for decision-making support (Haag, Baltzan & Phillips 2008, p.103; O'Brien & Marakas 2011, p.390). Providing information and support for all levels of management decision making is no easy task. For example, by surveying 4,000 senior executives of across the world, the researchers from The Economist Intelligence Unit identified three most important areas information systems needs to improve upon for better management decision making (reported in The Economist Intelligence Unit 2005): (1) getting the right information at the right time; (2) ensuring access to information anywhere (and any time); and (3) sending instant alerts on things going wrong.

In a McKinsey Global Survey of 864 executives from different industries and regions (reported in Roberts & Sikes 2011), the lack of required data is identified as the most frequently cited barrier to data-driven decision making, and other mentioned barriers include (in the order): firm's culture of prioritizing experience over data, the lack of skills in translating and synthesizing the results of data analysis for decision-making, the lack of analytical skills required to carry out analyses, litter or no interest in changing decision-making processes, and the unawareness of available data in the company. Therefore, information systems must be designed to produce a variety of information products to meet the changing needs of decision-makers throughout an organization.

What is the value of information? The answer to this important question varies depending on how the information is used (Haag, Baltzan & Phillips 2008, p.104). Two people looking at the exact same piece of information could extract completely different value from the information depending on the tools they are using to look at the information. Consider what characteristics would make information valuable and useful to you? One way to answer this question is to examine the attributes of information quality. Quality information is accurate, timely and easy to understand (O'Brien & Marakas 2011, p.323).

Meanwhile quality information is very critical. Without quality information, making right decision is a mission impossible. Some characteristics of quality information include (Haag, Baltzan & Phillips 2008, p.387): accuracy (determining if all values are correct), completeness (determining if any values are missing), consistency (ensuring that aggregate or summary information is in agreement with detailed information), uniqueness (ensuring that each transaction, entity, and event is represented only once in the information), and timeliness (determining if the information is current with respect to the business requirement).

Some sources of low quality information include (Bloomberg Businessweek Research Services 2011; Chui & Fleming 2011; Haag, Baltzan & Phillips 2008, p.388; Mayer & Schaper 2010; Milley & Wood 2010; The Author's Own Knowledge): (1) errors in collecting information (e.g., customers intentionally enter inaccurate information to protect their privacy), entering information (e.g., call centre operators enter abbreviated or erroneous information by accident or to save time), and data collection design (e.g., asking wrong questions to wrong targeted groups); (2) information from different systems with different information entry standards and formats; (3) missing information as a result of wrongly designed systems; (4) inconsistent and inaccurate information from various external and internal sources in different formats; (5) potential valuable not shared information, which is trapped in the organization silos; (6) the loss of information lost in transit from one system to another or lost in poorly integrated systems; and (7) presenting information in user unfriendly formats.

9.2 Information Systems for Decision Support

O'Brien and Marakas (2011, p. 393) suggest that the types of information required by directors, executives, managers and members of self-directed teams are different, and are directly related to the levels of management decision making involved (i.e. strategic, tactical and operational levels) and the structure of the decision situations they face (i.e. unstructured, semi-structured and structured). Laudon and Laudon (2005, p.91) have a similar view and believe that organisations should use different kinds of information systems at the various organisational levels to support different types of decisions.

Various technologies and systems that people can use to help make decisions and solve problems are now available. Some widely adopted decision-making information systems include management information systems, decision support systems, geographical information systems, group decision support systems, data mining, online analytical processing, executive information systems, business intelligence, artificial intelligence, among many others.

Management information systems and decision support systems

Management information systems were originally developed to serve middle level managers' information needs and support their decision making (Laudon & Laudon 2018, p.76). Management information systems primarily provide information on the firm's performance to assist managers monitor and control the business operation and produce information products that support many of the day-to-day decision-making needs of managers and business professionals. They typically produce summary and exception reports based on data extracted and summarised from transaction processing systems.

O'Brien and Marakas (2011, p.397) define decision support systems as 'computer-based information systems that provide interactive information support to managers and business professionals during the decision-making process'. Although decision support systems also serve the middle management level of the organisation, there are differences between these management information systems and decision support systems in four dimensions (O'Brien & Marakas 2011, p.395):

• Decision support provided: information about the performance of the organization by management information systems versus information and decision support models (i.e., what-if analysis, sensitivity analysis and goal-seeking analysis) to analyse specific problems/opportunities by decision support systems.

• Information form and frequency: periodic, exception, demand and push information by management information systems versus interactive inquires and responses by decision support systems.

• Information format: pre specified and fixed format by management information systems versus ad hoc, flexible, and adaptable format by decision support systems.

• Information processing methodology: extracting and manipulating data by management information systems versus analytical modelling by decision support systems.

Geographical information systems

A geographic information system is a type of decision support systems, and it applies data visualisation technology and uses geographic databases to construct and display maps and other graphic displays that support decisions affecting the geographic distribution of people and other resources (O'Brien & Marakas 2011, p. 405). Some examples are calculating emergency response times, identifying the best locations for ATM machines, finding locations for a restaurant chain, among many others.

Data mining for decision support

Data mining software analyses the vast stores of historical business data that have been prepared for analysis in corporate data warehouses, and tries to discover patterns, trends, and correlations hidden in the data that can help a company improve its business performance (Haag, Baltzan & Phillips 2008, p. 82; O'Brien & Marakas 2011, p.410). As Data-mining often works with data warehouses. Some common types of data-mining analysis capabilities include: cluster analysis (a technique used to classify information into mutually exclusive groups), association detection (examining the degree to which variables are related and the nature and frequency of these relationships in the information), and statistical analysis (looking at functions such as information correlations, distributions, calculations, and variance analysis).

Online analytical processing (OLAP)

Online Analytical Processing (OLAP) applications assist managers and analysts in interactively assessing and analysing large amounts of data from multiple perspectives (O'Brien & Marakas 2011, p.401). Sometimes this is called multidimensional data analysis, which gives an unlimited view of multiple relationships in large quantities of data. An OLAP session happens online in real time and responds to managers' queries rapidly. Online analytical processing involves several basic analytical operations including (O'Brien & Marakas 2011, pp.406-407):

- Consolidation: Aggregation of data (e.g., sales office to region)
- Drill down: Displaying detailed data (e.g., sales by product)
- Slicing and dicing: Looking from different viewpoints to help analyse trends and patterns.

Group decision support systems

A Group Decision Support System (GDSS) is 'an interactive computer-based system to facilitate the solution of unstructured problems by a set of decision makers working together as a group' (Laudon & Laudon 2005, p. 427). The number of attendees is normally 4–5 but can increase while productivity increases. GDSS fosters a more collaborative atmosphere, increases the number of ideas generated, and can lead to more participative and democratic decision making. It employs software tools that follow structured methods for organising and evaluating ideas and preserving the results of meetings (Laudon & Laudon 2005, p. 429).

Executive information systems/executive support systems

Executive information systems/Executive support systems concentrate on meeting the strategic information needs of senior management by analysing external and internal aggregate data(such as gathering competitive intelligence, monitoring corporate performance) (Laudon & Laudon 2018, p.78). Some benefits of executive information systems (Laudon & Laudon 2018, pp.78-79) include:

- Flexibility in assisting decision-making: using the system as an extension of executives' own thinking process.
- The ability to analyse, compare, and highlight trends: allowing users to look at more data in less time with greater clarity.
- More easily monitoring organisational performance (e.g., via balanced score card systems) or identifying strategic problems.

- Very useful for environment scanning and providing business intelligence to help management detect strategic threats or opportunities from the environment.
- Improving management performance and extend upper management's span of control: overseeing more people with fewer resources.

Executive support systems can be configured to summarise and present key performance indicators to senior managers in the form of 'digital dashboard' or 'executive dashboard', which integrates information from multiple components and present it in a unified display (Haag, Baltzan & Phillips 2008, p.107; Laudon & Laudon 2018, p.79). Typically a digital dashboard will present all of the critical company information in a single screen view. The results can be displayed as graphs and charts in a web-page format, providing a page-view of all the critical information for executive decision-making (Laudon & Laudon 2018, p.78). A picture is worth a thousand words.

Many companies now are also implementing balanced scorecard systems to support their executives to make decisions. The balanced scorecard approach supplements traditional financial measures with measures from additional perspectives, such as customers, internal business processes, learning, and growth. Executives can use balanced scorecard systems to examine how well the firm is meeting its strategic goals (Laudon & Laudon 2018, p. 504).

The key for executive information systems is to help top management easily access important internal and external information for managing an organization, and they should be able to effectively deliver varying levels of details according to the demands (e.g., navigation facilities to zoom in and zoom out the many layers of information collected by various information systems). The current offering of providing top-line view of business only by many dashboard vendors is not sufficient in this regard.

Business Intelligence

Business intelligence basically refers to effectively analyzing collected and available data for assisting business decision making (Campbell, Kurtzman & Michaels 2011). The author of this book takes the view that Business intelligence is equivalent to business analytics/data analytics, which has been discussed extensively in Chapter 5. Business intelligence (or data analytics or business analytics) and artificial intelligence allow organizations to utilize data from some non-traditional and unstructured sources (e.g., sensors, cameras and devices of Internet of Things (IoT) networks and social media/networks).

9.3 Artificial Intelligence

Artificial Intelligence (AI) aims to develop computers that can think, reason, learn, see, hear, walk, talk, and feel (Haag, Baltzan & Phillips 2008, p.109; O'Brien & Marakas 2011, p.418). Although AI does not exhibit the breadth, complexity, originality, and generality of human intelligence, it plays an important role in decision making. O'Brien and Marakas (2011) suggest that artificial intelligence can be classified into three domains: cognitive science (e.g., expert systems, learning systems, fuzzy logic, genetic algorithms, neural networks, intelligent agents); robotics (e.g., visual perception, tactility, dexterity, locomotion, navigation); and natural interfaces (e.g., natural languages, speech recognition, multisensory interfaces, and virtual reality) (O'Brien & Marakas 2011, pp.422). Some common AI applications are expert systems (looking at imitating the reasoning process of human experts), neutral networks (modelling after human brain's mesh-like network), and intelligent agents (such as search engines). On a related note, the key difference between AI and data analytics is the former is able to make consumption, test and learn autonomously (Reaive 2018).

AI market will grow from $8 billion in 2016 to more than $47 billion in 2020 (Press 2017); and by 2030, AI could deliver additional global economic output of $13 trillion per year (Cheatham, Javanmardian & Samandari 2019). The rapid recent development could attribute to factors such as availability of Big Data, Internet of Things (IoT) development, improvements in computing power, cloud computing advancement, and better algorithm (Pollard et al. 2017, p.15). AI can provide organizations such benefits as: improved sales and customer engagement, operational efficiency enhancement, better products (with embedded AI applications), new insights and new business models (Pollard et al. 2017, p.11).

Meanwhile PwC suggests (reported in Rao & Verweij 2017) that more than 55% of labour productivity improvements for the period of 2017-2030 will come from AI and North America and China will see the greatest GDP gains from productivity gains from AI. In addition, AI will have impact on industries, and the impact will vary (in the order): healthcare, automotive, financial services, transportation & logistics, technology, communications & entertainment, retail, energy, and manufacturing (Rao & Verweij 2017). Some leading sections of AI adoption are: financial services and high tech & telecommunication, which have been early adopters of digital technologies (Allas et al. 2018). Furthermore, the AI ecosystem consists of (from the top): the experience layer (including interface, device or application), the intelligence layers (including AI algorithms, process middleware, software ecosystem), the data layer (including systems of record, IoT sensors, cameras & connectivity, data metadata from other sources), and the infrastructure layer (including cloud, data center, networks) (Pollard et al. 2017, p.18).

Some popular AI technologies include: natural language generation, speech recognition, virtual agents, machine learning platforms, AI-optimized hardware, decision management, deep learning platforms, biometrics, robotic process automation, and text analytics and natural language processing (Press 2017). Some key AI vendors are: Amazon, Microsoft, Google, Alibaba, Baidu, IBM for AI platform-as-a-service; SAP, Oracle, Microsoft, Salesforce, Adobe for enterprise software; SAS, SAP, Oracle, Tableau, Mathworks, Qlik, Palantir, IBM, Informatica for data analytics; Clarifai, Kore, Aspect, IPSoft, Iflytek, Sensetime for Specialist AI; GE, PTC, SAP, Amazon, Software AG for industrial IoT + AI; and Accenture, IBM, Capgemini, Atos, Cognizant (Pollard et al. 2017, p.11).

According to a RAGE Framework survey of 132 senior executives (reported in RAGE Frameworks 2017, p.6): some important AI capabilities in the enterprise are (in the order): reasoning & traceability, natural language, natural language processing, machine learning, robotic process automation, natural language generation, computer vision, and speech recognition. Meanwhile some key types of AI applications for organizations include (in the order): solutions for decision-making/recommendation, process automation, virtual personal assistant/chatbots, embedded AI in products, and self-learning mechanical robots (Pollard et al. 2017, p. 25).

What are some concerns/issues holding AI back in the organization: a shortage of AI talent, lack of AI strategy, lack of strategic directive from senior management, lack of AI-ready infrastructure, challenges in quantifying value derived from AI, lack of understanding of AI algorithms, lack of funding, increased vulnerability and disruption to business, lack of transparency, governance & rules to control AI, trust issues and moral dilemmas, potential disruption to society, security and privacy concerns, governance issues, potential risks & liabilities, integration issues, lack of adequate regulations, and lack of clear understanding of AI (Pollard et al. 2017, p. 8 & p. 32; Rao & Cameron 2018; Rao & Verweij 2017).

What are employees' views of using AI in the work? According to a PwC study (reported in Baccala et al. 2018), 78% of employees would work with AI if meant more balanced workload, 65% think AI would free them from menial works, 64% believe AI would offer them new opportunities, and 50% would follow AI systems if they are effective.

Some areas they should look at when they are embarking on AI include (Agrawal & Kirkland 2018; Baccala et al. 2018; Bughin, Chui & McCarthy 2018; Burkhardt, Hohn & Wigley 2019; Chui, Manyika & Miremadi 2018; Chui, Wigley & London 2019; ITI n.d.; Manyika et al. 2018; Pollard et al. 2017, p. 8 & p. 32; Rao 2017; Rao & Cameron 2018; Stancombe et al. 2017; The Author's Own Knowledge):

• Having clear AI strategy that is aligning with your overall business strategy and roadmap/action plans.

• Clarifying how AI applications could support business objectives and company values.

• Examining data issues (e.g., data accessibility, data quality, data volume, data labelling, data availability, data integration).

• Knowing what you want to achieve via AI.

• Allocating sufficient funding and resources for AI initiatives.

• Working on required organizational adjustments and process improvements.

• Developing enterprise-wide AI capability.

• Winning the support and commitment from senior management.

• Clearly defining roles of AI initiatives (e.g., who is responsible for soliciting requests needs? who is responsible for development? Who is responsible deployment? who is responsible for translating the results? who is responsible for risk management & governance? who is responsible for education and training?).

• Appointing a chief AI officer or similar role to lead the AI initiatives.

• Having both business and technology people in the AI project teams.

• Starting with areas/use cases where AI can create significant and visible benefits.

• Ensuring the scalability of AI applications from initial cases.

• Establishing definitions and metrics for evaluating AI for bias and fairness.

• Putting a skills development and talent management strategy in place.

• Having appropriate data acquisition (e.g., how to get massive amount datasets for training), cleansing, conversation and use strategy and policies.

• Being able to explain the functions and performance of AI applications by adopting simplest performance model, latest explainability techniques, and understandable languages well as education and training.

• Actively promoting the success of AI initiatives.

• Embedding AI capabilities in your organization (e.g., business processes, platforms & systems, decision-making culture).

- Building trust towards AI and Trusting the machines when AI applications are properly designed and deployed.
- Setting up effective protection measures for dealing with security and privacy threats.
- Managing the learning loop (for manager's decision-making process and the AI's learning and for interaction between them).
- Closely monitoring evolving regulations.
- Closely monitoring emerging AI technologies.
- Implementing a clear AI governance framework.
- Ensuring interpretability, consistence performance and data integrity.
- Promoting responsible development and use (e.g., safety and controllability, robust & representative data and interpretability).
- Paying close attention to the sustainability and responsibility issues of AI (e.g., impacts and benefits to the society and abilities to address misuses).
- Following a process of AI development and deployment: designing AI with social impact consideration, testing extensively before release, using AI transparently, monitoring AI performance rigorously, developing required talent and skills, dealing with privacy issues, defining data use standard, and establishing tools and standards for auditing algorithms.

What are some predications about the future of AI? Garner (cited in RAGE Frameworks 2017, p.1) provides the following observations: (1) "By 2019, more than 10% IT hires in customer services will mostly write scripts for bot interactions; (2) Through 2020, organizations using cognitive ergonomics and system design in new artificial intelligence projects will achieve long-term success four times more often than others; (3) By 2020, 20% of companies will dedicate workers to monitor and guide neural networks; (4) By 2019, startups will overtake Amazon, Google, IBM and Microsoft in driving the artificial intelligence economy with disruptive solutions; and (5) By 2019, artificial intelligence platform services will cannibalize revenues for 30% of market-leading companies". Meanwhile it is argued that in the next decade, AI/Machine Learning will has the greatest impact on the firm (Pollard et al. 2017, p. 15). Some anticipated future AI applications include: robot musicians, augmented movie script writing, autonomous mining, legal e-discovery, personalized medicine, automated machine translator, self-driving vehicles, doctorless hospitals, creative art engines, self-navigating drones, automated 3D Bio-printing, artificial wildlife habitats, scientific discovery, among many others (Rao 2017).

9.4 Summary

In this chapter, we covered a range of systems developed to assist in decision making, including management information systems, decision support systems, executive information systems, business intelligence, artificial intelligence and other applications. While managers need to effectively use information systems to support their decision-making, they need to understand the danger of overreliance on electronic communication. We may have more connections via networks today, but fewer relations, less physical interactions, and insufficient "soft information" (e.g., gestures, tone of voice) (Mintzberg & Todd 2012). In addition, it should be emphasized that even though information systems could providing support to our decision, it is We-human beings- are making decision; and our intuition, experience, sense and judgment, which are essential for effective decision making, will not be placed by machines and systems.

One related note is a number of studies have indicated that the always-on and multitasking working environment, which is typical to many business executives, is so distracting and causing productivity loss (Davenport 2010). Furthermore even though organizations should pay more attention to fact-based/data driven decision-making as a result of Big Data and the available advanced analytics tools, it is argued that intuition based on working experience is still the driving factor of business decision, while the level of contribution by business intelligence could be varied as per the organizational context (e.g., from the rate of 60%/40% for traditional mix of intuition/fact-based decision making to less 60% but bigger than 50% for intuition/bigger than 40% but less than 50% for data-driven) (Bloomberg Businessweek Research Services 2011). In the next chapter, how organizations can manage their information systems operations/functions will be discussed.

References

Agrawal, A. & Kirkland, R. 2018, 'The economies of artificial intelligence', *McKinsey Quarterly*, April 2018, pp. 1-7.

Allas, T., Bughin, J., Chui, M., Dahlstrom, P., Hazan, E., Henke, N., Ramaswamy, S. & Trench, M. 2018, 'Artificial intelligence is getting ready for business, but are businesses ready for AI?', *McKinsey Analytics*, June 2018, pp. 7-22.

Baccala, M., Curran, C., Garrett, D., Likens, S., Rao, A., Ruggles, A & Shehab, M. 2018, *2018 AI Predictions: 8 Insights to Shape Business Strategy*, pp. 1-24.

Bloomberg Businessweek Research Services 2011, *The Current State of Business Analytics: Where Do We Go from Here?*, Bloomberg 2011, pp. 1-14.

Bughin, J., Chui, M. & McCarthy, B. 2018, 'How to make AI work for your business', *McKinsey Analytics*, June 2018, pp. 51-54.

Burkhardt, R., Hohn, N. & Wigley, 2019, 'Leading your organization to responsible AI'', *McKinsey Analytics,* May 2019, pp. 1-8.

Campbell, J., Kurtzman, K. & Michael, A. 2011, 'Crafting Best-in-Class Business Intelligence', *Strategy + Business*, Issue 63, Summer 2011, pp. 1-3.

Cheatham, B., Javanmardian, K. & Samandari, H. 2019, 'Confront the risks of artificial intelligence', *McKinsey Quarterly*, April 2019, pp. 1-9.

Chui, M. & Fleming, T. 2011, 'Inside P & G's digital revolution', *McKinsey Quarterly*, November 2011, pp. 1-11.

Chui, M., Manyika, J. & Miremadi, M. 2018, 'What AI can and can't do (yet) for your business', *McKinsey Quarterly*, January 2018, pp.1-11.

Chui, M., Wigley, C. & London, S. 2019, 'The ethics of artificial intelligence',*Podcast Transcript*, January 2019, pp. 1-14.

Davenport, T. H. 2010, 'Rethinking knowledge work: A strategic approach', *McKinsey on Business Technology*, Number 21, Winter 2010, pp. 26-33.

Haag, S., Baltzan, P. & Phillips, A. 2008, *Business Driven Technology*, 2nd edn, McGraw-Hill Irwin, Boston, USA.

ITI n.d., *ITI AI Policy Principles: Executive Summary*, Online, Available at: https://www.itic.org/public-policy/ITIAIPolicyPrinciplesFINAL.pdf (accessed on 19 June 2019).

Laudon, K. C. & Laudon, J. P. 2018, *Management Information Systems: Managing the Digital Firm*, Fifteenth Edition, Pearson Education Limited, Harlow, England.

Manyika, J., Bughin, J., Chui, M., Silberg, M. & Gumbel, P. 2018, 'The promise and challenge of the age of artificial intelligence', *Briefing Note, Prepared for The Tallinn Digital Summit*, October 2018, McKinsey Global Institute, pp. 1-8.

Mayer, J. H. & Schaper, M. 2010, 'Data to dollars: Supporting top management with next-generation executive information systems', *McKinsey on Business Technology*, Number 18, Winter 2010, pp. 12-17.

Milley, A. & Wood, A. 2010, *Business Analytics Essentials*, SAS Institute Inc., pp. 1-2.

Mintzberg, H. & Todd, P. 2012, 'The Offline Executive', *Strategy+Business*, July 16, 2012, Online Available at: http://www.strategy-business.com/article/00121?pg=all&tid=27782251 (accessed July 18, 2012).

O'Brien, J. A. & Marakas, G. M. 2011, *Management Information Systems*, 10th Edition, McGraw-Hill, New York, USA.

Pollard, S., Rajwanshi, V., Murphy, M. R., Auty, S., Huang, T. T., Anmuth, D., Yao, A., Hariharan, G., Willi, A. & Coster, P. 2017, *An Investor's Guide to Artificial Intelligence*, Global Equity Research, J.P. Morgan, 27 December 2017, pp. 1-112.

Press, G. 2017, 'Top 10 Artificial Intelligence (AI) Technologies, *Forbes.com*, Jan 23, 2017, Online, Available at: https://www.forbes.com/sites/gilpress/2017/01/23/top-10-hot-artificial-intelligence-ai-technologies/#3ff062192878 (accessed on 10 August 2018).

RAGE Frameworks 2017, The Road to Enterprise AI, pp. 1-17.

Rao, A. 2017, 'A Strategist Guide to Artificial Intelligence', *Strategy+Business*, Issue 87, Summer 2017, pp.1-10.

Rao, A. & Cameron, E. 2018, 'The future of artificial intelligence depends on trust', *Strategy+Business*, Autumn 2018 issue, pp.1-5.

Rao, A. S. & Verweij, G. 2017, Sizing the prize: What is the real value of AI for your business and how can you capitalise', *PwC*, pp. 1-27.

Reavie, V. 2018, 'Do you know the difference between data analytics and AI machine learning?', *Forbes Community Voice*, August 1, 2018, Online, Available at: https://www.forbes.com/sites/forbesagencycouncil/2018/08/01/do-you-know-the-difference-between-data-analytics-and-ai-machine-learning/#10c264d65878 (accessed on 6 June 2019).

Roberts, R. & Sikes, J. 2011, 'How IT is managing new demands: McKinsey Global Survey results', *McKinsey on Business Technology*, Number 22, Spring 2011, pp. 24-33.

Stancombe, C., Thieullent, A-L, KVJ, S., Chandna, A., Tildo, R., Buvat, J. & Khadikar, A. 2017, *Turning AI into Concrete Value: The Successful Implementer's Toolkit*, Capgemini Consulting, 2017, pp. 1-27.

The Economist Intelligence Unit 2005, *Business 2010: Embracing the Challenges of Change*, The Economist Intelligence Unit 2005, pp. 1-32.

Chapter 10

Information Systems Operation Management

This chapter will discuss the importance of effectively managing enterprise IS/IT operation/function, review information systems governance & service management as well as responsibilities of CIO, look at information systems skills management, highlight the roles of information systems in mergers & acquisitions, discuss recovering information systems in a disaster, and present discussion on outsourcing options and global information system management as well as virtual workforce management.

10.1 Enterprise Information Systems Operation Management

Information systems are not only an essential component of business success for companies today but also a vital business resource that must be properly managed. There are many questions that require answers, such as (O'Brien & Marakas 2011, p.595):
- How should information systems resources be managed?
- Should there be only one information systems function? Or dispersed within functional areas?
- Decentralised or centralised computer resources?
- How much should we spend on information systems?
- Which business processes should receive our information systems dollars?
- Which information systems capabilities need to be companywide?
- How good do our information systems services really need to be?
- What security and privacy risks will we accept?
- Whom do we blame if information systems fail?

These kinds of questions have to be properly addressed for the successful information systems management by the senior management.

Managing information systems is not an easy task. Many businesses have not been successful in managing their uses of information systems. We have seen many information systems project failures, and information systems have not always delivered. O'Brien and Marakas (2011, p.593) suggest the following reasons for failures of information systems:

(1) Information systems are not being used effectively (e.g., using primarily to computerise traditional business processes, rather than creating innovative business processes).

(2) Information systems are not being used efficiently (e.g., providing poor response times, frequent down times, and inappropriate management of application development projects).

Some other reasons include: a lack of understanding of the current situations & the needs; failing in consulting with all stakeholders; not understanding the cost structures; going cheap on security and privacy measures; over-reliance on vendor and vendor lock-in concerns; not having effective talent management strategy and action plans; not following rigorous systems development process for key/core systems development; a lack of strategic information systems planning; a lack of top management's involvement in the planning process of information systems strategy; a lack of understanding between end users, information systems professionals, and management; the inability to manage information systems specialists, end users and projects; and technology-driven solution (e.g., having too much faith in magical technological solutions) instead of business-driven technology approach (Dylan 2017; Edwards 2018; The Author's Own Knowledge).

Keep in mind that there are no quick and easy answers for the problems in IS/IT management. However O'Brien and Marakas (2011, p.594-595) argue that extensive and meaningful involvement by managers and end users, backed up by favourable policies and governance structures, is vital to the success and performance of information systems. With the participation of managers and end users, organisations can achieve better value of investments in information systems and enhance people's acceptance and use of information systems.

Fred and Stoddard (2004) suggest three principles of successful information systems management:

• A long term plan: need a long-term, disciplined, strategic view, and a focus on achieving the company's most fundamental goals or corporate goals. To achieve this, a good approach of information systems demand management, which has been adopted by Toyota for managing and improving its information systems function, could be very useful (reported in Cooper & Nocket 2009). This approach basically manages information systems projects as per the overall corporate needs rather than focusing on disparate needs and treating each business unit as an independent effort that creates lot of duplications and drives up unnecessary costs significantly (for example in Toyota only systems that fit with its strategic direction will be given green light)

• A unifying platform to connect and integrate various systems, applications, technologies, and data sources. Sufficient discipline and resources are needed to develop such platform.

• A high-performance information systems culture: A cohesive and pro-performance culture with clearly defined rules and sound performance management system.

Roberts, Sarrazin and Sikes (2010) suggest a dual-model approach for information systems management. Their suggested model includes "Factory information systems" and "Enabling information systems' models/parts. The former emphasizes improving productivity and cost performance by utilizing lean management techniques and adopting advances & computing technology and software development (such as cloud computing and agile development), and the latter pays close attention to building organization's innovation, learning and value creation abilities by embedding flexible and focused information systems workgroups.

Lean management approach aims at creating an environment, in which initiatives such as improvements of performance and skills, waste & inefficiency reduction, and elimination efforts occur continuously. Lean management approach powers information systems management via (1) standard work practices to improve quality, consistency, and response times; (2) performance transparency for bettering measuring project progress, prioritizing tasks, and meeting targets thus developing better visibility and trust between information systems and business; (3) demand management to better utilization of resources and fewer interruptions; and (4) skills development for information systems employees and knowledge sharing among information systems employees (Bensemhoun, Chartrin & Kropf 2011). Measures such as performance management, feedback sessions, user experience surveys, formal rewards, and people development are important factors for shaping people's continuous-improvement mind-set (Chartrin 2011).

Factory information systems model is working on taking advantage of scale, standardization, and simplification of information systems in the organization to drive efficiency, operational excellence and cost savings while enabling model of information systems is looking at making organizations more effective in responding to changes/uncertainties and developing competitive advantages through innovation and growth. The bulk of the information systems management activities should be in the aspect of Factory information systems management, and the cost savings achieved by Factory information systems model could be used to fund Enabling information systems management. The Google's rule of 80/20 (Google allows employees to spend 20% of their time in pursuing their interested projects) for time allocation could be a good starting point for the distribution of the resources for these two information systems management models (i.e., 80% resources for Factory information systems management and 20% for Enabling information systems management).

In addition, for large organizations, having a tech-savvy board is important to the success of information systems (Leatherberry et al. 2019). A tech-savvy board engages in such perspectives of performance (e.g., financial performance, business operations, talent), strategy (e.g., growth & innovation, data & insights, customer experience, ecosystem engagement and leveraging), and risk (e.g., cyber risks, regulatory matters, industry & technology disruptions).

10.2 IS Governance & IS Service Management

Information systems governance, which is a very important concept for effective information systems management even though its importance is only recognized by many organizations in recent years, is a subset of Corporate Governance. It looks at strategy & policies for deploying IT resources within an organization, specifies the decision rights and framework for accountability to ensure IT support the organization's strategies and objectives, and focuses on (1) how IT can add value to business strategy (alignment of business and IT), (2) the need to effectively and efficiently develop & deliver IT products /services and manage IT resources (effectiveness and efficiency of the deployment of IT resources, (3) preventing IT failures (risk management), (4) avoiding poor performance (performance management), and (5) investment evaluation and benefit realization (Laudon & Laudon 2017, p.97; National Computing Centre 2005; Kogekar 2010).

Leading information systems governance researcher Peter Weill suggests (Weill 2004, p.5) information systems governance looks at such perspectives as:
• Information systems principles: high level statements about how information systems are used in the business.
• Information systems architecture: an integrated set of technical choices to guide the organization in satisfying business needs. The architecture is a set of

policies and rules for the use of information systems, and plots a migration path to the way business how information systems matters (such as data, technology, and applications) will be done.

• Information systems infrastructure strategies: strategies for the base foundation of information systems (both technical and human).

• Business application needs: specifying the business needs for purchased or internally developed information systems.

• Information systems investment and prioritization: decisions about how much and where to invest information systems projects (including project approvals and justification techniques).

Meanwhile information systems decisions are made by stakeholders such as (1) business monarchy including a group of, or individual, business executives (e.g., CXOs) and communities comprised of senior business executives (may include CIO but exclude information systems executives acting independently); (2) information systems monarch including individual or groups of information systems executives; (3) feudal including business unit leaders, key process owners or their delegates; (4) federal including C level executives and at least one other business group (e.g., CXO and business unit leaders)-information systems executives may be an additional participant (something like in Australia and the U.S., the federal government works with state governments to run the country); (5) information systems duopoly including information systems executives and one other group (e.g., CXO or business unit leaders), and (6) anarchy including each individual user (Weill 2004, p.5). Meanwhile business and information systems have to be strategic partners-information systems people should be "business strategists" and "You are in this with me, Mr or Ms Business. Let us work together to manage and deliver your project") (Cooper & Nocket 2009, p.3).

Through effective information systems governance, organizations can address problems such as: (1) disconnection between information systems strategy and business strategy; (2) information systems not meeting or supporting compliance requirements; (3) poor information systems investment management; (4) information systems service issues and operational concerns; (5) information systems staff issues (e.g., insufficient number of staff, inadequate skills); (6) outsourcing issues; (7) knowledge management challenges; (8) lack of agility/development problems; (9) insufficient disaster recovery or/and business continuity measures, and (10) security and privacy threats (Applegate, Austin & Soule 2009, p.413).

Some popular IS/IT governance approaches and frameworks include Control Objectives for Information and Related Technologies (COBIT) and Information

Technology Infrastructure Library 4 (ITIL 4) (Pearlson & Saunders 2013, p.255). On a related, there exist confusions about the differences between information systems governance and information systems service management (Laudon & Laudon 2017, p.97; National Computing Centre 2005; Kogekar 2010; Watts 2017; Wikipedia 2019). The former has emphasis on the strategic importance & implications of information systems, alignment between business & information systems, and value creation for stakeholders; meanwhile the latter looks at information systems services delivery and operations of information systems functions.

Some characteristics and success factors of good information systems governance consist of (Kogekar 2010; National Computing Centre 2005):

• Information systems investments are assessed in a manner similar to business investments. And information systems is managed as a strategic asset.

• Top management participation in key information systems decisions and commitment to information systems governance.

• There is board oversight of information systems investments and executives are held accountable for realizing benefits.

• Information systems is essential part of corporate planning and strategic planning. Information systems understands the business dynamics and contributes to the development of business strategy. IT and business work together to identify opportunities.

• Treat information systems governance initiatives as on-going project and support it with sufficient resources and make it an integral part of the organization.

• Top information systems risks are considered within the enterprise risk management framework and receive periodic high level oversight.

• Information systems performance is regularly measured and benchmarked.

• Information systems focuses on transparency and clear communication of decision-making process.

• An enterprise wide approach is adopted.

• An agreed information systems governance framework is chosen.

• Required organizational adjustments and changes for information systems governance implementation are put in place.

• Expectations are managed properly. And people understand that the success of information systems governance takes time and requires continuous improvement.

10.3 Information Systems Skills and Talent Management

Another critical dimension of successful information systems operation management is information systems staff planning (i.e., recruiting, training and retaining good information systems staff). One emerging trend is to hire and develop digital workforce, who have the skills to access, organize, understand, analyse, communication, and utilize the large volume of data for decision-making and for creation of new ideas (Chui & Fleming 2011; Manyika 2009).

In line with the rapid development of computing technologies, the wide penetration of the Internet, and the large scale adoption of digitization (by individuals, businesses, communities, governments), the demand for information systems skills and talent will be no doubt increasingly dramatically, and we need more information systems skills and talent. The shortage of information systems skills and talent has not been commonly recognized, which could be a major hindering factor for our future developments. The survey of 3,169 respondents from 105 countries by IDG Connect (2011) has highlighted this concern, and most of the participants of the survey indicated there is a lack of senior technical skills in the market. The survey also asked the respondents' opinions for information systems employment problems in their area, some reasons identified from the survey include:

*   Economy uncertainty: in bad times, hiring is always slow.
*   Poor training: the results of the survey indicate information systems training issue is more for of an issue for participants from developing countries in Asia, Middle East, Africa, and South America. In fact, many universities and colleges around the world that used to offer information systems training programs downsized or even closed down their information systems faculties/departments after year 2000.
*   IT talent brain-drain issues: the survey results indicate it is a major issue (more than 50% participants believed) for Africans, South Americans and Asians. It has been an on-going issue for developing countries. Their best information systems talent prefer to go overseas for better pay or/and working conditions. But in recent years, to some extent, it has changed. For example, many information systems talents in China now would stay in China as a result of rapidly rising pay and much more opportunities in China.
*   The challenge of updating skills constantly as a result of a very changing information systems industry: this issue is really making people in Asia to think twice when they are planning to embark on information systems careers. In additional, the need for soft skills (e.g., interpersonal & communication, project

management, language skills) was also pointed out by some respondents. It is, in fact, really true in reality. In addition, the challenge of updating skills constantly coupling with factors such as poor information systems training and information systems talent brain-drain could lead to the identified shortage of senior technical skills.

• Generation Y work ethics: the majority of respondents across all regions agree that Generation Y information systems professionals (at the entry level) have different work ethics to older generations.

According to a recent Harvey Nash CIO Survey (reported in Red Hat 2016), some IS/IT functions having skills shortages (in the order) include: Big data/analytics, Project management, Business analysis, Development, Enterprise architecture, Change management, Mobile solutions, Technical architecture, Security & resilience, IT strategy, Testing, Business relationship management, Digital, Service management, Infrastructure/operations, Social media, ERP, Compliance, and Outsourcing. Another concern associated with information systems skills and talent management is the lack of soft skills among the information systems people who highly (if not overly) enjoy their technical skills. But information systems people don't work alone in the organization, and they are there to work with business side of the organization and are an integral part of the organization. Organizations could equip information systems people with such skills as effective working habits, better emotional intelligence, and enhanced skills of persuading and influencing people to make them more communication-minded. Some top attractive countries for digital talent include (in the order): the U.S., Germany, Canada, Australia, the U.K., Switzerland, France, Spain, Japan, and Italy (Strack et al. 2019, p.5).

Some factor influencing the talent's decision of joining and staying in a particular company include (Agarwal et al. 2006; Bauer et al. 2016; Red Hat 2016; Strack et al. 2019, p.7; The Author's Own Knowledge)

• Great job: opportunities to work on cutting-edge project, career advancement opportunities, interesting work, job security, coaching mechanism, freedom and autonomy to create and innovate, strong team work and sharing spirit.

• Attractive compensation: salary, bonuses, stock options.

• Great leaders who have the vision, are approachable, are open-minded, and can be the role model.

• Great company: good reputation, good culture supporting shared values & beliefs and team work, makes contribution to the society, good working environment with modern technology, looks after people's wellbeing.

- Emphasis on individuals (e.g., ensuring people who are feeling that are part of something greater than themselves; coaching, mentoring, mentoring; good work-life balance; work being appreciated).
- Great work environment (e.g., good relationships with colleagues and managers; creative and innovative work environment).
- Fostering community building.

Some talent management strategies and actions organizations could look at include (Agarwal et al. 2006; Allas, Chambers & Welchman 2019; Cable & Vermeulen 2018; Casey 2019; Pflügler et al. 2018; Pratt 2018; Red Hat 2016; Stract et al. 2017; Taylor & Joshi 2018; The Author's Own Knowledge):

- Using social media and speaking events to find and engage top talent.
- Becoming a part of open source community to identify and network with top talent.
- Working on affiliations with universities/colleges and having joint events with them (e.g., innovation hubs, hackathons).
- Presenting clear offers and keeping your promises.
- Providing a good and attractive work environment.
- Making work meaningful (e.g., reducing anonymity, assisting people understanding the impact of their work, recognizing & rewarding good work, and connecting work to a higher meaning).
- Building a talent pipeline.
- Stablishing internal job market.
- Re-employing previous employees.
- Accessing crowdsourcing workforce.
- Supporting flexible and mobile workforce.
- Conducting post-entry and exit interviews.
- Developing diversity in talent management (e.g., gender balance).
- Gaining leaders' support in adopting talent management strategy and best practices.
- Systematically investing in internal learning and capacity building.
- Building strong collaborative relationships between IT and HR department and between the organization and third-party HR services.

10.4 Roles of Chief Information Officer

Chief information officer (CIO) plays critical role in the success of IT in supporting and enabling the business. Boochever, Park and Weinberg (2002) suggest CIO should have four roles in the organization:

• A strategist who is a member of senior executive, and contributes to the development of business strategy (and associated information systems strategy), especially via leveraging on opportunities and dealing with risks associated with technologies.

• A business advisor who works closely with business unit leaders and translates information systems capabilities for business processes and operations.

• An information systems executive who is responsible for skills, training, assets, investment, performance of information systems.

• An enterprise architect who creates an enterprise-wide information systems infrastructure architecture for exiting systems and future systems to support business operations, business growth, and cooperation & collaboration with external parties.

Wood (2012) suggests similar view by arguing that chief information officers in the 21st century must be both technology and business experts and must be able to link technology with competitive business benefits, and he further proposes a number of questions to be asked when organizations are looking for or looking at their chief information officers:

• Can CIO directly correlate business value against information systems spend?

• Dose CIO know how your firm's information systems spend compares with that of competitors?

• Is information system function/operation a cost effective business partner?

• Can information systems promises be trusted in terms of it will deliver what it promise?

• Can security and risk issues be properly managed?

• Is there a clear strategy and path for de-commissioning old technology?

• Does CIO know technologies for business growth and competitive advantages?

• Do and How can we have the right and sufficient information systems talent in the organization?

In fact, chief information officer, who represents the information systems part of the organization, has to be a member of the organization's senior executive team and must have a say to the development of business strategy and to the strategic allocation of organizational resources, otherwise it is very difficult for information systems function/operation to effectively present business cases for information systems investments, to have effective input into the organization's strategic planning process, and to have full demonstration of the benefits and impacts of information systems projects/investments to the organization (especially the bottom line of the organization).

Chief information officers also could develop a technology roadmap for the whole organization, which looks at establishing a development roadmap path for making information systems more strategic (of course with good contribution from business side). Some aspects when they are developing a technology road map include (Alvarez & Raghavan 2010):

• Good understanding of business operations and value creation of the business.

• Good understanding of business needs regarding required information systems capabilities.

• Good evidence-based demonstration of return on information systems investment.

• Good evidence-based demonstration of the contribution of information systems capabilities to business strategy.

• Clear understanding of the gap between the current information systems status and required new information systems capabilities for business operations and business growth.

• Assurance of a joint effort between business and information systems when developing a technology roadmap.

• Agreement on using the developed technology roadmap for capital and resource allocation decisions.

• Assurance to have the roadmap followed via governance mechanism.

• Good skills and knowledge in evaluating information systems strategic initiatives.

• Good understanding of the need for consistently refreshing the roadmap and updating the architecture as well as upgrading systems as needed.

On the other hand, people like Charlie Feld, former CIO of Frito-Lay and a great IS/IT leader argue (cited in Cooke & Baker 2011) that Chief Integration Officer could be a more appropriate title than Chief Information Officer since the important skills for today's information systems leaders should be system thinking skills: the ability to see the system (that is the company), identify dynamic patterns, and build information systems infrastructure and applications which are dynamic, relevant, and connected to the larger ecosystem including your organization's employees, customers, suppliers, partners and other relevant parties. They also suggest information systems leaders should be versatile, multidisciplinary and multicultural; and they should be responsible for creating a culture/environment in which people are working for the common goal, and team-works & peer relationships (e.g., most people do well because they don't hurt their relations with peers and let other team members down) are really encouraged. They further point out that the performance of leaders including information systems executives should be reviewed by taking into consideration of how they lead, manage, and develop people.

According to CIO.com's recent global CIO suvery (reported in Collett 2018), some biggest issues CIOs face are (in the order): Security management, Aligning IT initiatives with business objectives, Improving information systems operations and performance; Cultivating business and IT partnership; Cost control; New system and technology implementation; and Leading change management. Meanwhile the results of Harvey Nash/KPMG 2017 CIO Survey (reported in Heneghan, Snyder & Symons 2017) indicate that CIOs are expected to play an important role in fostering and leading innovation efforts in the organization. On a related note, the focused areas of emerging roles of Chief Digital Officer are digital innovation, data analytics, and customer engagement (Tumbas, Berente & Brocke 2018) and some key required skills include: digital pioneering skills, inspiring skills, and change management skills (Singh & Hess 2017).

10.5 Roles of Information Systems in Mergers and Acquisitions

Mergers and Acquisitions have been often used for the purposes of growth, market dominance, entering into new sectors/industries/markets and new areas/regions/countries, and acquiring required expertise and knowledge. Information systems can play an important role in mergers and acquisitions. As organizations increasingly rely on information systems for their operation, growth and competitive advantages, the problems in information systems in the mergers and acquisitions could be very costly. Sarrazin and West (2012, p.34) state that "Many mergers don't live up to expectations, because they stumble on the integration of technology and operations". They also point out more than 50% of the synergies and integration in a merger are strongly associated with information systems. Some examples are: lowering information systems infrastructure costs, reducing information systems human resources costs, information systems procurement cost savings, integration of functional systems, and synchronizing data from different sources.

In order to play an effective role in the mergers and acquisitions, information systems operation/function has to be a part of the team from the very beginning. They should be an active player during the due intelligence process to identify information systems issues and insufficiencies as well as potential risks and liabilities in the target company by examining perspectives of applications and technology, information systems infrastructure, information systems skills & talent management, outsourcing activities, information systems demand management, and information systems operation/function management & governance. And hard decisions of which systems need to be maintained and integrated and which systems should be ceased have to be made once the scanning of IS/IT in the target company has been completed. Meanwhile if the acquiring firms' IS/IT infrastructure is flexible, scalable and adaptable, then integration in the mergers and acquisitions would become a much less issue. In addition, Henningsson and Kettinger (2016) provide some suggestions for dealing with information integration risks in acquisitions: educating senior management to understand when to call on IT (e.g., should be early stage of acquisition and not later than due diligence stage), integrating only what needs to be integrated, reducing complexity where possible, having room for adjustment when embarking for high-risk integration project, and understanding your limitations.

10.6 Recovering Information Systems in a Disaster

One unusual perspective of information systems operation management is recovering information systems in a disaster. Without careful preparation for unexpected disasters (e.g., hurricanes, earthquakes, floods, and other natural disasters), information systems operations will be seriously damaged or completely destroyed. Hurricane Katrina (reported in Junglas & Ives 2007), which happened in the U.S. in 2009 and caused serious damage to information systems infrastructure of affected areas, has taught us lessons: (1) keeping data and data centers away from locations threatened by potential disasters; (2) Not assuming the public infrastructure will be available; (3) planning for civil unrest; (4) assuming some employees/people will not be available; (5) working with your suppliers on implementing a contingency and recovery plan; (6) expecting the unexpected; (7) being prepared for unexpected; (8) having a strong leadership position as a part of contingency and recovery plan; (9) empowering decision making in the uncertainty and disastrous situation, in which needs quick responses based on the circumstance and prior arrangements and pre-established decision hierarchies will not be followed; and (10) working on opportunities arising from the disasters (e.g., developing better and more advanced infrastructure to replace damaged and legacy infrastructure).

10.7 Outsourcing

Outsourcing is "an arrangement by which one organization provides a service or services for another organization that chooses not to perform them in-house" (Haag, Baltzan & Phillips 2008, p.444). One major benefit of outsourcing is that an organisation can focus on its core competencies or core strengths, which allows an outsourcing provider to take over all non-core competencies. When organisations look at outsourcing as their choice, they face the choices of in-sourcing, outsourcing, offshore outsourcing, multi-sourcing, and partnership. Each of these has its own advantages and disadvantages (see Table 10.1). A systematic, balanced and integrated decision-making approach, taking into consideration various issues (e.g., costs, benefits), should be followed.

Table 10.1 Comparison of in-sourcing, outsourcing and offshore outsourcing of systems development

Systems Development	Advantages	Disadvantages
In-sourcing	Improves requirements determination; Has complete control of intellectual property and project delivery; Increases knowledge worker participation and ownership; Increases speed of systems development.	Inadequate internal expertise leads to inadequately developed systems; Lack of organizational focus creates "privatized" systems; Insufficient analysis of design alternatives leads to sub-par systems; Lack of documentation and external support leads to short-lived systems.
Outsourcing	Focuses on unique core competencies. And outsourcing non-core processes allows businesses to focus on their core competencies; Exploits the intellect of another organization; Better predict future costs; Acquires leading-edge technology; Reduces costs; Improves performance accountability;	Reduces technical know-how for future innovation; Reduces degree of control; Increases vulnerability (e.g., privacy and security issues) of strategic information; Creates Interoperability and integration issues; Increases dependency on other organizations.

	Has access to tailored services; Increases quality and efficiency; Reduces exposure to risk; Access to outsourcing service providers' economies of scale and expertise and best-in-class practices.	
Multi-sourcing	Increased competition among suppliers; Access to best-of-breed services; Reduced risks (e.g., over-reliance on one particular vendor); Better opportunities to find the best-fitting supplier.	Reduced incentives for suppliers; Reduced incentives for client to male vendor-specific investments (e.g., relationship building, knowledge, technology); Increased management and transaction costs (e.g., arising from managing multiple relations).
Offshore Outsourcing	Could realize saving quite significantly (e.g., labour cost savings); Attainment of higher service levels; Could access to a larger talent pool in other countries; Freeing up of in-house management to focus on strategic management as opposed to daily operational issues.	Could have not been proven on large scales; Could have the risks of instability of the offshore countries; Needs to deal with language, culture, and time zone issues; Could have reduced degree of control; Could lose training opportunities to internal staff; Creates interoperability and integration issues.
Partnership	Enhances collaboration with partners; Reduces cost and time of learning; Utilize each other's strengths and result in win-win situation; Could realize more benefits than working alone.	Could not have shared vision and willingness to share the information; Could have intellectual property disputes; Could have difficulties in establishing trust among partners; Could lead to lose-lose situation.

(Source: Aubert et al. 2016; Haag, Baltzan & Phillips 2006, pp. 157–160, 290–293; McKeen & Smith 2015, pp. 122-139; Pealson & Saunders 2010, pp.192-196; Pearlson & Saunders 2016, pp. 208-224;)

While enjoying some benefits of outsourcing, organisations also face challenges (Haag, Baltzan and Phillips 2008, pp. 453–454):

- contract length – most outsourcing contracts span several years.
- competitive edge – loss of competitive advantage resulting from loss of effective and innovative use of IT.
- information confidentiality issues.
- problems in defining scope.

However organisations can avoid the risks by considering some of the following activities (Mckeen & Smith 2015, pp.136-138; Pearlson & Saunders 2010, p.197; Pearlson & Saunders 2013, p. 271–272):

- Develop a sourcing strategy.
- Do not negotiate solely on price.
- Have good understanding of cost structures.

Carefully examine your own firm's capabilities

- Thoroughly look at the provider's capabilities and select an outsourcer whose applications complement yours.
- Make a choice on cultural fit as well as technical expertise.
- Examine whether a particular outsourcing relationship produces a net benefit for your company.
- Develop full life cycle service contracts that occur in stages.
- Establish short-term supplier contracts.
- Hire multiple, best-of-breed suppliers.
- Build up skills in contract management and make contract as tight as possible.
- Consider hiring legal experts
- Create a risk mitigation strategy and a governance strategy.
- Have open communications of your sourcing strategy to all stakeholders to mitigate political risks
- Manage bottlenecks to deal with time zone issues
- Decide on full or selective outsourcing models.

So how can an organisation choose the best outsourcing approach? Organisations can choose any of the four outsourcing approaches after evaluating advantages and disadvantages of different outsourcing approaches and taking into consideration their organisational circumstances and requirements. Alternatively a combined outsourcing approach also can be pursued. On a related, the discussion of various outsourcing options of cloud computing can be found in Chapter 6.

Critical capabilities for offshore outsourcing of information systems

By studying 18 firms, Ranganathan and Balaji (2007) identify four major outsourcing capabilities: (1) systemic thinking on offshore outsourcing (capability to strategize and offshore readiness); (2) global information systems vendor management (vendor selection, contract facilitation and relationship governance); (3) global information systems resource management (human resource management, knowledge management and distributed work management); and (4) information systems change management (managing user-related change and dealing with organizational change). They also put forward five lessons learned/suggestions for effective offshore outsourcing management: (1) taking a systematic approach to developing offshore outsourcing capabilities; (2) working on the entire outsourcing lifecycle; (3) acknowledging the dynamic nature of capabilities; (4) investing in structure and people; and (5) regularly auditing offshore outsourcing capabilities.

10.8 Global Information Systems Operation Management

With the assistance of information technology, many companies throughout the world are attempting to transform themselves into global players (O'Brien & Marakas 2011, p.598). The changes in the marketplace, the rapid adoption of the Internet and development of Internet technologies have presented organisations with new opportunities (e.g., reaching global customers, establishing global supply chains) and challenges (e.g., political, cultural, geo-economic challenges). The management issues are enormous and need to be carefully evaluated if organisations wish to reap the full benefits of the global market. Like any other business operations an essential part of global information systems management is to explore the impacts of cultural, political and geo-economic realities in different business locations. In addition, organisations also need to pay a lot of attention to such issues as establishing global business information systems strategies, managing global business application portfolios, building global information systems platforms, dealing with global data resources, and working on global systems development (O'Brien & Marakas 2011, pp.601).

One area needing particular attention is cross-border data access and transmission since cross-border data flows may be viewed as violating a nation's sovereignty for the reason it avoids customs duties and regulations. Other issues concerning cross-border data communication include: laws protecting the local information systems industry from competition, laws protecting local jobs, and privacy legislations. Some key issues of cross-border data communication include (O'Brien & Marakas 2011, p.606): (1) networking management issues (e.g., operational efficiency of networks, data communication security issues); (2) regulatory issues (e.g., cross-border data flow restrictions, international communication regulations, international politics); (3) technology issues (e.g., network infrastructure across countries, international integration of technologies, applications, systems); and (4) country-oriented issues (e.g., national differences and characteristics, international tariff structures).

Information systems can play an important role in developing a faster, more agile, and innovative global organization. To effectively and efficiently support global operations, organizations need to take a combined approach of decentralization (to look after local information systems needs and unique requirements and skills) and centralization (to leverage the scale of information systems globally and take advantages of the power of centralized computing (e.g., best of breed and standardized technologies, common platforms, and shared services for application development and infrastructure for the sake of efficiency and cost saving).

One good example of such approach is Ford's information system transformation in recent years, with evidence of Ford's latest SUNC and my Ford Touch innovations. By applying centralized federated information systems management model (Ford's name for the combined approach), Ford has simplified, centralized and delivered information systems as a service across its globe operations while allowing sufficient room for localization and customization (Dignan 2012; Hiner 2012). The drive behind this is Ford's emphasis on new product developments and sales: any information systems initiatives are not contributing to these goals will not be approved or will be stopped. In addition, Ford's information systems operation has been focused on four priorities: integrating applications, supporting growth, enabling collaboration, and improving internal efficiency. One particular point of integration is integrating BYOD (bring-your-own-devices) into the corporate computing infrastructure in line with the popularity of mobile computing and enterprise mobility. When implementing the combined approach at the local level, the acceptance and cooperation of local leadership is very critical. Local leaders have to be included in the process and be consulted, and benefits of the implementation (especially to the local operations) and the impacts of not-implementing (especially to the local operations) should be clearly communicated to local leaders. Otherwise they will feel the threat (that headquarter will have more control) and don't have the feeling of ownership.

In addition, Benni, Muto and Wang (2011) suggest three essential management skills for implementing global enterprise resource planning projects, which are generic in nature, could be applied to other global information systems projects. The three suggested essential management skills are:

• Setting and steering company-wide priorities to define the target operating model of the global project: including activities such as developing priorities with management and other stakeholders via workshops; agreeing on the level of consolidation, standardization, and automation needed to align with identified priorities; and establishing project teams with commitments and tangible support from top management to clear the potential political hurdles.

• Translating the target operating model into an information systems architecture: including activities such as developing an architecture as per the agreed target operating model with the room for localization and customization, aligning and ensuring the expected business outcomes with the suggested architecture, and adjusting information systems operation/function (internal organizational changes within information systems operation/function) to be ready for the transition to the target operating model.

• Fine-tuning change management approach: including activities such as clearly communicating every aspect of forthcoming changes (e.g., when, why, how the changes are going to happen?, what is expected from people?, and who will be change champions?); refining and reinforcing change management processes; assigning task forces to drive changes; and emphasizing the change management is focusing on business transformation (so communication and negotiation are critical) rather than basic information systems implementation.

Managing global virtual teams

Global virtual software development teams have often been used by organizations to utilize firm's global-wide in-house expertise, but the lack of face-to-face interactions has made working together virtually a difficult task. Siebdrat, Hoegl and Ernst (2009) argue virtual collaboration has to be managed in specific ways and provide some suggestions based on their studies of 80 software development teams from 28 Labs worldwide:

• Emphasizing social and teamwork skills: team members from different cultures and different functions have to be able to effectively communicate and work together. When forming global teams, organizations can not solely look at candidates' expertise and availability, but also social and teamwork skills.

• Promoting self-leadership and developing self-sufficiency: experienced team leaders should be assigned to the global team whenever possible and sufficient training should be given to team members to ensure each team member could contribute fully and complete their assigned tasks by overcoming geographic dispersion and cultural diversity issues on his/her own.

• Providing face-to-face meetings: A project kick-off face-to-face meeting and/or social gathering before the project starts is necessary for establishing a common ground in the beginning of the project. Of course periodic face-to-face meetings will be required as well.

• Fostering a global mind-set: every team member should see him/her as a part of international networks, and recognize the international nature of the organization. Approaches for developing global mind-set include short-term international assignments at overseas locations of the organization and inter-cultural training.

On a related note, Eckhardt et al. (2019) propose a stage model for establishing virtual workforce:

• Stage 1: Preparation: hiring people with right skills, increasing awareness of change in work situation, and providing sufficient training on working virtually.

• Stage 2: Implementation: providing right and reliable technologies and tools to virtual employees, providing training for using the technologies and tools, establishing mixed virtual/office teams, mentoring provided by experienced employees, and providing virtual working opportunities throughout the organization.

• Stage 3: Virtualization: having regular face-to-face meetings, developing virtual trust, and monitoring performance of virtual employees.

10.9 Summary

Information systems can play a very important role in the success of organisation's competitive strategies. However competitive strategies alone cannot create magic. The success of such strategies heavily relies on good information systems management. In this chapter, some important aspects of information systems management, namely enterprise information systems operation, IT governance, roles of CIO, outsourcing, and global information systems, were discussed.

References

Agarwal, R., Brown, C. V., Ferratt, T. W. & Moore, J. E. 2006, 'Five mindsets for retaining IT staff', *MIS Quarterly Executive*, Vol. 5, No. 3, pp. 137-150.

Allas, T., Chambers, L. & Welchman, T. 2019, 'Confronting overconfidence in talent strategy management, and development', *McKinsey Quarterly*, June 2019, pp. 1-7.

Alvarez, E. & Raghavan, S. 2010, 'Road Map to Relevance: How a capabilities-driven information technology strategy can help differentiate your company', *Strategy + Business*, Iss. 61, pp. 1-6.

Applegate, L. M., Austin, R. D. & Soule, D. L. 2009, *Corporate Information Strategy and Management: Text and Cases*, 8th Edition, McGraw-Hill, USA.

Aubert, B.A., Wiener, M., Saunders, C. Denk, R. & Wolfermann, T. 2018, 'How Adidas realized benefits from a contrary IT Multi-sourcing strategy', *MIS Quarterly Executive*, Vol. 15, No. 3, pp. 179-194.

Bauer, H., Burkacky, O., Kupferschmidt, J. & Rocha, A. 2016, 'From hardware to software: How semiconductor companies can lead a successful transformation', *Semiconductors*, McKinsey & Company, December 2016, pp. 1-8.

Benni, E., Muto, K. & Wang, K. W. 2011, 'Tailoring IT to global operations', *McKinsey on Business Technology*, Number 24, pp. 2-7.

Bensemhoun, D., Chartrin, C. & Kropf, M. 2011, 'Tracking the roots of underperformance in banks' IT', *McKinsey on Business Technology*, Number 24, pp. 22-27.

Boochever, J. O., Park, T. & Weinberg, J. C. 2002, 'CEO vs CIO: Can this marriage be saved', *Strategy + Business*, Iss.28, pp. 1-10.

Booth, A., Roberts, R. & Sikes, J. 2011, 'How strong is your IT strategy?', *McKinsey on Business Technology*, Number 23, Summer 2011, pp. 2-7.

Cable, D. & Vermeulen, F. 2018, 'Making work meaningful: A leader's guide', *McKinsey Quarterly*, October 2018, pp. 1-9.

Casey, K. 2019, 'AI Skills: 5 ways to build talent individually', *The Enterprise Project*, January 21, 2019, Online, Available at: https://enterprisersproject.com/article/2019/1/ai-skills-5-ways-build-talent-internally (accessed on 2 March 2019).

Chartrin, C. 2011, 'Brining learn to a Skilled workforce: An interview with Thierry Pécoud of BNP Paribas', *McKinsey on Business Technology*, Number 24, pp. 28-31.

Chui, M. & Fleming, T. 2011, 'Inside P & G's digital revolution', *McKinsey Quarterly*, November 2011, pp. 1-11.

Collett, S. 2018, 'The biggest issues CIOs face today', *CIO*, July 11, 2018, Online, Available at: https://www.cio.com/article/3287913/the-biggest-issues-cios-face-today.html (accessed on 6 November 2018).

Cooker, M. & Baker, E. 2010, 'Helping the CIO lead', *Strategy + Business*, December 13, 2010, Online Available at: http://www.strategy-business.com/article/00055?gko=ebedc (accessed Aug 2, 2012).

Copper, B. & Nocket, K. 2009, 'Toyota's IT Transformation', *Strategy + Business*, Iss.55, pp. 1-3.

Dignan, L. 2012, *Four IT management lessons from Ford*, Online Available at: http://www.zdnet.com/four-it-management-lessons-from-ford-7000000520/ (accessed July 20, 2012).

Eckhardt, A., Giordano, A., Endter, F. & Somers, P. 2019, 'Three stages to a virtual workforce', MIS Quarterly Executive, Vol. 18, No. 1, pp. 19-35.

Edwards, J. 2018, '8 IT cost cutting mistakes you need to avoid', *CIO*, October 4, 2018, Online, Available at: https://www.cio.com/article/3309400/8-it-cost-cutting-mistakes-you-need-to-avoid.html (accessed on 1 March 2019).

Fred, C. S. & Stoddard, D. B. 2004, 'Getting IT right', *Harvard Business Review*, February 2004, pp. 72-79.

Haag, S., Baltzan, P. & Phillips, A. 2006, *Business Driven Technology*, 1st edition, McGraw-Hill Irwin, Boston, U.S.A.

Haag, S., Baltzan, P. & Phillips, A. 2008, *Business Driven Technology*, 2nd edition, McGraw-Hill Irwin, Boston, U.S.A.

Heltzel, P. 2019, 'The 11 biggest issues IT faces today', *CIO*, February 15, 2019, Online, Available at: https://www.cio.com/article/3245772/the-12-biggest-issues-it-faces-today.html (accessed on 8 June 2019).

Heneghan, L., Snyder, M. & Symons, C. 2017, 'The route to digital business leadership', *Insight*, KPMG, 7 September 2017, Online, Available at: https://assets.kpmg/content/dam/kpmg/xx/pdf/2017/09/the-route-to-digital-business-leadership.pdf (accessed on 1 May 2019).

Hennongsson, S. & Kettinger, W. 2016, 'Managing IT integration risk in acquisitions', MIS Quarterly Executive, Vol. 15, No. 1, pp. 1-19.

Hiner, J. 2012, *How Ford Reimagined IT from the Inside-out to Power its Turnaround*, Online Available at: http://www.techrepublic.com/blog/hiner/how-ford-reimagined-it-from-the-inside-out-to-power-its-turnaround/10671 (accessed August 2, 2012).

IDG Connect 2011, *IDG Connect Special Report: The Global IT Skills Landscape*, Summer 2011, IDG Connect International, pp. 1-8.

Junglas, I. & Ives, B. 2007, 'Recovering IT in a disaster: Lessons from Hurricane Katrina', *MIS Quarterly Executive*, Vol. 6, No. 1, pp. 39-51.

Kogekar, H. 2010, 'Think Tank: Better IT Governance', *CIO from IDG*, Online Available at: https://www.cio.com.au/article/345139/think_tank_better_it_governance/?pp=2 (accessed on 30 October 2017).

Laudon, K.C. & Laudon, J. P., 2017, *Management Information Systems: Managing the Digital Firm*, Fifteenth Edition, Global Edition, Pearson, U.K.

Leatherberry, T., McCormack, D., Kark, K. & Lamm, R. 2019, 'The tech-savvy board: Engaging with CIOs and management on strategy, risk, and performance', *Deloitte Insights 2019*, pp. 1-15.

McKeen, J.D. & Smith, H. A. 2015, *IT Strategy: Issues and Practices*, Third Edition, Pearson Education, United Kingdom.

Manyika, J. 2009, 'Hal Varian on how the Web challenges managers", *McKinsey Quarterly*, January 2009, Online available at: https://www.mckinseyquarterly.com/Strategy/Innovation/Hal_Varian_on_how_the_Web_challenges_managers_2286 (accessed July 23, 2012).

National Computing Centre (U.K.) 2005, *IT Governance: Developing a successful governance strategy-A Best Practice Guide for Decision Makers in IT*, Online, Available at: https://www.isaca.org/Certification/CGEIT-Certified-in-the-Governance-of-Enterprise-IT/Prepare-for-the-Exam/Study-Materials/Documents/Developing-a-Successful-Governance-Strategy.pdf (accessed on 30 October 2017).

O'Brien, J. A. & Marakas, G. M. 2011, *Management Information Systems*, 10th Edition, McGraw-Hill, New York, USA.

Pearlson, K. E. & Saunders, C. S. 2010, *Managing and Using Information Systems: A Strategic Approach*, fourth edition, John Wiley & Sons, USA.

Pearlson, K.E. & Saunders, C.S. 2013, *Managing and Using Information Systems: A Strategic Approach*, fifth edition, John Wiley & Sons Inc.

Pearlson, K. E. & Saunders, C. S. 2016, *Managing and Using Information Systems: A Strategic Approach*, sixth edition, John Wiley & Sons, USA.

Pflügler, C., Becker, N., Wissche, M. & Krcmar, H. 2018, 'Strategies for retaining key IT professionals', *MIS Quarterly Executive*, Vol. 17, No.4, pp. 297-314.

Pratt, M. K. 2018, 'How to build the next generation of IT leaders', *CIO*, August 06, 2018, Online, Available at: https://www.cio.com/article/3294697/how-to-build-the-next-generation-of-it-leaders.html (accessed on 2 February 2019).

Ranganathan, C. & Balaji, S. 2007, 'Critical capabilities for offshore outsourcing of information systems', *MIS Quarterly Executive*, Vol. 6, No. 3, pp. 147-164.

Red Hat 2016, 'IT Talent Crisis: Proven advice from CIOs and HR leaders', *Harvard Business Review Analytic Services*, pp. 1-12.

Roberts, R. Sarrazin, H. & Sikes, J. 2010, 'Reshaping IT management for turbulent times', *McKinsey on Business Technology*, Number 21, pp. 2-9.

Sarrazin, H. & West, A. 2010, 'Understanding the strategic value of IT in M&A', *McKinsey on Business Technology*, Number 21, pp. 34-39.

Siebdrat, F., Hoegl, M. & Ernst, H. 2010, 'How to manage virtual teams', *MIT Sloan Management Review*, Vol. 50, No.4., pp. 63-69.

Singh, A. & Hess, T. 2017, 'How Chief Digital Officers promotes the digital transformation of their companies', *MIS Quarterly Executive*, Vol. 16, No. 1, pp. 1-17.

Strack, R., Dyrchs, S., Kotsis, A. & Mingardon, S. 2017, 'How to gain and develop digital talent and skills', *The New Way of Working Series*, The Boston Consulting Group, pp. 1-15.

Strack, R., Antebi. P., Kataeva, N., Kovacs-Ondrejkovic, O., Lopez, A. & Welch, D. 2019, *Decoding digital talent: What 27,000 digital experts in 180 countries tell us about their mobility and work preferences*, The Boston Consulting Group, pp. 1-12.

Taylor, J. & Joshi, K.D., 2018, 'How IT leaders can benefit from the digital crowdsourcing workforce', *MIS Quarterly Executive*, Vol. 17, No. 4, pp. 281-295.

Tumbas, S., Berente, N. & Brocke, J. V. 2017, 'Three types of Chief Digital Officers and the reasons organizations adopt the rule', *MIS Quarterly Executive*, Vol. 16, No. 2, pp. 121-134.

Tylan, D. 2017, 'The 8 biggest IT management mistakes', *CIO*, December 11, 2017, Online, Available at: https://www.cio.com/article/3240943/biggest-it-management-mistakes.html (accessed on 10 July 2019).

Watts., S. 2017, 'What's the Difference Between ITIL and COBIT?', *BMC Blogs*, May 15, 2017, Online, Available at: https://www.bmc.com/blogs/cobit-vs-itil-understanding-governance-frameworks/ (accessed on 22 July 2019).

Weill, P. 2004, *Don't just lead, govern: How top-performing firms govern IT*, Working Paper No, 341, Center for Information Systems Research, Sloan School of Management, Massachusetts Institute of Technology, pp. 1-21.

Wikipedia, 2019, *Corporate governance of information technology*, 21 February 2019, Online, Available at:
https://en.wikipedia.org/wiki/Corporate_governance_of_information_technology (accessed on 22 July 2019).
Wood, D. 2012, 'Does you CIO have what it takes', *Forbes*, 05072012, Online Available at: www.forbes.com/sites/danwoods/20120705/does-your-cio-have-what-it-takes/print/ (accessed July 9, 2012).

Index

Printed in the United States
By Bookmasters